Wakefield Press

Beyond the Books

Heather Robinson is a writer and researcher specialising in the cultural history of the twentieth century. She is also a creative producer with thirty years of experience across the Australian GLAM sector and public service. In 2020, Robinson completed a PhD at Flinders University, exploring the creative industries policy impacts on cultural institutions and their communities. She is an Honorary Research Associate of Flinders University and the Los Angeles County Museum of Natural History, an avid reader, Darwinian gardener, and passionate motorcyclist.

Praise for *Beyond the Books*

This is an urgent, important book. Our cultural institutions have been held to ransom by bean-counters for too long and Robinson provides a detailed and persuasive case that there is a better way – or in fact a myriad of better ways – of valuing them. This book should be required reading for all policy-makers and economists.

– **Gillian Dooley**, Author and researcher,
Honorary Librarian, Royal Society of SA,
Special Collections Librarian,
Flinders University (1999–2015)

For anyone concerned with Australian culture, this book provides a wealth of commentary on problems of value, public policy and the common good . . . Accessible, compelling and timely, *Beyond the Books* is a succinct, thought-provoking attempt to get us to "count" publicly what we value privately, and to allot to cultural institutions the respect they deserve in Australian society.

– **Julian Meyrick**, Professor of Creative Arts,
Griffith University

Beyond the Books provides a compelling and delightful account of the social value we place in our libraries, and how it is that our governments keep failing to value them enough.

– **Danielle Clode**, Author & Associate Professor,
Creative Writing,
Flinders University

Public libraries are a crucial part of our collective lives, and absolutely essential to any democratic society. This book asks the pointed question as to why it is that they have been so marginalised by many contemporary governments, and how we might re-centre them as part of a revitalised, forward looking South Australia.

– **Justin O'Connor**, Professor, Creative Economy,
UniSA

This book is about so much more than one cultural institution, one state and one sector; it gets to the heart of the problems of why it has been so challenging to communicate the value of arts and culture to the different groups that support, use, fund and care for cultural legacies.

– **Tully Barnett**, Associate Professor,
Creative Industries,
Flinders University

Beyond
the Books

Culture, value, and why
libraries matter

Heather Robinson

Wakefield
Press

Wakefield Press
16 Rose Street
Mile End
South Australia 5031
www.wakefieldpress.com.au

First published 2025

Text designed and typeset by Jesse Pollard, Wakefield Press

ISBN 978 1 92304 289 6

A catalogue record for this
book is available from the
National Library of Australia

Wakefield Press thanks
Coriole Vineyards for
continued support

Contents

Acknowledgements

I would like to thank the members of the public, especially Natalie Harkin, for contributing their time and stories that comprise the heart of this book. A very special thanks go to Geoff Strempel, Lucy Guster and all at the State Library of South Australia for enabling my research, their ongoing belief in this book, and for the opportunities to share it with their community. I am very grateful to Assoc. Prof. Tully Barnett, for her friendship and encouragement, and for the Flinders University Laboratory Adelaide Project's contribution towards the publication of this book. Thanks to Michael Bollen and Wakefield Press, for seeing the value of this publication for South Australia and for securing a place for it amongst their publications. Thank you also Elizabeth Ho and Michael Jacobs, for the testing of ideas, valuable insights and encouragement when my compass strayed. My colleague Peter Beaglehole was an invaluable early reader and trusted BS detector. And my gratitude is also carried over to all my beloved PhD Buddies – Stefano Bona, Madeleine Regan, Melanie Prior, Piper Bell, and Piri Eddie. I am grateful for the editorial guidance of Penelope Curtin. Thanks also to Gillian Dooley, Justin O'Connor, Julian Meyrick and Danielle Clode for their support.

I would also like to acknowledge Sarah Long, Rob Ray, Margaret Brown and other passionate advocates defending the value of qualitative research across all sectors and disciplines. For my extended blended family and friends for their encouragement and excitement that I was finally writing a book. Thank you – it's done! My husband John Long is my constant inspiration and occasional taskmaster. I could not have written this without his insights from years of research and museum leadership, for lighting the way when my outlook turned bleak, and for that wonderful trip to Arezzo. Avanti!

This book is dedicated to my dear Dad, Randall Ormond Robinson, who taught me how to read, and showed us what really matters. And to the staff and volunteers of the South Australian Public Library Service, for their tireless community service, care of the collections, and for supporting members of the public in their ongoing pursuit of knowledge and understanding.

Foreword

As Director of the State Library of South Australia, and having worked in the library profession for decades, I am familiar with the constant discussion around the "value" of libraries, along with the value of the 'cultural sector' in general. During this time, I have seen the attempts to use various forms of economic value theory to justify libraries when compared to other 'public good' expenditure and the use of public money.

I don't think there is any debate that libraries create value through a range of opportunities including supporting researchers who create new knowledge or in people finding new meaning in their lives, or from the pleasure of reading for pleasure, engaging with an exhibition or just sitting and enjoying the environment. But there is a deeper question as to the value such cultural institutions provide to society just by existing over centuries.

In this context I was delighted when Heather Robinson met with me to discuss her intended area of study for her PhD; understanding the issues of 'meaning' and 'cultural value' in the context of the GLAM sector, and more particularly that she had chosen the State Library of South Australia as her case study! What could be better than having a very experienced arts practitioner wanting to undertake some deep research into our institution and its cultural value to our community?

I enjoyed engaging with Heather as she developed her research methodology, engaged with our customers and began to draw conclusions from her research. And here in this final output I am delighted to see all of this come together in an engaging and compelling way.

Heather takes us on a journey which explores how the arts became an industry, where quality and meaning were replaced with measurement and control, before reaching back to explore the historical and societal context which gave rise to libraries in the UK and how this gave birth to the aspirations of the early South Australian colonists. This early history is an important consideration as it helps to set the context for what the Library was and what it has become.

Using a combination of well-structured qualitative research, illustrative anecdotes and a combination of the general and specific Heather uses the voices of the public to illustrate how they value their experiences, and the fact that an institution such as the State Library exists. To quote Heather in summarising her engagement with interview subjects,

> *"They also spoke of how the institution builds trust in the community, supporting their sense of identity by reinforcing both personal and collective memory."*

Heather has reworked her PhD thesis to provide this very readable work which includes her own personal insights and passion for the State Library, libraries in general and the GLAM realm more broadly. And she has distilled what libraries are in a way that I have rarely seen before. I am thinking of getting this quote turned into a plaque on my desk, or perhaps the footnote to my correspondence with Arts bureaucrats and policy makers.

> *". . . libraries are a community's secret weapon in the war against ignorance and isolation. They are also sites of pleasure and entertainment, and of rich cultural experience, knowledge transfer and social connection."*

As Heather asserts and demonstrates, it is impossible to measure this cultural value in dollars alone.

I look forward to this work providing great insights for those who grapple with the 'value' question in a cultural context, those who work in and make policies about 'the Arts', and those who are looking to ensure that such institutions are nurtured, regarded and funded to continue to contribute deeply to the fabric of our communities.

Geoff Strempel
Director
State Library of South Australia

Introduction

How an artwork saved a town

As a researcher and arts worker, I've spent a great deal of time thinking, writing and talking about what is meant by the term 'cultural value'. In 2015, I chanced upon what turned out to be a lightbulb moment. Since then, when people ask me about the 'problem' of cultural value, I tell them the following story.

Early in 2015, I met Jane Gleeson-White, a writer visiting Adelaide from Sydney to discuss her new book, *Six Capitals: The revolution capitalism has to have – or can accountants save the planet* (2014). It was the subtitle that caught my attention. How could accountants possibly save the planet? Curious, and conscious of the gaps in my knowledge, I bought both *Six Capitals* and her earlier book, *Double Entry: How the merchants of Venice shaped the modern world – and how their invention could make or break the planet* (2012). In *Double Entry,* I was fascinated by the following anecdote.

In 1944, as the Allied armed forces headed north through Italy in pursuit of the retreating German army, a unit of the Royal Horse Artillery took up position outside Sansepolcro, a town established in the tenth century in eastern Tuscany, nestled in a valley near the northern headwaters of the River Tiber. The Allied forces had systematically razed townships en route to drive out enemy forces prior to their entering on foot. The officer in charge of the Sansepolcro unit was Anthony Clarke. As his gunners prepared to bombard the town, Clarke surveyed the area for signs of enemy forces. Sansepolcro – the town's name rang a bell in his mind. As the first shells rained down on the town, the art-loving Clarke recalled an essay he had read by Aldous Huxley. It was titled 'The best picture', and it concerned a fifteenth-century fresco by the Renaissance master painter and mathematician Piero della Francesca. And that fresco, *The Resurrection of Christ* (1458), was in Sansepolcro.

Risking court martial for disobedience, and despite never having seen the work, Clarke ordered his gunners to cease fire. The calls came in from his commanding officers, demanding to know why the shelling had stopped. Clarke stalled, eventually convincing them that there was no sign of the enemy, no real target, and therefore no need to destroy the town. Sansepolcro was liberated the following day with little damage done to most of the creamy stone architecture, including the town hall, inside which Piero's *Resurrection* had inspired and, some say, protected civic leaders for more than five hundred years.[1]

Piero spent most of his life in Sansepolcro, mastering his painting and the principles of mathematics, and writing a treatise on the use of perspective in art, a work which influenced generations of Renaissance artists and all who followed in their footsteps. One of his companions and pupils was another resident of the town, Luca Pacioli, the accountant who imported double-entry bookkeeping practices from the Middle East to Italy. This revolutionary accounting system, which enabled the early merchants of Venice to track their wealth, underpinned the capacity of the great banking houses, including the legendary Medici family, to fund the boom in trade. As the Italian states' economies grew, the Medici bankrolled the Renaissance boom in the arts and cultural patronage, supporting the defining successes of the world's best-known and most influential artists of the day.

After reading the story of Clarke and Piero's *Resurrection*, I joked that if Piero had been expected to provide a statement about his work's anticipated impact – a requirement of today's funding and acquittal processes – no one would have believed him if he had said that, one day, his painting would save the entire town from destruction.

This story demonstrates a number of important issues relevant to the assessment of cultural value: there are many ways to calculate the value and impact of a cultural artefact or experience; this value and the extent of its impact are often unknown at the time of its creation; and how that impact will be realised and by whom are unpredictable.

This book looks at how we value culture today, focusing on the value we place on one of Australia's best-loved institutions, the State Library of South Australia. Through this detailed example, I will investigate the commercialisation of the cultural sector, a situation that led people like me, with the best of intentions, to believe that it was important to 'walk the commercial talk' when we spoke about what we produced or delivered as workers in the arts sector. In so doing, we inadvertently contributed to the minimisation of society's fundamental need for the arts, and underestimated the societal role of the cultural institutions to which many of us have dedicated our professional lives. To survive, to remain employed, to develop credibility and to demonstrate our transferrable skills, everyone in the cultural sector – and indeed the sector itself – has become hostage to a commercial ideology that (at best) merely regulates and limits our cultural expression, expectations and access; and (at worst) inadvertently destroys everything we would like to think we stand for, such as free access to knowledge, our relationships with our audiences and our so-called participatory democracy. For those of us who work in the sector, much of the value of the work we do is seen every day in the reactions of people who connect with and are moved by a cultural experience. The problem arises when that eye-witness testimony cannot be easily recorded on a spreadsheet. What is more, as the story of Piero's *Resurrection* illustrates, some elements of value cannot be recognised until after, maybe long after, the spreadsheet has been deployed in its destructive work.

How does the opening story relate to the cultural value of the State Library of South Australia, located on the far side of the world from Piero's *Resurrection*? Founded in 1834, two years before colonists left England for Adelaide and the lands of the Kaurna people, the State Library remains the keeper of stories that have been collected for generations. Like artworks in Tuscan town halls, these stories and objects may have been collected or created with one particular purpose in mind, although their purpose may have evolved or increased in importance as the world itself changed. Likewise, something that was once thought unimportant could have gained in critical, personal, artistic, symbolic or social significance over time, depending on the hands into which it fell. These are events beyond the creator's control. Yet this capacity to understand, appreciate and communicate the value and meaning of culture to individuals and communities in non-financial terms is being eroded. We are in danger of losing the language to describe why and how culture matters to us, as individuals, communities and nations. That loss of language is contributing to a lack of understanding of the role culture plays in our lives. This is not a conspiracy theory, and it's not just happening in the arts and cultural sector.

Who am I?

I am a creative producer with broad experience in the cultural sector, designing and delivering exhibitions and public events in museums, galleries, festivals and libraries across Australia. I've spent some time in the public service working in digital education and funding programs. I've also completed a doctoral thesis on the topic of cultural value, this book being the public version.

Like many of my colleagues in the arts sector, I have enjoyed a variety of roles in cultural heritage and collecting institutions, drawing on the rich collections and the professional expertise of these institutions to design and deliver informal education programs and events for the general public. These roles were based in or supported by government, providing valuable insights into the institutional challenges prompted by the policy shifts that come with changes of government and other major redevelopments. I also came to understand the close and proprietary relationship the public has with 'their' gallery, museum or library. Some members of the public were part of my daily life as much as the institutions were a part of their lives. We were bound together by common interests based in and around the physical site of the institution. Each of us played our part in the institution and its community throughout the year or years, contributing to its economic resilience and long-term institutional value.

More recently, I have worked with a variety of festivals, which are more short-term or episodic cultural experiences. On these occasions, the public is amorphous and temporary, attracted to the concepts underpinning the experience rather than to a particular site or collection. However, the powerful effect the experience had upon them is no less significant. Many like me, nervously watching from up the back, become astute judges of whether an audience has engaged and enjoyed the experience. (There is little doubt when they have not.) I gained friendships, professional insights and satisfaction through random interactions with members of the public, building and rebuilding the connections each time through sharing thoughts and personal stories. I still remember conversations with a couple of visitors who came to one of the events in which I was involved 20 years ago; they attended simply because they were curious or were accompanying a friend, but left with a changed worldview. At the conclusion of productions, we would make notes, record feedback – the good and the less so. I remember positive, albeit anecdotal, feedback described by one administrator as the 'warm fuzzy file', which rarely made the final report. The most important details of our work and the public experience both needed to fit on a limited number of pages prefacing extensive spreadsheets designed to reflect numbers and profit. Although good numbers were always celebrated, the most memorable and rewarding public insights were often lost.

That said, I have no argument against financial reporting or reporting obligations to partners. Ideally we work together as a team and financial accountability is something the arts does very well. We can make a dollar go further than many other sectors, simply because we must. If the cultural sector has a 'problem' with managing money, it's because we are expected to produce more with less in increasingly competitive environments. While balancing the books is an essential component of professional arts practice and reflects our responsibilities to our partners and our public, perhaps it would be more useful if the numbers and narrative in reporting were more evenly balanced, to address the interests of all involved, and to ensure all expectations, achievements, and goals are not just met, but recorded equally.

This book explores how those public narratives can be reclaimed to demonstrate precisely what our cultural institutions provide in return for government support, and what culture means to the community, beyond dollars and numbers. I will share anecdotes from my own experience working in the sector, as well as my research and findings from my doctoral thesis, a case study of the rich cultural value of the State Library of South Australia.

Supported by a great number of experienced and credible theorists, academics, friends, librarians and cultural practitioners, this book presents a roadmap for how we might be able to reinstate this 'balance'. I've chosen to tap into the public's perspective of what cultural institutions like the State Library of South Australia delivers to them, the tax-paying members of the public, and will explain why this matters. The voice of the public and the accounts of their experiences resonate for longer in the memories of cultural practitioners and echo more loudly down the halls and corridors of cultural institutions for far longer and more roundly than mere numbers on a spreadsheet. Why not with policy-makers?

This book does not propose a single method of measuring the value of the State Library or any cultural institution. Instead, I wish to explore how we need more than one approach by which to identify where value can be found, what it looks like, and what goes into its creation. I hope to reflect both the complex nature of a major cultural institution and the long-term perspective required to appreciate how cultural value accrues over time. Identifying how the public perceives value and meaning in their relationship with an institution may be the most appropriate and authentic means for understanding how that institution contributes to the life of a community, a city, or a state. This approach requires an investment in audience relationships, which takes time, one of the most precious commodities for many in the sector. As a doctoral student, I had the time and capacity to sit with members of the public and discuss the many ways by which the State Library of South Australia supports their research, provides a safe and secure environment, and reconnects them with family experiences over generations. I include a range of warm, insightful and informed statements about the Library, which demonstrate what can be gained by spending a little time with the people institutions work for – the members of the public. These voices are presented here to assist other practitioners, policy-makers, and even account-ants, to understand what those of us working in institutions such as a library actually do, for whom, and why it matters.

Chapter 1

Culture and value

John Holden, one of the world's leading thinkers and researchers in the field of value, heritage and the arts, has written a great deal about culture, although he admits that 'No one would suggest that defining culture is easy'.[1] Holden did, however, make a fair attempt and came up with a practical definition, which I have used throughout this book. When I write or speak of culture in this book, I am using Holden's broad and encompassing definition of culture: 'the arts, museums, libraries and heritage that receive public funding'.[2] The inclusion of libraries in Holden's definition is crucial for my thinking about cultural value. Many see libraries as peripheral to arts and culture, as merely functional information-delivery services, a view that represents a limited approach to considering today's library spaces. In fact, libraries are a community's secret weapon in the war against ignorance and isolation. They are also sites of pleasure and entertainment, and of rich cultural experience, knowledge transfer and social connection. Holden's reference to public funding also carries with it a range of obligations and responsibilities that cultural collecting institutions must fulfil for their communities over time – as past, current and future taxpayers, and audiences. The term also emphasises all governments' obligations for ensuring the long-term sustainability of cultural institutions, as part of a long-standing social contract with their constituents to provide public services.

I think it's important that we are reminded of these contracts from the outset. The Australian cultural sector has struggled with the disintegration of understanding at the highest level of governments for more than a decade and has been discounted and ignored on the policy level. Compounding this is that the sector has been operating largely without a national cultural policy, one that acknowledges the role and nature of culture and what the sector provides communities. This has occurred within a market-focused environment of constant demands for evidence of value for money, and of ongoing threats of funding withdrawals. Although some governments make promises to rectify some of the damage of their predecessors, there are no guarantees. Many of us with experience in the sector can remember past disappointments.

This book covers the impacts of this breakdown in understanding and the importance of culture's contribution to the community – all communities – throughout Australia and across generations. It also records the public's appreciation of a long-standing institution, the State Library of South Australia, which is repeatedly asked to do more with less. It records how much is lost each time a much-loved role is made redundant, an archive remains unopened and inaccessible, or a visitor is turned away. I have captured the voices of the public and hope to encourage discussion of how we assess the value of cultural experiences by referring to those who benefit directly from them, and why this counts not only economically, but also socially, personally and historically. As Prime Minister Anthony Albanese said at the 2023 launch of *Revive*, Australia's first national cultural policy in more than a decade, 'Culture is the common ground in which we plant the seeds of our dreams'. I will demonstrate that the State Library is that fertile common ground and that it supports people from all walks of life and from all over the world to fulfil their aspirations – claims also applicable to cultural institutions across the country.

Most of the time, I consider 'cultural value' as public value within a cultural context, but because of its subjective nature, it can be almost impossible to pin down at any single time. Objects may lie dormant for decades before their potential value can be realised. Turning to Holden again, we can see how challenging it is to identify the value of a cultural experience or institution, when that value will not be the same to everyone. As Holden explains: 'Value is located at the encounter or interaction between individuals (who will have all sorts of pre-existing attitudes, beliefs, and levels of knowledge) on the one hand, and an object or experience on the other'.[3] Cultural value is a process not limited to a single person and point of time. It is also entirely dependent on access. When members of the public engage with an item housed in a cultural institution like the State Library, they activate the latent value in that collection. The opposite would also apply: if the public is prevented from accessing the collections, through lack of availability, neglect or regulatory process, the value of the collections will remain dormant, unrealised. This interaction and activation depend on 'institutional value', a form of value that has attracted less attention than other instrumental or intrinsic forms of value. However, I find this concept critical to how we think of the long-term value of the ongoing services, experiences and relationships that institutions provide over time, and how that value accumulates. I did not anticipate stumbling on the connection between institutional value and an institution's history, although I now believe that the two cannot and should not be separated. The term 'institutional value' is an apt way to describe the contribution and relationship built up over almost two centuries between the State Library and the South Australian community. This complex relationship continues to be a work in progress.

Culture's crisis of legitimacy

John Holden is best known for disassembling and standardising the three main forms of value generated by the arts and cultural sector, using terms that are accessible to both practitioners and policy-makers. After witnessing decades of creative industries policy, conferences and industry think-tanks in the UK, Holden concluded that the arts were viewed by policy-makers as a means to other ends. Culture was valued only for 'what it could achieve for other economic and social agendas . . . politics had mislaid the essence of culture, and policy had lost sight of the real meaning of culture in people's lives and in the formation of their identities'.[4]

Drawing on research from the fields of environmentalism, anthropology and accounting, which also questioned the limitations and applications of economic rationalism and the neoliberal measurement imperative, Holden explored 'ways in which to express the value of things that are difficult or impossible to measure'. In 2006 he suggested that language lay at the heart of the policy[5] and public service challenges associated with cultural value. To aid these discussions, he proposed that culture's value could be seen as encompassing three forms of value, linked but separated – intrinsic, instrumental and institutional. His 'Cultural Value Triangle' was the result, a construct that reduced a complex topic to more readily accessible categories for non-specialist stakeholders across different sectors. As useful as his work has been, it could also be said that this teaching tool inadvertently encouraged some to focus on just one form of value, perpetuating the problems Holden was trying to solve.

Policy-makers in particular did not seem to grasp the extent of the interdependence of each corner to the other.

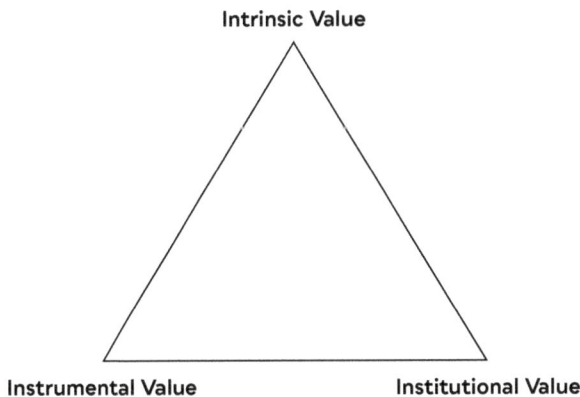

Holden's Cultural Value Triangle

What does each corner mean?

Intrinsic value is the subjective and individual experience of culture. Holden describes it as 'the capacity and potential of culture to affect us, rather than as measurable and fixed stocks of worth'.[6]

Included here is the impact of artworks or cultural experiences on audience members or visitors at the emotional, intellectual and spiritual levels in ways that cannot be replaced through other means.

Owing to its largely intangible and personal nature, intrinsic value is not merely the essence of cultural experience, it also represents the major challenge when culture is being held to account, or when impact is being questioned or measured. Each of us experiences art or culture internally, cognitively and differently, depending on our background, history, gender, age and so on. This impact – intrinsic value – is not only impossible to measure with any genuine accuracy, but is also more difficult to articulate, aggregate, compare or forecast. This poses major problems for administrators requiring impact statements.[7]

Instrumental value refers to subsidiary impacts, those generated through cultural practices that are not an artist's or company's *raison d'être*. Instrumental value is a consequence of a cultural experience, rather than being the primary objective. It's not their goal in undertaking their practice, but they coincidently manage to score it along the way. These 'spreadsheet' impacts are generally represented by numbers.[8] They include tourist dollars spent in the city during a period when an exhibition or festival is being staged, social or community wellbeing indices, and employment statistics (even if the dozens of new jobs recorded only last a few weeks). Instrumental value is favoured by many policy-makers because it may be more easily 'captured in output, outcome and impact studies that document the economic and social significance of investing in the arts'.[9]

Similar to intrinsic value, instrumental value alone is not an authentic or true indicator of cultural impact, nor is it without its challenges.[10] The problems associated with instrumental value include the capacity for arts organisations to demonstrate a causal link or a connection between their practice and the coincidental outcome; for example, an increase in interstate visitors arriving through the airport may be unrelated.[11] Governments are bound by the need to demonstrate success within an electoral cycle, yet it's next to impossible to provide evidence of an institution's impact within a government's three- or four-year term, beyond fluctuating numbers through the door. Collecting institutions like the Library operate on different time scales. Again, without adequate support and continuity of personnel and reporting processes, we cannot easily prove there are connections between cultural productions and wider societal shifts. The prevalent and not-always-successful use of instrumental impact statements as advocacy tools can also be a trap: the more arts companies struggle to prove connections with successes in other sectors, the less likely they are to be believed, especially if they cannot provide evidence of causal links between their cultural activity and the impact they claim to be the result of their work. They play a dangerous game when tying their success to events beyond their control.

It is hard to ignore the binary nature of debates over the primacy of intrinsic over instrumental value. Several scholars and advocates over the years, I believe, have missed the real point; that is, the *relationship* many people have with cultural sites and institutions, the constant, permanent and ongoing sites like galleries, museums and libraries. My professional experience working in the cultural sector is best reflected in Holden's description of *institutional value*:

> Institutional value sees the role of cultural organisations not simply as mediators between politicians and the public, but as active agents in the creation or destruction of what the public values. The responsible institutions themselves should be considered not just as repositories of objects, or sites of experience, or instruments for generating cultural meaning, but as creators of value in their own right. It is not the existence of a theatre or a museum that creates these values; they are created in the way that the organisation relates to the public to which, as a publicly funded organisation, it is answerable.[12]

Institutional value is reflected in the relationship between state-run cultural institutions and their public, the processes that facilitate their engagement, the behaviours and attitudes demonstrated at the point of encounter, and the delivery of services, whether it is the provision of access to collection items or welcoming people through the door. My roles as an arts worker have focused on the public experience: ways to improve audience engagement; intellectual and physical access; and supporting audience curiosity, comfort and values. These priorities aimed to ensure the ongoing relevance and integrity of the institution, as well as to cultivate positive relationships with the community at all levels. Some, though, would see these services as contributing to ticket sales and return custom, which is also valid but not our prime motivation.

That said, even Holden's descriptions fail to mention the somewhat fallible nature of institutional value: it is dependent on interactions between the public and the people delivering these services, actual humans facilitating the engagement with the institution, not merely on digital delivery systems, although these too provide invaluable points of engagement. The interpersonal interactions or performative behaviours by staff and volunteers inform the perception and co-creation[13] of value within the cultural sector. Members of staff and volunteers are also responsible for the ongoing dialogue that keeps well-managed institutions aware and responsive to their community's changing values and preferences, as seen in the evolution of collecting practices, object or exhibition interpretations and attendant internal policies. This ongoing conversation ensures the institution's relevance and authority in the eyes of the community. The appropriate access to and care of Indigenous collections within the State Library, an example which will be explored in later chapters, is a case in point. Changes like these require time, resources and institutional cultural shifts, yet such changes do occur, especially under the right leadership and within a supportive political environment.

Institutional value emerged from the ideal of political neutrality within the public service, whereby every member of the public can expect to be treated equally. This in turn engenders a civic environment of trust in government and acceptance within the community, which can work both ways. If, for example, an institution, and by extension a government, does not offer inclusive and non-discriminatory access, they risk damaging their relationship with their public. Institutional value is generated at the point where the government fulfils its social contract with the community, providing a public service in a way that adds value to the quality of life. Institutional value is:

> . . . all about the way that cultural organisations act. They are part of the public realm and how they do things creates value as much as what they do. In their interactions with the public, cultural organisations are in a position to increase – or indeed decrease – such things as our trust in each other, our idea of whether we live in a fair and equitable society, our mutual conviviality and civility, and a whole host of other public goods. So the way in which our institutions go about their business is important. Institutional value should therefore be counted as part of the contribution of culture to producing a democratic and well-functioning society.[14]

The 'way that cultural organisations act' is the most relevant to the function and meaning of the State Library in the South Australian community. Not only is this form of longitudinal or 'lifetime building' value diminished in importance in ongoing debates on instrumental and intrinsic values, but institutional value is also threatened by the short-term episodic 'eventalisation' of culture. This too will be explored in later chapters.

Since institutional value also underpins the two more frequently cited and debated forms of value – intrinsic and instrumental – it is surprising that more people are not taking more notice or care of it.

Making time and space for heritage
Along with culture, the definition of 'heritage' appears to be problematic, as does an understanding of its importance. Perhaps

this reflects the lack of public and policy interest in this highly specialist and complex field in recent decades. Similar to cultural value, heritage value accrues over time, making it very difficult to track on a spreadsheet. Based on data uncovered as part of my research, I will argue that the two are less about history, and far more about our future.

Not everything that is old is heritage: to be considered heritage, an object or site must have a symbolic relationship with the community around it, accrued over time, and it must have both shared meaning and value that extend beyond monetary value. When speaking to visitors about their experiences at the State Library, I found it impossible to ignore the way by which their past relationships with the institution had influenced how they experience and value the institution, a significance that extends beyond an appreciation of architecture or access to historical documents. The Library had become an important part of both personal and community identity. Monetary value barely rated a mention.

So, when speaking of heritage, culture and their symbolic value for communities, I borrow from a former colleague at the National Gallery of Victoria, Professor Derek Gillman, who has spent a career in museum and heritage institutions around the world:

> *Cultural symbolism derives from relationships between people, values, practices, places, events, memories, records, stories and objects; consequently, particular objects may have symbolic but not monetary value ... Without notable historical context, a mid-eighteenth-century English bronze bell would command relatively little on the market ... But if the Liberty Bell itself came to auction, institutional and private bidders would compete vigorously for this principal symbol of democratic freedoms.*[15]

The symbolic value of the State Library connects users to the history of South Australia and their community identity, in both positive and negative senses, engendering a meaningful relationship between the community and the institution. As I'll discuss

later in this book, this is how heritage becomes a major component of cultural value. Like institutional value, heritage is based on
relationships with community over time, with the public's appreciation of the Library's continuity being one of the most interesting
aspects identified through this research. Including a chapter on the
history of the Library in a book about its cultural value therefore
provides some fascinating and important context, in that it helps
to make sense of what I found when I interviewed and surveyed
the public.[16] Although a complete history of the Library is beyond
the scope of this book, an examination of its roles during two time
periods – British colonisation and today – will demonstrate, first
of all, the origins of the institution, specifically the values that
informed its early development, and, secondly, how these values
can still be observed in the experiences of today's public.

Relevance is everything. However much the Library may have
been hampered by lack of funds or by political priorities, the institution has through both necessity and design evolved with the times.

Quantity over quality

Well before the global pandemic arrived in 2020, the arts sector
was under pressure to provide evidence of impact to account for
public investment. For decades, the role and value of the cultural
sector, and the investment of public moneys in the arts, has been
questioned:

> Even in countries that spend relatively large amounts of public
> provision or subsidy of culture, the cultural budget is only a
> small proportion of government spending, often less than one
> per cent of the government budget . . . However, cultural policy
> and public expenditure on culture are often controversial,
> attracting attention that is disproportionate to the amount of
> money involved.[17]

A trend towards evaluating cultural experiences and institutions,
in line with measures derived from the commercial sector, has now
become an imperative. A range of library scholars suggest that in

many instances public investment in libraries is made based on economic, rather than social, impact studies, which used to be more common.[18] Libraries have also experienced additional pressure to justify their presence and function in a digital world.[19] This view was confirmed by a State Library team member, who suggested that: 'Our main competitor for visitor numbers is Google'. This perception of competition from digital experiences and a sense of looming redundancy coming from someone inside the institution is sad. My findings presented here demonstrate that this perception is also wrong.

Quantitative approaches take precedence in Australian cultural reporting structures, allowing for 'numerical evidence to replace experience as the arbiter of sense, creating thin understanding at policy level'.[20] I recognise that balancing the books and keeping track of visitor numbers has and should always be a significant part of any cultural institution's evaluations; however, I will show why this approach cannot be the only form of evaluation if the institution's real value is to be understood. The focus on quantitative reporting and evaluation methods diminishes public voices in reports: what the institution or the experience means to them and its value. Nevertheless, if we are to understand cultural value – the public return for public money spent on culture and the arts – we need to speak with and listen to the recipients of that value and the real source of those funds – the public.

Ticking the boxes but missing the point

Generally, all that is required as a record of an event or for an evaluation of the operations of an institution is quantitative data: numbers through the door, social media hits, books in and out, money raised and media engagement. Audience surveys tend to be designed around digital system capability, rather than what and how much organisations may wish to know. While once there may have been more room for feedback and reviews, that space has been reduced. Replacing that experiential feedback are questions about value for money and how much the audience spent as part of attending. Data collection is generally planned around the acquittal of sponsorship or government funding agreements, compiled in the time between the production and expiration of employment contracts, particularly in festival environments. Data is collected quickly to meet the obligations to sponsors, be they government or commercial, and compiled before the staff contracts run out. While the impact data (those tourism spikes and individual spend data) can expeditiously capture the perceived instrumental consequences of what was produced, the more complex conversations on what motivated the production, how it was received by the audience or what the artists hoped to achieve in terms of practice and quality are neglected. Little 'presence' of the public appears in cultural reports, with their voices rarely heard or stories of impact included, be they emotional, intellectual, spiritual even. Sometimes, that impact may even be beyond words. I've often thought it a pity that such stories are not included in most reports and therefor do not make it through to board members, sponsors, bureaucrats and policy-makers. This is the chasm this book hopes to bridge.

In South Australia, the State Library, the Art Gallery, and the Museum are obligated to include a breakdown of negative public feedback in their annual reports to Treasury. There is no similar obligation to reflect positive commentary. Exit interviews, participant testimonies or summary reports may be written for internal purposes, but it is difficult to determine whether these have any influence. The focus on statistics and financial-reporting requirements begs the question of whether the positive achievements of our cultural institutions are fully appreciated and recognised. Half the story is missing.

My experiences of Australia's cultural institutions in recent decades reflect the rise in the sector's 'crisis of legitimacy'. We have become dependent on complex commercial management tools to plan, deliver, promote, communicate and acquit cultural projects in order to be considered professional, accountable or 'legitimate' in the eyes of many commercial and government partners.[21]

Such tools are powerful in the right hands, and it helps to have a common language and understanding with partners. However, rarely does the onus to communicate in another professional language run both ways.

These issues around measurement and accountability are prevalent across the GLAM (galleries, libraries, archives and museums) sector – although many in the education, science and health sectors are confronted by similar pressures. While these essential services are often placed in opposition to the cultural sector as more urgent, vital and legitimate areas of government expenditure, they also face the same challenges in meeting efficiencies and providing evidence for intangible and unpredictable outcomes. As Carol Scott argues in relation to museums, this need for evidence has grown to the extent that it's not just about accounting for public monies; it's become about justifying our existence:

> *Accountability . . . is a requirement of our professional practice. Governments, policy-makers and other funders require more evidence that there is a return on their investment. But in an economic climate where the total amount of public funding is declining, museums in many countries find themselves fighting to maintain a position as essential public goods in competition with other necessary services. We are no longer just accounting for public monies. Providing evidence that museum work results in public benefit is now crucial to our survival.*[22]

Audience evaluation has become a hotly contested domain across academia and the cultural sector, as consultants and external organisations promise new means of capturing or reflecting the impact of the public's experience as the return on government investment. But what is the most authentic, cost-effective and legitimate way to capture and convey culture's worth to preserve the relationship with the public and satisfy the reporting imperatives of government? This deceptively simple question has troubled the cultural sector and others in social services, health and education for decades.

My hope is that this book will stimulate meaningful conversation about and within the cultural sector, increasing understanding of the sector and celebrating culture's valuable role within communities. My aim is to demonstrate that arguments based on slogans such as 'health or heritage', or the need for efficiency dividends in one sector, but not others, are no longer acceptable to the public, and that this should be reflected in changes at policy level.

Changes at the policy level were instrumental in creating this imbalance, meaning that, with enough support for and commitment to culture's value to the community, the opportunity for change will arise. First, though, we need to understand how modern life has become dominated by an inexorable pressure to measure.

Chapter 2

How the arts became an industry

One of my interview subjects (who prefers to remain anonymous) noted wryly that if you were to stack all the top-quality international research confirming the cultural value and the positive contribution made by libraries, the resulting pile would be taller than the State Library itself, one almost certainly hard to ignore, and yet it rarely makes a difference to policy or budget decisions.

Much of this research reflects how some cultural institutions are evaluated in ways that ignore their institutional missions and responsibilities, to the extent that their sustainability is jeopardised. In recent decades, some funding bodies have insisted on the sector's use of new evaluation methods, promoting the hope that the next cutting-edge approach or innovative technology will enable the cultural sector to flourish and contribute to a thriving economy (even more than they currently do). Yet, despite this energy and endeavour, arguments concerning how and why cultural institutions are valued, or what role the arts fulfil in communities to justify public subsidy, have not significantly advanced. If we are not at an impasse, we are at best stuck in a stalemate.

Culture, control, and tight fiscal policy

To understand how the arts were recast from a public service to an industry, we must first come to terms with what we mean by 'the arts', and by 'culture', and how arts and cultural institutions have been impacted by the pressure to measure their value in numbers – dollars or visitors through the door to reflect a return on government investment. This will involve understanding how governments have changed over the last 40 years or so, and how this is reflected in changes to arts and cultural policies, with a focus on Australia, the UK and parts of Europe.

Arts policy, like other policies, is a strategic tool of government, used to accomplish goals informed by party ideologies. John Pick, a British academic specialising in arts administration, wrote in 1988 that government funding policies 'are often at best political constructs, thinly disguised control systems', which do little to reflect the quality of government:

> The percentage of GNP [gross national product] which a government chooses to give in grant-aid to the arts is no real indication of the government's civilization, nor of its generosity of spirit . . . the most liberal and democratic of governments of the twentieth century have given little and had no arts policies; the most vicious and inhuman have had arts policies . . . and have been extremely kind and generous towards their opera houses, museums, galleries and concert halls . . . Therefore, arts policies are only real when they are economic policies, and artistic aims are therefore necessarily subordinate to managerial aims.[1]

Language is always a critical factor in these conversations, and Pick, amongst many, opposed the political realm's reconceptualisation of the arts and cultural sectors as a single homogenous industry rather than a rich and varied creative network. He described the changes made in the 1980s to English policy terminology as nothing more than a 'pervasive fallacy'.[2] Around this time, the New Public Management model (NPM) was adopted in the UK, altering the language of government and introducing evidence of value for the public dollar as the preferred indicator of responsible financial management. Pick suggested that the arts and cultural sector had not previously been under as much pressure to produce instrumental or quantifiable (and preferably economic) outcomes. Instead, the focus of evaluation had been on the creation of public value, which is far more difficult to assess. The arts came to be evaluated against instrumental measures, such as improved liveability or wellbeing indices, which Pick suggested would carry significant challenges for the arts sector. For example:

> *The risk in saying that 'the arts attract business' is that you come to define the arts as being only those activities which do attract business . . . policy making will boil down to being a simple question of how the 'arts industry' is to be 'funded'. Then all questions about the nature of creativity, about interpretation and criticism, about freedom and complexity, about diversity and choice, about value and excellence will take second place to the supposed high truths of economics.[3]*

Numbers now dominate the reports of cultural institutions, at the expense of critique or public feedback related to quality, variety, reception or significance. This shift of reporting focus reflects the historical and contemporary challenges within the cultural policy domain since the late twentieth century; namely, the changing economic imperative driving policy-makers' preferences for short-term results and immediate (tangible) impacts. This abbreviated approach in public sector reporting and goal setting converts the traditional qualitative language and expertise of the arts world into 'jargonese' for a 'narrow bureaucratic construct', subject to the political preferences of the day. Art:

> *. . . is no longer subject to genius, creativity, interpretation and criticism, but simply economics. Bureaucrats cannot recognise or control genius or creativity, and they fear criticism, but economic forces, they can control. Therefore, art has to be seen as something which is 'like everything else', subject to economic laws.[4]*

Pick's fears over the industrialisation of the cultural sector and its reductive effect on the relationship between the sector and government have been realised, first in the UK and subsequently in Australia. As evidenced by the *Arts and Culture Plan South Australia 2019–2024*, and as forecast by commentators like Pick, culture is now expected to be more 'like everything else', subjecting the complex value offering of the arts to the vagaries of not only political persuasion but also the vacillating economic drivers of scarcity, demand and competition. The sector is being judged and valued according to measures beyond its control, expertise and compass.

The marketisation of cultural value and public services coincided with the emergence in the 1980s of neoliberalism worldwide, which 'claims that unrestricted competition, driven by self-interest, leads to innovation and economic growth, enhancing the welfare for all ... The reality is rather different'.[5] The tone and expectations of today's arts policy environments are now governed by economic rationalism. Public institutions like the Library are subjected to competitive forces and evidence-based funding arrangements. (There is no coincidence that this is also the same period in which cultural value has been problematised.) This commercial management focus in government portfolios sets agencies in charge of cultural institutions against other departments in a competition for funding, whereby economic impact is used as the yardstick of success. They must prove they are worthy of government funding and are forced to compete against each other for the available resources. In the process, the requirement for several government agencies – health, education, culture – to deliver public services is ignored. As a result, government services have become focused on compliance and evaluation, rather than on delivery of cultural value and satisfaction for the public.

Economists and observers suggest that the colonisation of the arts and cultural sector by economic impact analyses has created a regulatory policy environment, reducing the sector's contribution to society and our way of life to evidence-based evaluation and short-term funding processes. These management frameworks keep institutions and the teams employed there continually on their toes – operating with a pervasive sense of uncertainty, acquiescence, and the occasional anxiety about their employment. And it's hard to be truly creative and representative under such scrutiny.

This sense of precarity is not limited to only those working in the arts. Economist Mark Blyth also suggests that, rather than being a tool to serve the common good, the economies of nations have been positioned by proponents of neoliberalism within governments to create the impression of recurring budget emergencies, with these matched to election cycles.[6] The cuts to policy areas not aligned with government priorities are communicated to the public as austerity measures. By election time, governments previously on this course suddenly open the coffers and announce additional funding for major projects in, coincidentally, marginal electorates. This questionable approach to economic policy design, popularly known as 'pork-barrelling', leads to short-term policy development and design, as well as a preoccupation with economic spending for the sole purpose of re-election.[7] This has dramatic impact on cultural institutions' ability to plan and work: they operate on a much longer timescale.

Austerity has become a common catch-cry, acting as a virtue-signalling premise to rationalise ongoing funding cuts to the cultural, education, health and social services sectors.[8] Before the pandemic, and since, budget cuts to fund policy priorities came in the form of 'efficiency dividends' and they have been regularly imposed upon the cultural sector. They are an invidious tool, rolled out during times of so-called austerity. In 1987 the Australian Prime Minister Bob Hawke introduced efficiency dividends as part of the reform of the Australian Public Service.[9] Initially a three-year proposition, over recent decades these savings measures have increased from the original one per cent to four per cent, and extended to the core funding allocated to agencies, rather than targeting administration and travel.[10]

Efficiency dividends have become an inappropriate but effective mechanism for reducing government spending in the cultural sector. Far from being a savings measure, this outdated strategy reduces the amount of public funding distributed to Australia's national cultural institutions. Successive federal and state governments have made it clear that there will be no return to the previous levels of government funding to support their core operations. To maintain the expected level of service provision, institutions are encouraged to limit access to the public or explore other income-generating opportunities. These other avenues of revenue include sponsorship from the business community, as also encouraged by the *Arts and Culture Plan South Australia 2019–2024*. However, these relationships are neither easy to establish or maintain. They can also be entailed with attendant challenges and responsibilities:

> *Sponsorships are not philanthropic donations – they are business investments from which the company wants a return that can be managed and measured . . . Competition for the sponsorship dollar is always intense and arts organisations need all their skills in matching the return to the investment . . . Yes, they'll still want measurables and deliverables and audience synergy with simpatico brand values, but they'll also want some of your charisma and cultural capital.[11]*

Once again, the arts are expected to produce measurable impacts, impacts that may be beyond their sphere of operations, or even their expertise. In this instance, though, the cultural sector is 'encouraged' to partner with organisations whose motivations may be less concerned with cultural value, collections and artistic development and more with image management and access to new markets – for someone else's economic benefit at the expense of taxpayers. This is neither fair nor sustainable, more so in a city the scale of Adelaide, which is home to very few major companies and where the quest for sponsorship is highly competitive. Economist Richard Denniss uses the example of BHP's partnership with the Australian War Memorial to illustrate this paradoxical and fraught relationship between private funding sponsorships and public sector institutions:

> *Neoliberalism has trained us to thank our sponsors, not our fellow citizens, for what we have collectively achieved. But many of those generous sponsors work hard to minimise the generosity of their tax bill. The Australian Tax Office is currently chasing BHP for around $1 billion in underpayment of*

*tax. If the company paid its taxes in full and ditched the corpo-
rate sponsorship, we . . . would be far better off.*[12]

In 2018, the Australian Major Performing Arts Group found that, while corporate sponsorship is 'incredibly important to the arts sector', it is also 'a volatile source of revenue', subject to the fortunes and vagaries of the commercial sector and is not without its own challenges:

> *Cash sponsorship is more beneficial to major performing arts
> companies as it provides greater financial flexibility and is more
> readily quantifiable, but it is becoming increasingly harder to
> obtain and more difficult and expensive to service.*[13]

The costs of servicing sponsorship also point to a disadvantage for many in the arts sector: by deed of inheritance, scale and capacity, major arts organisations are better placed to garner and service major sponsorship from either the government or commercial sectors than companies in the small-to-medium cultural sector. Sponsorship is also highly dependent on relationships, which are difficult to maintain for an organisation that may employ most of its teams for six to 12 months at a time. Such relationships also perpetuate the need for evidence to prove a return on the sponsorship investment, which is generally tied to the priorities and performance indicators of the *sponsor*, rather than the company. The need to prove a return on investment for sponsors also adds another layer of work to what the company is funded to deliver.[14]

Over the last ten years, austerity cuts to state government funding have been an ongoing challenge for not only the State Library, but all cultural institutions in South Australia. In 2016, the state government announced a $6 million reduction to the State Library's budget over three years, leading to the loss of 20 members of the Library's staff. The reason given to the public was 'simply budget cuts':

> *The Library has already shed jobs, we've lost a lot of casual
> jobs already and now the permanent staff are being targeted.*

We're looking at jobs going which include librarians, adminis-
tration and support staff, and supervisors and managers and
our members are now assessing what this will mean for public
services.[15]

Although unpopular, and with few alternatives, the Library considered job cuts to be the most effective means of meeting the
required efficiencies; they had nothing to do with poor performance or service delivery. This course of action prompted a
restructure of the workloads for the remaining 70 full-time staff,
which, as a government spokesperson claimed, would ensure
'structural and financial stability and sustainability while still
being able to deliver on the priorities outlined in its strategic
plan' (2016).[16] Operations had to adapt to the new level of funding.
Working in the arts means doing more with less, in a way that
other government departments are rarely called upon to do.

Job cuts and tight financial times are not new to the State
Library or most arts organisations of significant scale and longevity. What is different now, however, is the extent to which
external economic and political performance measures are being
used to regulate the operational capacity of public institutions,
enforcing a competitive environment and sense of 'frustration,
envy and fear'.[17] Moreover, the rhetoric of neoliberalism excludes
the measures and informed judgement, characteristic of the
cultural sector, in favour of reductive commercial language and
homogenising processes, devoid of nuance and expertise; hence,
the dominance of numbers through the door and dollars on
the balance sheet over critical feedback and public narratives
of value.

In pursuit of whole-of-government reporting and management
strategies, policy-makers in both Australia and the UK have also
experimented with aligning the arts and cultural sectors with
other unrelated departments. This approach created new industrial models, making sense for the economists but driving the
arts sector even further from its original purpose. Rather than
being concerned with the delivery of public services, creativity

and cultural experience, the cultural sector would be rebranded and managed as an industry.

Creative industries: policy boomerang or backfire?

In 1994 the Creative Nation federal arts policy was introduced, representing a turning point for the Australian cultural sector which was already responding to changes in public attitudes and transforming from a supply-led to demand-led enterprise. The market would guide its future directions. Institutions would be obliged to react to these external preferences and expectations, rather than setting their own course. This change of direction was intended to provide the 'means to link the audience with the art'.[18] Inclusivity and public responsiveness are indeed good things, but could it really be that simple for institutions to succeed?

The phrase 'culture industry' originated in the UK in 1979, when it was engaged as a deliberate oxymoron to illustrate its contradictory nature.[19] The UK's New Labour government, however, was oblivious to the ironic and binary nature of the term, and instead applied the concept to 'invent' the creative industries as a policy platform, in the process borrowing heavily from Australia's Creative Nation policy.[20] In 1998, under the Blair New Labour Government, the Department of Digital, Culture, Media and Sport (DCMS) released the *Creative Industries Mapping Document*, a new policy, which consolidated under a single banner a range of disparate policy areas. These included the booming UK film industry, businesses associated with the digital economy and online gaming development. These formerly separate commercial enterprises were affiliated with keepers of cultural collections and arts producers in a single portfolio. This smorgasbord of loosely creative businesses and institutions were believed to be aligned because of their association with burgeoning new technologies and the potential capitalisation of ideas. All would be covered by the single new policy.

By the time the Creative Industries policy had been adopted by New Labour in the early 2000s, the tone of discussions surrounding culture and the arts in the UK had switched from one

encompassing intrinsic arts concerns and priorities, to one rig-
idly focused on income and evidence-based decision-making to
inform and justify government spending. Economic rationalism
became a whole-of-government ideology for evaluation, and the
UK cultural sector became subject to the same reporting mechanisms as every other government department, in that they were
forced to demonstrate a return on the government investment of
public monies.[21] The alignment of the cultural sector with portfolios that were more politically and economically influential was
intended to produce a range of benefits for all involved, mainly a
greater financial return and exchange of ideas.[22] Culture and creativity were seen as critical components along the assembly line
of innovation, the magical fuel of the fast-paced and profitable
digital economy.[23] Under the one policy structure, culture, heritage and archives were evaluated using the same tools, timelines,
language and philosophies as online gaming and screen production – as a set of inputs, outputs, growth and competitive edge.
Such techniques were antithetical to cultural practice, long-term
value and even classical economics. Even though the arts were
also expected to benefit from the new policy context, the impact
on creative practice and individual artists was confronting, regulatory and largely detrimental:

> In many of these industries, in idealized terms, economic
> potentials and material existences were clearly conjoined to a
> practitioner's own valued capacities to express and articulate
> their lived cultural experience, including, often, the production
> of oppositional meanings and social critique. But as demon-
> strably cultural – with the duality of culture and economy finely
> balanced in productive tension – these activities obtained a
> less positive evaluation than the emergent and favoured kinds
> of 'new' creative entrepreneurialism that appeared to privilege
> commerce primarily, and culture secondarily, if at all.[24]

Rather than offering support to artists and cultural institutions,
the creative industries policy deprived many in the sector of their

voice and agency, impacting on their willingness and capacity to represent the community, their contemporary discourse, or indeed any form of dissent. If they could not show a financial return on their investment by the time the acquittal was due, then their activity was not considered of any value to the government. The arts sector was instead encouraged, and therefore expected, to become less concerned with advancing exploratory arts practice or interrogating current community concerns and the public's experience of them; instead, the sector was refocused on generating revenue and public benefits beyond their control, capacity and, interestingly, beyond their funding level. In effect, the new policy environment seemed to question the cultural sector's very existence.

Academics across the UK questioned the intentions of policy-makers.[25] On the one hand, government departments were insistent that the intrinsic values of the arts 'were at the very heart of what we do'. On the other, they were simultaneously requiring more evidence of instrumental impact in areas such as wellbeing, jobs growth and community development.[26] As early as 2004, Eleanora Belfiore, a professor in cultural policy, observed that:

> In the last decade, arts organisations in the United Kingdom have been reinvented as centres of social change. They have been expected to contribute actively to urban regeneration and to the government's fight against the plight of social exclusion.[27]

Despite similar criticism across the GLAM sector and mounting evidence of the negative consequences of the UK Government's cultural policy settings, the creative industries platform and the instrumentalisation of culture proved itself to be remarkably entrenched and had a range of negative effects. Criticism of the new policy direction continued to grow. Despite this, so did its influence. Culturally specific language, authority and evaluation processes were lost in environments dominated by economic impacts, the needs of more influential policy domains, and imperatives to demonstrate instrumental outcomes. This disruptive influence occurred while policy-makers kept insisting that such alignments were made to ensure the sustainability and resilience of the sector.

Return above service

Although accountability had always been part of arts practice and cultural management, this new emphasis on economic return contradicted the traditional focus on delivering cultural value, artistic and social returns. Quantity over quality. Some of the basic tenets of public service were challenged by the new focus, which in turn challenged its 'publicness' – the features of impartiality, distinction from the private sector, and traditional commitments to equality, longevity and representation – all elements usually found in every cultural institution's charter. Instead, the focus of government activity both in the UK and Australia became more commercial in outlook, driven by instrumental outcomes, and politically strategic and short-term in focus. And it was not simply isolated to the management of the arts. The nature of the public service was forever altered.[28]

As both a practitioner and researcher in recent decades, I have experienced these impacts on the Australian cultural sector and the cultural workforce. Although many of the policy decisions were made at a federal level or overseas, they exerted a trickle-down influence on how all organisations of all scales in receipt of public monies operated.

In parallel with the Australian GLAM sector, the State Library of South Australia has experienced similar changing policy impacts. By presenting the State Library, a cultural collecting institution of long standing, as a case study of cultural value, we gain a clear idea of how these policy decisions impacted on similar institutions, such as museums and art galleries. The cultural policy literature is replete with research examining the ways by which public cultural institutions are now managed and evaluated. Under the banner of 'economic rationalism', three decades of widespread public sector reform in the UK and in Australia have seen the imposition of commercial language and practices across all areas of government. The main feature of the new approach was a simplified and singular focus on economic norms and values, rather than 'broader political concerns, sector-political goals, professional expertise, different rights and rules, the interests of societal groups and so on – making the conflicts and tensions between different considerations more evident'.[29]

The disparity between commercial or corporate-style evaluation approaches and public service accountability in qualitative frameworks has also been observed across Western Europe and Scandinavia. Serious concerns have been raised over its impact on democracy and concepts of citizenship.[30] Some have argued that the New Management Model's focus on measurement 'can lead to several unintended consequences', which 'may not only invalidate conclusions on public sector performance but can also negatively influence that performance'.[31] These 'unintended consequences' include the increase in cost for external auditors and government auditing divisions, 'market-type mechanisms' such as the outsourcing of public services to private contractors and competitive tendering for government contracts. These were accompanied by the introduction of 'performance indicators', which were found to 'lead to ossification, that is, organizational paralysis'. Expertise was imported on an 'as needs basis' rather than cultivated within the government department.[32] Specialist portfolios, such as those covering state arts and cultural institutions, were handed over to administrators with little experience or qualifications in the area, but glowing reputations for compliance, economic management and political fit. Innovative and inspiring cultural leadership was not the outcome of this approach; rather, it created: 'Tunnel vision, which can be defined as an emphasis on phenomena that are quantified in the performance measurement scheme, at the expense of unquantified aspects of performance'.[33]

In the early 2000s one of Australia's leading arts writers and advisors, Jo Caust asserted that 'Industry models that have no direct relevance to the arts should not be used to monitor/evaluate this sector'.[34] Sadly, by the time her research had been published, the public sector reforms that had begun with the NPM had spread across both British and Australian governments. In a pattern that will be repeated over the first decades of the twenty-first century, and despite the genuine concerns regarding the fallibility and misapplication of the NPM approach, project management and the measurement imperative have become standard practice in the public service. The alignment of a quantifiable approach with digital tools created a level of co-dependence and mutual fascination between government and the technology sector, a relationship that has permeated the public service and embedded whole-of-government management and reporting strategies.

The twenty-first-century public service shift towards econometric methods and language was not an entirely comfortable fit for the management of cultural institutions. Observers noted how 'economic rhetoric reverberates throughout public policy', creating frustration over its misapplication in fields and practices for which it was not designed, such as arts and cultural institutions.[35] As Australian cultural policy and economics analyst Christopher Madden notes, 'These are more than harmless misinterpretations; they impact the real world through the actions of politicians, public servants, and others with command over resources'.[36] Madden refers to the inappropriate application of economics tools and approaches (like economic impact statements) in the cultural sector as examples of 'misinterpreted authority',[37] which distracts from the cultural sector's natural strengths and expertise, and may actually work against the sector:

> The greatest practical risk in adopting 'economic' impact studies for [arts] advocacy . . . is that governments might actually take notice of them . . . 'Economic' impacts invite governments to intervene in art and culture for financial gain, and the results can be disastrous . . . Mediocre 'economic' impact

numbers may dispatch arts and cultural policies further to the periphery of government interests, or encourage the view that cultural policy is a mere adjunct to policies aimed at wealth or job creation.[38]

The use of economic impact studies and statements during the opening decades of this millennium has meant that instrumental approaches to evaluating arts and cultural institutions has become embedded practice. Their prevalence in the sector reflects government demands attributable to the rise of 'economic rationalism' in politics.[39] Professor David Throsby, one of Australia's highly regarded scholars of cultural value and economics, describes how these financial modelling tools can be 'useful' if done well, but the 'pitfalls are many' and well documented:

There have been a number of dubious applications of the technique over the years; it seems that poorly executed studies are particularly likely to arise when the motive is advocacy rather than objective economic analysis.[40]

Throsby suggests that non-economists, as most arts administrators tend to be, may not always be as effective as they believe when attempting to justify the value of their organisation in economic terms, particularly since they are using tools and techniques they may not fully understand. The adoption of balance sheets made cultural institutions intelligible to policy-makers with little or no experience in the arts sector and allowed for the institution's value to be (mis)interpreted as primarily an economic one, rendering the contribution comparable to (and thereby competing against) other government services. 'Misinterpreted authority' could therefore be said to run both ways: both sides of the funded and funding body dichotomy were bringing the wrong measurement tools to the job at hand. Recent research also indicates that arts management courses have not kept up with developments in the fields of performance measurement, accounting and finance.[41] Despite the calls for 'new calculative processes', the field 'has so far been unable to propose a theoretical framework for a contextualized, in-depth study of the practice of evaluation in the arts and cultural sector'.[42] By promoting increased economic impact as the primary and most appropriate evidence of success, organisations have become more tightly bound by traditional market imperatives, such as competition and expectations of perpetual growth, over which they have next to no real control (for example, museums expected to show an increase in numbers through the door while receiving less funding for new exhibitions).

In Australia, much of the dissatisfaction over the new focus on measurement stemmed from the NPM's encouragement of its characteristic 'top-down, regulatory environment'.[43] The traditional 'arms length' principle of the public service was eroded. Funding for public institutions, including those in the cultural sector, became even more dependent on delivering government policy, 'which was increasingly pragmatic, "instrumental" and unashamedly interventionist'.[44] Researchers in the UK tracked the 'trend of arts policy and funding to measure and ascribe to the arts "instrumental" qualities such as reducing crime, increasing tourism or increasing literacy rates'.[45] Even though the arts sector is expected to report against these broader indicators of impact, they are beyond the scope or capacity of most arts organisations to manage or influence. Such policy indices are the responsibility of government portfolios overseeing policing, foreign policy or education. Those few cultural organisations that can show causal links between their artistic practice and instrumental (and largely economic) outcomes tend to be rewarded with funding increases. Issues arise when successful organisations are expected to maintain those coincidental impacts, an added expectation that feeds an unhealthy appetite for growth and creates a trap for organisations: a disjunction between purpose and performance, between actual arts practice and outcomes that may in reality be the responsibility of other areas of government – departments that are probably better funded, equipped and capable of delivering in these areas.

By adopting increased economic impact as the primary evidence of success, cultural organisations have also become tightly bound to the vagaries of market realities – quantifiable financial gain, competition, and expectations of perpetual growth – over which they may have little understanding or control. This is the brick wall upon which arts workers regularly bash their heads. Many in government, with or without an understanding of cultural practice, public engagement and artistic motivation, have come to consider economic impact as *the only* valid indicator of success in the cultural sector. Economic impact is also frequently misunderstood on both sides of the reporting relationship. It is a complex field, one difficult to calculate and variable in its priorities and methods and one which may not be readily implemented by non-economists.[46] Nonetheless, the financial contribution made by the arts sector has become the key criterion when considering the value of investment in arts and cultural infrastructure, both in the assessment of funding applications and at the acquittal stage. The requirement to assess cultural experience according to instrumental outcomes is reflected in the prominence arts organisations give to economic impact when announcing favourable outcomes. Tourism dollars, as well as increased box office revenue (the smashing of box office records has become a predictable headline), are hailed as markers of success, before any mention is made of the quality of artists or the experience of local audiences.[47]

> The rational institutional response is to supply governments with whatever information they demand or whatever information moves them. If governments have found 'economic' impacts convincing, arts and cultural advocates have merely responded accordingly.[48]

This is not necessarily what the organisation either believes or prefers, although regrettably it is what they must present to be deemed successful and credible in the eyes of government.

Are cultural institutions part of an industry?

Cultural and other forms of social institutions have been perplexing classical economists for some time, largely due to their persistence in defying the traditional imperatives on which economic theory is based; namely, competition, scarcity and efficiency, which remain the keystones of modern industrialisation.[49] As a result of the 'creative industries' policy framework, cultural institutions such as the State Library of South Australia have been inappropriately subjected to processes designed to collect evidence of their value in numerical or financial terms. This approach ignores or disregards the longevity of their relationships with the community and their responsibilities as the keeper of the state's collective memory. As one former colleague told me, they are 'being measured by the wrong bloody yardstick'.

This tension between institutional purpose and externally derived performance measures is nothing new. Writing almost three decades ago, the economic historian Douglass North addressed the challenges that arise from the application of tools and techniques from one field to another unrelated to the discipline for which they were designed. He observed 'a persistent tension in the social sciences between the theories we construct and the evidence we compile about human interaction in the world around us'.[50] These traditional social interactions take the form of institutions. North defines institutions as 'the rules of the game in a society or, more formally . . . the humanly devised constraints that shape human interaction'.[51] Examples of these agreed behaviours and 'rules' create expectations and include staying quiet in a library or haggling over certain goods in a marketplace. The sites where these behaviours are enacted are dependent on such interactions and are based on mutual trust, respect and cooperation. The interactions come to shape, define, or even govern an institution, especially a cultural institution like a gallery or a library. They need these behaviours for their continued relevance and existence.[52] Libraries are commonly understood to be institutional (social, interactive), rather than industrial (competitive, commercial, measurable) complexes. To escape the 'persistent tension' North describes, is it not reasonable to expect that institutional and industrial complexes require different forms of evaluation and understanding (that is, sociological, qualitative)? The public expects more than merely financial management from their institutions. And if the government is answerable to the public for their financial management, then it's not unreasonable to expect that the public's sense of value should also be taken into account. As we will see, quality, shared values and memory are also very important considerations for members of the public. This is a long-term relationship, not just a short-term encounter. Nor is it a transaction devoid of value.

Cultural institutions are complex organisations and continue to exist, although uncomfortably, in creative industries policy frameworks, 'serving multiple purposes supporting multiple masters'.[53] Aligning cultural policy to 'other' policy areas has rarely delivered the expected instrumental benefits for either the cultural sector or their new policy bedfellows. Despite the best of intentions, these relationships encouraged in the UK under the creative industries rhetoric were usually proved to be inequitable:

> *Cultural policy, in practice, is in a weak position in comparison with other policy sectors that have greater access to claims of policy necessity, centrality, legitimacy or priority than does the cultural sector . . . In these circumstances, it is not surprising that the cultural policy sector tends to be seen as an embattled arena of political actions whose claims of policy centrality and importance are simply not accepted as relevant in their own right, but only in so far as they actively contribute to governments' other policy ambitions.[54]*

Regardless of this well-documented juggle between cultural or artistic aims and achieving measurable instrumental impacts, the ongoing focus on accountability and return on government investment has seen the introduction of a standardised form of quantitative language for the evaluation of cultural institutions, which can be understood by administrators and policy-makers who have little or no experience or comprehension of arts and cultural practices. This emphasis on finance-based evaluation initiated an 'audit explosion' in the UK and the inauguration of an 'audit society' across the arts and cultural sector.[55] The creative industries scholar Eleanora Belfiore has highlighted the consistently selective use of evidence of economic and instrumental impact to inform arts and creative industries policy. Even though institutions provided evidence of positive economic impact and balanced books for the auditors, it did not stop budget cuts. Eventually Belfiore called out what many in the sector have thought more than once, declaring the situation to be 'Bullshit'.[56]

Since the early 2000s a general uneasiness with financial reporting pressures has pervaded Australian cultural institutions. Kevin Fewster, then Director of the Powerhouse Museum of Applied Arts and Sciences in Sydney, noted that the economic imperatives imposed by government kept the museum focused on quantifiable up-front services, 'whether it be exhibitions, programs, the web and other things'. Fewster also suggested that government support indicated an acceptance that policy-makers and the society they represented considered 'that the role we serve is worthwhile and important to the community'.[57] Government funding does not just keep the lights on and the doors open: it is a source of validation that the institution performs a critical role in the civic life of a community. However, it's also logical that the opposite would apply: the withdrawal of government funding indicates that policy-makers no longer believe cultural institutions to be worthwhile, even if they are able to provide evidence of positive social, cultural, and economic impact. Therein lies the *contradiction* at the heart of the cultural value conversation. Institutions are forced to accept and adhere to instrumental outcomes they may not control to justify their worth in the eyes of government. For their part, governments are more inclined to see this level of success as evidence that institutions can survive with less government funding, so they withdraw it, forcing the institutions to become more dependent on commercial funding, which is tied to market realities, or the mercurial nature of sponsorship relationships. External funding then becomes essential for maintaining operations, not an optional extra to be dedicated to special or optional projects. Sponsorship thus becomes a priority area for the institutions, perhaps even at the expense of authentic cultural relevance, heritage values and collections management – their core business. As the British scholar and arts practitioner Ben Walmsley summarised: 'the arts have increasingly become subjects to the benchmarks of incompatible disciplines and practices in order to meet the demands of instrumentalist policy-makers'.[58]

The South Australian context

Since the early 1990s, the South Australian Government has considered the arts sector an industry, one whose role is to contribute to the state economy, with somewhat less regard for 'the essential nature of arts and cultural activities or of their broader social role'.[59] In recent decades, several studies and sector-wide consultations have been conducted to address the role of the arts and culture in the state's development. Unfortunately, as Jo Caust describes, these initiatives 'did not necessarily translate into promoting arts practice or arts development'. Instead, since the 1990s, the South Australian policy-makers decided that Adelaide would be positioned both publicly and politically as a 'cultural destination' rather than 'a cultural producer'.[60] The state's funding arrangements and cultural infrastructure have subsequently been geared towards importing national and international acts, artists and experiences, rather than developing an authentic local cultural identity and audience for and within the state. Hence, South Australia is promoted as the 'Festival State': a dazzling array of festival options are on offer, largely featuring imported acts, usually happening simultaneously. This festival calendar is designed to maximise marketing and tourism opportunities to showcase the best of the state for visitors. The numbers of travellers arriving at the airport rise, while bookings at restaurants and hotels skyrocket, all of which represent commendable numbers of visitors seeking an enriching art experience. Notably, these figures are also easily counted and recalculated to reflect a return on the government investment. If only it were as simple as that to quantify the impact of the Library.

As in the health and education sectors, there is a growing expectation that the South Australian cultural sector will deliver instrumental benefits, particularly economic and social impacts, as evidence of success and value, an expectation made explicit in the 'SA Arts Plan 2020–2024'. Following months of detailed consultation and submissions from across the sector, it was proposed that arts and cultural organisations, including the State Library, will 'take a whole-of-government' approach to ensure that the benefits of the arts 'are able to be realised across the range of sectors where the community interacts with government'. No additional funding was allocated to realise this goal. Ergo, the cultural sector is again expected to do more with less. To make up the shortfall, the arts plan encouraged the sector to explore opportunities 'facilitating engagement between Arts and other government departments, particularly Tourism, Multicultural Affairs, Communities and Education, along with other levels of Government and also the corporate and philanthropic sectors'.[61] These strategic policy goals have little to do with creative or cultural practice; they lack qualitative nuance and are beyond the operational capacity of institutions already running on reduced budgets.

Since the introduction of the arts plan in late 2019, the cultural sector in South Australia has been in transition. The plan, which is notable as much for its positive appraisal of the sector's potential as for the lack of funding to realise it, could not have anticipated a global pandemic. As seen across the globe, the impacts on the South Australian creative sector were immediate. Given the years of budget cuts and diminished ministerial backing, few resources were available to see many in the sector through the crisis. Policy decisions made before the pandemic led to the dismantling of Arts South Australia, the department for the arts. The essential expertise had already been lost, and other voices had greater claim on the public purse. The responsibility for managing state cultural institutions was absorbed into the Department of

Premier and Cabinet. That said, during the pandemic, it was the health, education, and the cultural sectors – essential community services – that rallied to adapt and maintain some sense of normalcy and connection for the public.

Perhaps it is an old-fashioned concept, but most arts professionals and volunteers I have worked alongside are motivated to contribute to the 'public realm' through their personal preference, professional interest and love of the arts. The public realm, or common ground, is used for the engagement, leisure and pleasure of the public, but it is also where people become active citizens within a democracy, not merely consumers.[62] This places us at odds to some of the behavioural assumptions that underpin cultural policy and market economics. We don't contribute our time, intellects and labour primarily for the money – we do it for the public good, and to share our love of cultural collections and experiences. These are significant motivations for people drawn to cultural vocations, such as those who become librarians. Nevertheless, even though we don't pursue these careers for financial gain alone, the cultural sector makes a significant contribution to the federal economy. Research conducted in support of the Australian Federal Government's *Revive* arts policy found that cultural and creative activity contributed $63.7 billion to the Australian economy, or 2.5% of Australia's GDP in 2022-23. These are good numbers.[63] As we will explore in the coming chapters, that economic impact is not the only return on government investment.

The ramifications of South Australia's outdated and underfunded cultural policy decisions have been devastating for the local sector, both major and emerging organisations alike. Perhaps the biggest losers, though, are local audiences. Without reliable and substantive funding in recent years for local infrastructure and development strategies for local audiences and artists, South Australian stories rarely make it into the public domain.

It must be challenging to be a local institution of any scale in a state that prides – if not defines – itself according to its festival calendar. Adelaide's festivals are indeed wonderful experiences: world-class, well-marketed, pre-packaged forms of entertainment. We are lucky to have them. It's difficult not to enjoy such high-quality, well-promoted world-class encounters. For most of the year, however, local South Australian companies such as the Adelaide Symphony Orchestra and State Theatre Company compete for access to venues, sponsorship and marketing budgets. Without funding for appropriate infrastructure and the promotional power that comes with government investment, local productions that do get off the ground struggle to register with potential local and interstate audiences. Unfortunately, what this well-established emphasis on major festivals has created is a city in which, for many, culture and the arts have become a special event for certain times of the year, separated from normal life; something contained (you could say 'regulated') and ultimately tied and measured by economic rather than unique artistic outcomes.

Festivals, by their nature, have a sporadic and hedonistic relationship with the public. They are created as a form of fleeting entertainment rather than as a tool for the cultural or artistic development of a specific community over time. Consequently, the success of a festival is also easily measured. Individual artists or performers may indeed tackle contentious societal topics or challenge public figures, but how many of them directly address the local South Australian case? In the 1970s, cultural historian Derek Whitelock wrote that 'Adelaide people take themselves, their city and their Festival rather seriously. Many of them feel themselves to be experts in the arts, or at least on the Festival.'[64] Many would agree that this passion for the festivals is as strong today as it was 50 years ago. The pre-eminence of the Adelaide Festival and, increasingly, the Adelaide Fringe in the South Australian cultural ecology is attributable to the decades-old government arts policies continuing into the twenty-first century.[65]

The rise of festivals to cultural dominance in Adelaide's cultural landscape coincided with the rise of neoliberalism, evidence-based arts policy-making and the 'crisis' of cultural value experienced by collecting institutions. Collections-based organisations such as museums, libraries and galleries operate continuously and over decades. They are destination institutions throughout the year and curate, exhibit and conserve both physical and intangible items in perpetuity. Although they do have goals associated with occasional events, their continuity and service-based relationship with the public mean that economic measures are an uncomfortable fit. Furthermore, the impact of public investment made today may not be evident for some time. These organisations are often quiet reflective places, filled with people reading or talking in whispers amongst objects that require careful handling and the complex specialist knowledge of experts to curate, research and conserve over decades. By comparison, festivals – discrete, readily measurable – fit the economic rationalist mindset: numbers through the door, ticket sales data, media spend, tourism visitor data and social network hits all mean that festivals are relatively simple to evaluate. These quantitative indicators provide an impression of both social and economic impact – outputs and outcomes – which funding bodies consider to be markers of success and evidence of return on investment.[66] Good numbers and much easier to show on a spreadsheet. The relationship between the public and the State Library of South Australia is entirely different from the relationship between a festival and its audience, a factor that could easily be overlooked or at least misunderstood when assessing the two types of cultural investment (festivals vs state cultural institutions) via the same quantitative reporting techniques.

The public's relationship with the State Library and the state's other cultural institutions – and how they perceive and value their experiences – extends well beyond the books, the artefacts, the artworks and the buildings, and into the city around them. As I've found, to appreciate the value of this relationship takes a lot of work and an entirely different approach. Communities of shared meaning and creativity form within and around the bricks-and-mortar of cultural institutions. Understanding is born through recognition of shared values. Across Australia, and indeed worldwide, the experience of individuals collectively supports both major cultural institutions and smaller local arts organisations, 'bringing them to life' and releasing their 'capacity for shared meaning making'.[67] The prioritisation of tourist numbers and the estimated economic impact in reporting and evaluation clouds the public and political perception of what also matters: the positive social, cultural, and creative benefits *for the people who live, work and dream in South Australia*. The evaluation procedures imposed by governments on both festivals and institutions exemplify commercially driven numbers-based approaches, which 'equate value creation predominantly with profit rather than society'.[68] This jeopardises institutions' ability to convey the value and meaning delivered for their users, irrespective of the numbers that come through the door or login online. If quantifiable estimates and outcomes are all that seem to count, how can we communicate the State Library's role, meaning and value to the community it serves throughout the year in a way that will also make sense to the decision-makers who hold its future in their hands?

Without a narrative context to balance the numbers, most of the story is lost.

'Whose value is it anyway?'

If the prevailing view is that public institutions are accountable to the public, then we should be asking the public to recognise what they value most about their public institutions. Walmsley proposed an approach, one designed to identify and capture the value generated by cultural organisations; To centralise the audience, artist or visitor perspectives of value to the strategic planning and evaluation of a cultural institution:

> There appears to be a growing awareness of the inability of market economics to reflect the social value of organisations and their resources ... makes the case for the adoption of alternative neo-institutionalist (i.e. sociocultural and practice-based) models of value based on the real-life experiences or praxis of artists and audiences.[69]

'Neo-institutional value', as Walmsley defines it, identifies the stakeholder experience and expectations as the most appropriate set of goals to be met by a cultural institution, to be used in tandem with quantitative measurement and evaluation. He does not suggest that cultural institutions should no longer report their finances and demonstrate accountability for public money, merely that this is not the *only* form of reporting to be taken seriously when considering what institutions actually produce or provide with that public money. The neo-institutionalist approach struck me as a strategically balanced perspective from which to understand what the State Library, and by extension the cultural sector, provides to the community: how 'value' is perceived and articulated by those who engage with it, and what it means to members of the public as one of the state's longest running and influential cultural institutions.

This approach rang true with my experiences working with the public and understanding the cumulative process of value creation in a cultural context, especially the reciprocal nature of the relationships between an institution and its public. While echoing North's descriptions of the propensity for institutions to confound economistic thinking,[70] Walmsley's neo-institutional approach also addresses 'misinterpreted authority' – the term used to describe the inappropriate use of economic tools and approaches in the cultural sector – by drawing on the natural language of the public and their relationships with cultural institutions. Walmsley's research was grounded in qualitative data – thematic, narrative-based profiles and case studies. He drew on an anthropological approach known as 'Deep hanging out' – spending time with audiences (in a cultural context) to understand what they derived from an experience, as they were experiencing it.[71] Walmsley explains that, by engaging with audiences directly, it is possible to tell the story of a particular arts company's value, using the voices and perspectives of their most important stakeholders. This information can then be used to plan the future and judge the success (or otherwise) of the institution from the audience's perspective, rather than from external third-party stakeholders. Walmsley discovered that companies had a much greater sense of what their audiences would or wouldn't like because *they had asked them*. Following a survey of commercial and traditional arts marketing approaches to evaluation, Walmsley concluded:

> There is perhaps a circle to square here: namely that arts organizations should place audiences at the heart of their missions and strategic objectives and evaluate their performance accordingly.[72]

Walmsley's findings aligned with my experience as a practitioner in the cultural sector: if the needs and expectations of the public are regularly met, or even occasionally exceeded, the public would be more likely to return or recommend the particular institution/event/exhibition to others, thereby also increasing the numbers through the door, the takings in the till and the overall sustainability and relevance of the institution to the public. It is good public and customer service that builds community and audiences year-round, rather than relying solely on tourist numbers at certain times of the year. Treat people well, listen to them, provide what they need, and they will come back for more – all of which the arts sector already does very well. Could understanding cultural value be that simple?

Capturing the public's perspective of cultural value is challenging, which could explain why their voice rarely makes it into today's evaluation of the State Library. That said, I believe it is more likely that their absence is related to the types of assessment preferred by funding bodies. In many instances, public servants under pressure to meet targets prefer to receive information in numbers and graphs, as a quick and efficient means of reporting results. Ministers are often too busy to read, while arts administrators are under pressure to present something that will tick the current policy boxes to keep the doors open for another year. Confronted by time, workload and financial pressures, many responsible for funding cultural institutions literally do not know what they are missing. Incorporating the public's views on the value and the rich community benefits that accrue from cultural experiences offers context and meaning for quantifiable data, acting as a counterbalance to regulatory financial reporting requirements. Embedding the quantitative and financial data into a qualitative – narrative – framework also means that the data are less susceptible to politicisation or being leveraged against changeable strategic goals or policy shifts. It tells the whole story, interpreting the data rather than leaving it to be inferred, clouded, or misinterpreted.

Despite his critics, John Holden had a similar, and powerfully simple, suggestion for identifying the value of culture: 'what you want to know is the value that people collectively place on culture. And so you must ask them'.[73] This approach, like Walmsley's, seems like sound and sensible advice for establishing the cultural value of the State Library of South Australia, so I took their suggestion: What would a random sample of visitors share with me about their experience of the Library and what does, in their words, cultural value mean? Whatever I thought I might find, nothing really prepared me for the simple beauty of the stories shared with me by strangers, stories linking today's experience at the State Library not only to the ideals behind the institution's history and origins, but also to what makes us human.

Chapter 3

Libraries, literacy and a distinctive state of mind

Not surprisingly, the history of a public institution like the State Library of South Australia mirrors the history of its people.[1] The historical context of the late eighteenth and nineteenth centuries that gave rise to the formation of the State Library also saw the spread of literacy amongst the general population of Great Britain. No longer the preserve of the elite, reading and public discussion drove the establishment of public libraries and mechanics institutes, mutual improvement societies, public reading rooms, and subscription and circulating libraries across England, Scotland and Wales. The values and ideals underpinning this movement – democracy, universal education and knowledge exchange – were deliberately transferred to the new colony of South Australia, despite facing some predictable obstacles, such as the lack of secure financing and political support. Today, the Library is promoted as an agent facilitating social inclusion and identity, although for much of its early existence it was exclusive and discriminatory. Access to the spaces and resources was originally limited solely to white men of the elite social order. (There is evidence that even dogs were allowed in, before women and non-Caucasian members of the community.) However, traces of the founding ideals and democratic values associated with universal access to education and library resources survived and still inform the public experience of the State Library.

The rationale for a library in the colony of South Australia arose from the nineteenth-century appeal of libraries as social, educational, and cultural sites in the new urban industrial centres of

England. The high literacy levels of aspirational migrants made this imperative for the new colony. The idealised institution was intended as an instrumental mediator of British values, a tool by which 'civilisation' could be transplanted from one side of the world to the other. The early history of the State Library of South Australia, with its challenges and the fierce public debates on access and funding, reveals three important factors: the relationship between the inhabitants of the new colony and their distant imperial government; the expectations and rights of citizens to access their cultural heritage; and the extent to which today's institution has evolved from these conflicted origins.

Not everyone is familiar with the colonisation and heritage of South Australia. This state's intriguing history goes some way to explaining the South Australian character, community and identity, which is held to be more progressive and distinct from other Australian states.[2] This brief overview of South Australian history is essential to understanding how the public connects their experiences today to the heritage of the State Library site on North Terrace. This chapter also introduces two of the key arguments of this book: that the success of cultural institutions is inseparable from the vagaries of their economic and political contexts, and that fundamental to an understanding of culture's value is the role played by time.

Conversations about the role and functions of the State Library, along with the arguments about how it should be funded and by whom, are as old as the institution itself – indeed, older than the city of Adelaide. With its deliberate planning and entrepreneurial ambitions, 'South Australia was very pleased to see itself as a new start, with land sales, immigration of respectable people, education, religion, no convicts, indeed a paradise of dissent. It may just as appropriately be called a paradise of deception'.[3] For all the persistent claims to its uniqueness and difference, we need to remember that South Australian history remains a deeply contested space, one in which the familiar patterns of colonisation, the disenchantment of colonists, and the displacement and destruction of Indigenous cultures played out with tragic predictability. The aspirations of the South Australian enterprise and how that plan was realised on the ground 'may have had some impact on the cultural and artistic development of the state'.[4] Perhaps the stop-start nature of the early State Library's development set the tone for decades to come, but the original dream survived and eventually prevailed – largely due to the will and needs of the public.

Later in this chapter, I give an overview of some of the history and the ideals that were part of it, although it is far from being an in-depth historical account of South Australia's history and every step taken towards a truly public state library in South Australia.[5] I have drawn out certain strands of that history because they cast light on something that I have found fascinating: how today's public relates to the Library and its history; and how the early aspirations that informed the Library's development still inform the present-day experience, more than 150 years later. This continuity and civic pride are a significant part of the institutional value of not only the Library, but all institutions that comprise the North Terrace Cultural Precinct.

The temper of the times

The story of the State Library begins with the plans for the colonisation and settlement of South Australia by a group of British entrepreneurs in the mid-nineteenth century. This enterprise was born from the tumult of the early decades of the nineteenth century when Great Britain was at the centre of an expansive colonial empire. However, it was also grappling with a melange of forces disrupting traditional ways of life: the Industrial Revolution, the spread of Enlightenment ideals, the perceived influence of the French Revolution, and an explosive birth rate. The social, economic, political, intellectual and geographic landscapes were being transformed in ways that could not have been foreseen a century earlier, and which many believed required support and regulation.[6] For the price of a subscription fee, early public libraries across Great Britain provided reading materials, lectures and comfortable rooms in which members of the public could gather, discuss and explore the innovations in science, technology, literature and politics that were changing their world around them. Libraries formed and adapted 'neatly with the ebb and flow of Victorian social crises' and were also promoted 'as a panacea for social instability'.[7] 'Keep calm and read a book' might have been the mantra. Libraries also played an instrumental role in social regulation. They were sites where the public were required to abide by acceptable standards relating to dress, behaviour and noise levels (thus was created the shushing librarian). They 'have rarely been socially uncontroversial institutions':

> From their inception in 1850 public libraries were presented by librarians, reformers and benefactors as vehicles for social integration and harmonisation. Behind this façade of neutrality, however, the Victorian public library was value-laden and, far from acting as a passive provider of books and other reading materials, reflected (and contributed to) the tensions associated with nineteenth-century transformations.[8]

By the 1830s, literacy and the benefits of education had spread well beyond the wealthy elite of British society. The working classes of nineteenth-century Great Britain were far from illiterate and ill-informed; many had learned the basics of literacy and numeracy at church. Further instruction supported their roles as mechanics or farm labourers. Weavers, before the mechanisation of the industry, were 'legendary for their habit of reading at the loom'.[9] Libraries developed symbiotically alongside these rising literacy levels to supply reading materials to people who could not necessarily afford them. As the political landscape changed and new parties emerged advocating for increased access to the vote, many believed that 'no disenfranchised people could be emancipated unless they created an autonomous intellectual life', built on and nourished by access to quality reading material: 'the politics of equality must begin by redistributing this knowledge to the governed classes'.[10] Universal education became part of the government's responsibility to support an informed democracy.

The rise of literacy, literature and libraries in Great Britain explains the high level of importance that those emigrating to South Australia placed on the promise of a library. Literature and reading were a major part of their lives. These were not uneducated labourers being transported to serve yet another master. They were aspirational, enfranchised and reasonably educated colonists seeking better lives for themselves and their families. If anything, they were perhaps too idealistic, too trusting in the founding entrepreneurs, who were promoting the promise of freedom and independence in the new colony, but who would first secure their own wealth, advantages and social superiority. However, the dream of a utopian 'Paradise of Dissent'.[11] has survived the disenchantments and betrayals that took place in the early colony. The dream lives on in the experience and identity of the public today.

Colonisation

The planning and development of the Library was initiated two years before the first British colonists had departed from England. In August 1834, a group of communitarian entrepreneurs, religious idealists and Chartist radicals pushed through parliament a plan to establish a utopian society on the shores of southeastern Australia. The Provisional Committee of the South Australian Association (SAA) developed a plan for the transplantation 'not of a seedling, but of the full-grown tree of English society, root, trunk and branch'.[12] Provision for educating the colonists was considered as essential as defence and security. Education and literacy were viewed 'as a means of self-improvement and even a way of creating a better society'.[13]

Confident of their success, the SAA agreed that, in return for the granting of regal authority, the new colony would come at no cost to the British Government, even though the government stood to benefit from the creation of new markets, access to valuable tracts of land, and migration. The scheme was also seen as the solution to 'the problem of rural unemployment'.[14] The profits of land sales would fund the migration of skilled workers. These skilled (and literate) workers in turn could save to buy their own property, thus funding the transport of more settlers, increase the population and develop a sustainable economy.[15] Many wealthy Britons were able to get in early, purchasing vast tracts of arable land 'site unseen' in the belief that the investment would be 'money for jam'.[16] They would not need to leave the comfort of their homes in England to profit from their investment in a venture based on the other side of the world.

Potential settlers had been sold the concept of a utopian 'Paradise of Dissent', free of the class distinctions and convict stain that had marred the earlier settlements established in what would become Australia. By refusing to admit convicts and initiating protective measures for the Indigenous inhabitants, the SAA hoped to avoid the disastrous frontier catastrophes experienced in Sydney, Perth and Hobart.

The Adelaide Plains had been home to the Kaurna people for millennia. It is estimated that the Indigenous population numbered approximately 15,000 at the time of European contact.[17] Following the abolition of slavery in England in 1833, the leaders of the emancipation movement turned their attention to the treatment of Indigenous populations throughout the British Empire.[18] The question of Aboriginal rights was hard to avoid in both England and Australia.[19] The South Australian colonists were very much aware of violent conflicts over land ownership and authority, and the ongoing tensions between Indigenous people and British settlers in Western Australia, Tasmania and New South Wales. This awareness, however, did not impede the systematic colonisation of South Australia. To circumvent the property rights of all Aboriginal people, members of the SAA proposed establishing the colony on lands described as 'waste and unoccupied' and 'fit for colonisation'.[20] Colonel Robert Torrens, a prominent economist and then commissioner of the SAA, argued that 'the unlocated tribes had not arrived at the stage of social improvement at which a propriety right to the soil exists'.[21] The banks of the river that came to bear the name of Colonel Torrens was chosen as the site of colonial settlement. The Kaurna people know this river as Karrawirraparri, 'a sacred river', believed to be a mirror of 'the night sky – which represents . . . the afterlife'.[22] The banks of the river were important residential, hunting and ceremonial sites up to and during the time of colonial settlement. However, by denying the Indigenous community legal status and property rights, the settlers perceived no need to purchase the land. The colonial venture proceeded. The strategy was based on a lie and was entirely unethical; the Kaurna did not formally cede their land to the colonists. Gradually Aboriginal groups were dispossessed of their lands and removed from the urban site of Adelaide, first to the western edge of the settlement and sub-sequently, in later decades, to other parts of the state:

> The government provided homes for Aboriginal settlement, and the 'Native School', where Aboriginal children were trained in English language, the Bible and the kind of practical skills that would make them useful servants to Europeans.[23]

I have seen no evidence to suggest there was any provision to supply the Native School with secular books or other reading material, or to allow its students access to the colony's proposed library, the seeds of which were planted two years before the colonists set sail from England.

South Australian Literary and Scientific Association

Two weeks after the Royal Licence for the founding of the new colony was granted, and more than two years before the first colonists would depart from England, one of the founding members of the SA Association, the lawyer Richard Davies Hanson, delivered the inaugural address to the South Australian Literary Association (SALA) on 29 August 1834 in London. Within three weeks, the association changed their name to become the South Australian Literary and Scientific Association.[24] Hanson proclaimed that their consortium was 'engaged in a unique experiment; and that never before had such enlightened planning for the cultivation and diffusion of knowledge in a new country been developed'.[25]

During the planning of the South Australian colony, Western culture and education were considered civilising, regulatory social forces, and libraries were the vehicles intended to deliver this service. Therefore, the first iteration of the State Library was expected to fulfil a range of aspirational and instrumental goals: as a tool of education, acculturation, and social moderation for the proposed new society. The weight of expectation was enormous and, it could be said, doomed to failure. The proposed library was to suffer from scant consideration by the colony's leadership, who were distracted by land sales, law and order, and the search for a dependable source of fresh water. It would be years before most colonists would be allowed to access books collected on their behalf. Even less thought was given to what they would want to read.

The South Australian Literary and Scientific Association (SALSA) was a subcommittee of the South Australian Association and featured several members of the SAA Committee, notably its first Secretary, Rowland Hill, and the influential colonist Robert Gouger. The Scientific and Literary Association assembled a collection of books and pamphlets from its members to form the core of a library with a single object: 'the cultivation and diffusion of useful knowledge throughout the colony',[26] a mission reflecting the goals – and the name – of a well-established community-based educational movement, the Society for the Diffusion of Useful Knowledge (SDUK), the most influential and controversial educational program in early nineteenth-century Britain.[27]

The SDUK was created to support the universal emancipation of working men and represented an exercise in 'cooperative education', encouraging interested groups of men to meet and share reading materials provided by the SDUK:

> *In its classic form, it consisted of half a dozen or a hundred men*
> *from both the working and lower-classes who met periodically,*

sometimes in their own homes, but commonly under the aus-
pices of a church or chapel. Typically, one member would
deliver a paper on any imaginable subject – politics, literature,
religion, ethics, useful knowledge – and then the topic would
be thrown open to general discussion. The aim was to develop
the verbal and intellectual skills of people who had never been
encouraged to speak or think.[28]

The SDUK differed in several ways from mechanics institutes. Where the institutes targeted professions-based audiences and offered structured formalised courses, the SDUK espoused broader aims: to provide all sectors of society with the tools (through their series of publications) for exploring areas of common interest and pursuing their education on their own terms. Some supporters proudly claimed that the SDUK aspired 'to promote a love of freedom, and of peace, by educating the people and elevating their tastes'.[29] The SDUK committee would tour the country with its publisher Charles Knight to encourage small community groups to pool resources and share publications. Basically, they would sell reading materials to anyone who wanted them. If these were beyond the reach of an interested community, the committee would give them away, leaving publications at the local inns where people regularly gathered. Other committee members, acting in the spirit of philanthropy, bought texts and 'donated' them to institutes. There were no official teachers, syllabus or hierarchy; pupils would cooperatively support each other, contributing what they could to share, analyse and exchange knowledge to expand and build common understanding in their communities.

The SDUK and other self-improvement societies were also motivated by more pragmatic issues. If more people were to be allowed to vote, it would be best for everyone if were capable of making well-informed decisions. Some commentators saw this drive towards mutual improvement amongst the working classes as an effort to conform to middle-class sensibilities; 'a capitulation to bourgeois cultural hegemony' and part of the regulatory function of early urban cultural institutions. Others, from a working-class perspective, believed it was more 'a return of the oppressed'.[30] People who had previously had little say in how their country was governed were arming themselves for a social and political revolution.

Combining the working-class appetite for education and the philanthropic bent of progressive idealists, the SDUK, with its mutual improvement model of 'cooperative education' and shared resources, appealed to the SALSA committee members for important reasons: there was no generous budget for organised education – the colonists would have to take care of their own learning needs for some time, and the more they shared and the less opportunity they had to access new radical texts, which could foment dissent amongst the fledgling community, the better. By including the phrase 'the diffusion of useful knowledge' in its foundational documents, the Literary and Scientific Association committee aligned itself with the Society for the Diffusion of Useful Knowledge, an organisation already well known amongst potential migrants to South Australia. It is not surprising there-fore that these migrants also expected a similarly egalitarian ease of access to publications and learning opportunities. Such a dis-tributed model would have allowed the Scientific and Literary Association to fulfil its promise to provide educational resources in the new colony. However, the new colony lacked both a local government and any form of philanthropic sector to enable them to do so. This did not prevent a handful of bibliophiles amongst them from keeping the dream of a library alive.

Robert Gouger was one of the founders of the South Australian Association and the colony's first Colonial Secretary. In 1834 he began collecting books to be read by colonists during the voyage, which later formed the basis of the proposed circulating library.[31] These non-fictional 'handbooks' included accounts of exploration and settlement in Western Australia, New South Wales and Van Diemen's Land, as well as further afield, in India, New Zealand, Canada and Sierra Leone. Amongst the collection were texts examining the North American colonial experience: the memoirs and correspondence of Thomas Jefferson, *Comparisons Between England and North America*, *Manual for Emigrants to North America* and *A Moral and Political Sketch of North America* by Achille Murat.[32] Today, these and other surviving texts from the South Australian Scientific and Literary Association form the Gouger Collection and remain on display in the Mortlock Wing of the State Library of South Australia.

The Scientific and Literary Association and the SDUK shared committee members and founders who promoted lifelong learning and access to education. There were also some very strong family ties between the two organisations, which were transferred to South Australia and influenced the foundation of the State Library. Matthew Davenport Hill was a lawyer who rode the wave of political reform to become the first Member for Hull in the House of Commons. He was joined on the Scientific and Literary Association committee by his brother Rowland Hill. These brothers from Birmingham had arrived in London after having successfully published a treatise on public education reforms, which extolled a mutually supportive combination of students, self-sufficiency and personal responsibility. Crucially, it attracted the admiration of the renowned philosopher and reformer Jeremy Bentham. Through his subsequent association with Bentham, and as a new Member of Parliament, Matthew was introduced to Lord Brougham, who, in the 1820s, had contributed to the founding of the Society for the Diffusion of Useful Knowledge. Matthew Davenport Hill was one of the members of parliament who ushered the Bill to establish South Australia into law, devoting 'himself to the drudgery of making it known, and rendering its provisions acceptable'.[33] He did so 'on behalf of his brother Rowland's interests', describing him as one of the founders of the SDUK in 1826, along with Lord Brougham and publisher Charles Knight.[34]

Rowland Hill became the Secretary of the South Australian Association and arranged for the donation of SDUK publications, valued at 10 pounds, to the nascent library collection.[35] Today, Rowland Hill is also remembered for the development of the first postage stamp and the revolutionary Penny Postage system, implemented in 1837. His creation of pre-paid postage gave all classes access to affordable mail. Until this innovation, postage was paid on delivery by the recipient and was prohibitive for many in the working classes. Hill's monumental reform is credited with fostering literacy and communication across the British Empire.[36] His drive to improve the postal system began when he was 'still connected with the South Australian project', perhaps in contemplation of maintaining family and cultural ties between the colonists and 'home'.[37]

The Hill brothers have been described as exemplars of Victorian reform, who over time transitioned from libertarian ideals to an 'acceptance of regulation',[38] a description also applicable to many involved in the South Australian colonial experiment. Together, Matthew Davenport Hill and Rowland Hill contributed to the formation of the colony of South Australia and revolutionised the education of the working public via the distribution of accessible reading material throughout the then British Empire.[39] However, it would be their nephew John Howard Clark who ensured the establishment of the State Library of South Australia.

Amongst the collection of publications collected for the first library was a selection of pamphlets donated by the SDUK and organised by Rowland Hill. He delegated the selection of items to John Hindmarsh, the colony's first governor.[40] The donation from the SDUK brought the total collection to 'a little over 500 volumes, as well as some pamphlets, loose serials and maps'.[41] In 1836, this extensive collection was packed into a heavy trunk and loaded aboard the *Tam O'Shanter*, bound for the Gulf of St Vincent.

The members of the Scientific and Literary Association believed they were responsible for guiding the behaviour of the labouring classes of the new colony and ensuring they were not tempted by potentially dangerous political thought. Hanson, Gouger's fellow member of the SA Association, promoted the idea that:

> The real interests of all classes are identical . . . But it is obvious,
> that among those who go out as labourers we must expect to
> have many who are deeply imbued with the doctrines now

prevalent among the class to which they belong ... it will
therefore behove us to take care that an antidote is provided.[42]

Hanson expressed a genuine concern: the colony had little by way of military presence and limited capacity for law enforcement. With a stubbornly persistent class-based form of governance underpinning the colony and the French Revolution still a recent memory, the colony's leaders could not afford the dissemination of radical ideas. This prompted the leading colonists to initiate the regulation of workers' access to potentially inflammatory reading material. Hanson's antidote was one already accepted in Great Britain as having assisted in the transition of the rural population to new urban areas. The antidote to dissent was supervised learning, and for that there needed to be a library.

The original aims of the Literary and Scientific Association were indeed lofty. Their collection of books to enable settlers to share in the wealth of the new knowledge, to promote creativity and sustain the economic prosperity of the colony was very well-intentioned. However, the arrival of the *Tam O'Shanter* at Port Adelaide did not go according to plan, nor did it bode well for the precious trunk full of books and plans for learning in the colony:

> *Arriving at the Port river in December 1836, she first struck a*
> *sandbar and was tilted there on her side at a precarious angle*
> *by the flood tide ... The heavy iron box was taken ashore by*
> *boat but, in the process, it was inadvertently dropped over-*
> *board and had to be fished up from the riverbed.*[43]

To add insult to injury, once the trunk was landed, it was stored in a warehouse, where it lay undisturbed for two years. According to Bridge, this may have been due to a number of reasons: the colonists had more pressing matters of survival to attend to, the books were waterlogged and left to dry out, and no one could find the key.[44]

The earliest iteration of the State Library was designed as an instrumental mechanism for social regulation and education, and although intended for the many, it eventually became accessible to just a few. The first mechanics institute in Adelaide was funded by subscriptions, eventually failing with the colony's first economic crisis. In 1840 those colonists with the wealth and privilege entailed in prior land ownership, and a degree of imported cultural capital, chose to establish the library as an exclusive gentlemen's club, limited by exorbitant membership fees and regulations. Membership was available through invitation only, and no working men could join. Women were not eligible either, forcing them to rely on the men in their families to make selections on their behalf. These were not new forms of social and cultural discrimination: they replicated and reinforced the class and gender divisions that working settlers believed they had left behind. Many realised they had fallen for a utopian dream, waking up to a new reality, which was far more feudal.

Early Adelaide and the birth of a literary identity

The promises made about South Australia seduced a stream of working migrants 'who believed that they only needed the fuller and freer life of Australia to enable them to find an outlet for the energies of themselves and families, and a real chance of bettering their positions'.[45] The assisted emigrants from the UK, selected for their vocational capabilities, were both enterprising and literate. Four out of five were able to read, and of these, more than half could both read and write.[46] The new arrivals to South Australia had been led to believe they would be able to access a library of books to improve their education and foster their imaginations. Unfortunately, this was not their only disappointment.

British settlers faced a complex new reality and a challenging way of life in the Antipodes. Those who travelled to the Australian colonies were often considered to be voluntarily exiling themselves from acceptable British society, thus becoming forever associated with the perceived criminality and moral corruption of prisoners deported from England to penal colonies in Australia. According to the Adelaide historian Paul Sendziuk, the founders of South Australia felt the success of their colonial venture rested on maintaining a convict-free society – not for any philanthropic reasons but for economic advantages and social respectability.[47] The perceived danger of criminal corruption was so strong that the SAA incorporated prominent references to being a 'free state'. It was hoped that promoting this strategy in the marketing material would appeal to potential migrants wary of damaging their reputations at home and abroad.

Books played a galvanising role in promoting the 'rightness' of emigration, reassuring migrants that their actions and energies were contributing to the success of an expansionist British Empire:

> Settler readers were front-line agents, vehicles for the dissemination of ideas and values that normalised and neutralised their activities: the real-world activities of political domination, exploitation and cultural destruction. Proud of their Britishness, Australian settlers read books that organised and reinforced 'perceptions of Britain as a dominant world power' and 'contributed to the complex of attitudes that made imperialism seem part of the order of things' . . . But the colonial newcomers, as they set about creating another Britain from the social and institutional structures, technologies and skills, narratives and cognitive maps they carried over with them, also found themselves alienated from their homeland, and out of place in their new country.[48]

Removed from the familiarity of their surroundings and transplanted to the other side of the world, many migrants brought their collections of books, including favourite novels, with them. Others also turned to the promise of a library to maintain their cultural identity and their imaginary links with the people and places they'd left behind. Coping with the brutal realities of distance and dislocation, many colonists were looking for a wide variety in their reading diet. They expected more than 'useful information' from the library; they needed creative works to stimulate their imaginations. What they were seeking were comfort and solace, and by extension the confidence and reassurance of personal and community identity in the imaginative familiar, provided by the literary connections to their home culture – a comforting 'common ground' on which to build their dreams and construct their new society. However, their new society came to mirror many of the social and economic difficulties and structures they had hoped to leave behind, including a suspicion of novel-reading. The practice of reading novels had gained in popularity, as serialisation and cheap availability made them more accessible. By the early nineteenth century, the sympathetic reading of fiction had garnered a problematic reputation:

> *Working-class novel reading had become suspect by the 1830s ... Reading was likened to a disease and an addiction to which working people were naturally more vulnerable ... comparing working class reading to gin drinking, and the journal longed to 'extinguish this fever of curiosity' that manifested itself in popular reading.*[49]

At a time when the joys of being absorbed in a good book would have been a balm for weary dislocated souls, the promise of a library would have gained significance.

According to Australian historian Manning Clark, John Hindmarsh, the colony's first governor, was known to be a 'wild ass of a man'.[50] A-less-than-effective governor, he was also the *ex officio* President and local representative of the SA Literary Association and was expected to take an active interest in the collection of books that represented the colony's library. He appears, though, to have overlooked that point in his job description; instead, he 'made it plain that he would not support a library in South Australia: "What good will books do our colony?"'[51] The nascent State Library was over-burdened by expectations and unsupported by the financial or political means to deliver them.

As Carl Bridge, the author of the State Library's history, puts it: 'puffing in London about an ideal colony and library was one thing; establishing them on the shores of the Gulf of St Vincent was quite a different matter'.[52] The hoped-for library was deprived of an effective champion and devoid of an official representative to promote and implement the vision; nor was there a workable management model or any funding available to make a library a reality. The aspirational collection of 'useful knowledge', compiled by the SAA for the working settlers, became little more than unaccompanied baggage, which was eventually claimed by the new colonial elite and moved beyond public reach. Between the dunking of the trunk holding the Literary Association's collection of books as it was carried from the *Tam O'Shanter* and the neglect of the colony's first and subsequent governors, the Scientific and Literary Association did not survive the voyage out from England. The organisation had already been 'usurped . . . by a Conversazione Club which met on alternative Wednesdays in London to discuss Colonists' problems and to drink tea'.[53] The original members charged with championing the concept of a library had either lost interest or resigned from their positions of influence.

The working colonists, dislocated from their familiar environment and deprived of their promised opportunities of land ownership and culture, had to live with their disappointment or turn to each other for support. A free public library remained an intangible symbol of culture and education in the new colony. Decades would pass before the goals of the Scientific and Literary Association were realised in a public institution capable of delivering the instrumental benefits expected of the colonial administrators, and the intrinsic values demanded by Adelaide's early reading public.

A library too far away

With no government funding available, any proposal for a public library would be dependent on subscription fees, an approach that replicated the user-pays model underpinning the mechanics institutes in the UK. However, in the new colony, this model had little chance of success in times of economic hardship. During the early

1840s, when the economic fortunes of the colony were so dire as to call into question the venture's viability, subscriptions to the library plummeted and the first library folded. As the only asset available to the administrators, the collection of books assembled in London with the noblest of intentions was ignominiously deposited with a money lender to cover a debt of 20 pounds.[54] By 1845, the economic engine of the state kicked into life. Wheat sales picked up and copper had been discovered around Kapunda and Burra. This relative boom time boosted confidence and prosperity for both the local administration and some landowners. A private group of moneyed gentlemen, intending to form a private reading club, retrieved the Literary Association's books from the money lender.[55] Only carefully selected subscribers would be admitted to this new reading club. According to reports in the *South Australian* newspaper, this exclusivity incensed the public, many still struggling to scrape together a subsistence living:

> *Does it not occur to you or to the gentlemen who have the management of the institution . . . that there may be many to whom it would be most desirable to throw open the doors of the Subscription Library – who may not have, or who cannot afford the means? Is it not notorious that the class who would derive most advantage from access to the Library, and from whose lucubrations there the colony also would probably derive benefit, are not ordinarily much burdened with superfluous cash. To make no provision . . . is . . . very illiberal and exhibits the Muses in a very unsocial light.[56]*

As the fortunes of the colony ebbed and flowed, the private reading club sank in dire financial straits. For any form of library to survive, an alliance that spanned the class divide was essential: one side of the divide represented workers who demanded access to educational texts and opportunities to improve themselves, and the other represented the new elite – those enjoying their positions as major landowners. Both parties were passionate about establishing the library, yet disagreed about the purpose – reading for enjoyment or for education – and who should pay. A new coalition of administrators was formed and was granted access to government funds, on condition that they agreed to share resources, that the facility be made available to all men, and would provide educational opportunities for the public.[57] This version of the library was expected to provide access to books, as well as social and cultural exchange, rather along the lines of the institute format. However, some workers were more interested in access to classes, given that 'a few needed to learn to read first' before they could appreciate the collection of books or gain much from a lecture series.[58]

In October 1847, in rented rooms on Hindley Street, the combined Adelaide Institute and Subscription Library hosted a gathering to celebrate their official opening and launch a fundraising campaign for a purpose-built library. It sounds as if it was quite a night. There was:

A lengthy pointed, and eloquent address upon the advantages of education to the 250 Adelaideans assembled, mostly 'of the softer sex'. The walls were covered with pictures, including an engraving of the Duke of Wellington, taken from a daguerreotype likeness. Dr Kent's electro-magnetic battery, Mr Berry's model steam engine, and a seraphine, or reed instrument, made by a young man called Adamson, by trade a wheelwright, together with some geological specimens, were much admired. Mr Witton played music and refreshments were had for a shilling. All agreed it was a 'very brilliant affair', so much so that on the night Mr Stephens of the Bank promised to donate a piece of land to build an institution and six gentlemen between them promised forty-five pounds to start a building fund . . . Unfortunately, nothing came of it in bricks and mortar.[59]

Colonial Adelaideans, especially the women amongst them, were clearly avid consumers of culture, but not necessarily as eager (or able) to provide the required financial support. The combination of the two library models – subscription and public funding – was intended to unite social classes, span disciplinary interest and safeguard the collection. The appetite was there, but not the means. Within a year, the struggles of the Institute reflected broader societal and cultural clashes:

> *The mechanics and the gentlemen were not getting on with each other. Lectures were interrupted by 'ill-bred' persons 'stamping' and 'hissing' as in 'pot-houses' the Register complained; on the other hand, 'Quill' wrote to the paper that the Institute had been swamped by 'clergy, landowners and employers' and this new 'aristocratic tone' was discouraging to the 'people'.[60]*

The fate of the fledgling institution mirrored the standards and structures, behaviours and fears of the new experimental society developing around it. This has been the State Library's destiny ever since. What was required to establish an accessible and sustainable public library was an independent and active arbiter, to balance the interests of the moneyed subscribers with the educational needs and aspirations of the public. The library would also require the financial clout to ride out the colony's economic fluctuations. This was to be the role of a representative elected government, just as soon as the colony could get one.

Learning from history

Several factors were involved in the establishment of the first public library in South Australia, with these remaining relevant to the cultural value of the State Library today: time and persistence; the relationship between the public and their government; and government's responsibility to provide political and financial support for the Library.

History records too few of the people who passionately pursued the establishment of an accessible library in South Australia. There is one individual, though, who represents the connection between the first effective public library and its roots in the

Society for the Diffusion of Useful Knowledge. John Howard Clark arrived in the colony with his parents in 1850. He was not only a promising accountant, which would have been helpful in any new community; he was also the nephew of Rowland Hill and Matthew Davenport Hill. The son of Caroline Clark, the sister of the Hill brothers, he shared the family commitment to self-improvement through education. Clark's father Francis Clark had kept a journal of their voyage to Port Adelaide on board *The Fatima*, in which he recorded his longitude and latitude positions, sightings of birds, whales and constellations, as well as the number of pages he read out loud each day to his fellow passengers from the books accompanying him on the voyage.[61] The back pages of his journal, kept as part of today's SLSA Special Collections, are also filled with an inventory of the family's precious collection of books. Given this love of reading and education, it's not surprising that the family became involved in the conversations around the promised library for Adelaide.

John Howard Clark quickly gained a reputation as 'the most proficient accountant in the colony'.[62] He became both a successful businessman and a vocal advocate for a free public library in Adelaide. A fascinating polymath, Clark was drawn to the Institute and was elected its first secretary in 1851.[63] Indispensable for his financial management skills, political know-how and passion for public education, he remained associated with the Library and education sector of South Australia until his death in 1878.

The second factor contributing to the advent of the first public library was the establishment in 1857 of a democratically elected bicameral parliament, finally enabling self-government in South Australia, some 21 years after the colonists had arrived. A period of political instability followed, which would remain a feature for the remainder of the century.[64] However, a democratic South Australian government, even a mildly dysfunctional one, could still be effective – and responsive to community pressure.

Clark joined forces with two fellow library advocates to secure a sustainable future for a public library. Benjamin Babbage was an engineer and founder of the Adelaide Philosophical Society (the forerunner of the Royal Society of South Australia). Charles Mann, the Crown Solicitor, had been involved in the discussions around establishing a library in SA for 17 years. Together they lobbied members of the new parliament, convincing them that the government of South Australia should assume 'a permanent responsibility to provide a library for the public'.[65] This responsibility was enshrined in law by the colony's Board of Governors as the first Libraries Act, in 1856. This Act enabled the construction of a permanent building to house the South Australian Institute and its library on the corner of North Terrace and Kintore Avenue. It also established the government's responsibility to provide for the running costs for a reference library for the public. Those wishing to borrow would need to pay a minor subscription fee. This legislative rubber stamp ratified the role of government in the continuing responsibility for the provision of library services in South Australia.

This ongoing partnership, established over 160 years ago, is a critical component of the State Library's institutional value. It has also permitted a more democratic understanding of the Library's purpose. The often-heated arguments around the value of reading for pleasure, as opposed to the importance of reading for the self-improvement of individuals and society, continued. I even found while interviewing members of the public that those arguments persist. The most critical issue in these arguments was, and continues to be, *who* should pay for the use of the Library.[66] Then, as now, this tension is arbitrated by the government, and balanced by the institutional value created by the relationship between the institution and the public. This tension can be viewed as a colonial example of the current dichotomy between intrinsic and instrumental values: is investment in culture only worthwhile when it has positive economic impact, or can it be justified when spent on something intangible, such as a perceived improvement in a community's quality of life?

Until there was a representative government for the public in South Australia, there was no balance between the intrinsic concerns of the reading public and the anticipated instrumental benefits. Nor was there an independent body to speak for all citizens. These early conflicts reflected the power struggles arising from the colony's often dire economic circumstances, the commercial priorities of its early ruling elite, and the ongoing imperative of the colonists to be able to access books for both pleasure and education. The long-term financial commitment to the Library, sanctioned by the first Act of 1856, enabled the institution to evince a sense of confidence, fostering continuity, access, agreed behaviours and clear responsibilities. The Act legitimised the endeavour, fulfilling the institutional role of government to ensure the Library's continuity of purpose and providing a site and a service that belonged to all citizens. Although it still took time before all were permitted access and subscriptions were not required, this long-term commitment allowed for the beginning of 'the invisible work of culture formation'.[67]

Many scholars have observed in recent decades that the legitimising impact of government support for arts and cultural institutions cannot be over-estimated. In South Australia, the public–private partnership in 1856 sparked the development of what is now formally recognised as the North Terrace Cultural Precinct. By 1860, the South Australian Institute, as it was to be known, had been constructed and opened with the purpose of providing 'lectures, classes, and otherwise, to promote the general study and cultivation of all or any of the various branches of arts, science, literature and philosophy'.[68] From this building, various boards established the South Australian Museum and the first art gallery for South Australia. The building also became the venue for the first university exams (for those hoping to qualify for English tertiary placements). Seven years after the opening of the Institute, the demand for library and cultural services had outgrown the site, and the Institute's board was lobbying for more support to expand the premises. In the meantime, Clark had begun to address the need for rural access to library collections. Possibly inspired by similar schemes in early nineteenth-century England, and influenced by his uncles' roles with the Society for the Diffusion of Useful Knowledge, Clark conceived of a box system to circulate the collection across the regions.

> *The sturdy wooden boxes were lined with green baize and designed so that they had the appearance of a bookshelf when rested upright on one side. They were about three feet long, two feet wide, and foot high, with screw down lids. Each contained fifty or more volumes, mostly in the general literature category – essays, biographies, travels – with some popular science and standard novels.*[69]

The excitement for avid regional readers on the day these functional and aesthetically designed objects arrived in town can only be imagined. The first were sent out in September 1859. As simple as Clark's system for the diffusion of knowledge in South Australia may sound, it was revolutionary and actually 'in the forefront of library development in the world at the time'.[70]

The stalwart Institute Building still stands today, having outlasted several tenants – and the original commercial interests across the road. It embodies the ideals and values of the original South Australian Literary Association and, for many members of the public, has grown to become a daily symbol of the utopian aspirations that informed South Australia's progressive political legacy and community identity. The ongoing public desire to read, learn and exchange information, in combination with the legislative clout of the South Australian Government, drove the establishment of the State Library and, by extension, the culture of South Australia. This formative need, I would argue, was more successful than the early attempts by some colonial administrators to shape and regulate the library's public.

Both the concept of cultural value and South Australia's cultural policy environment have changed radically since the nineteenth century. However, the State Library remains in public hands and is a statutory authority, governed by the *Libraries Act 1982* and within the terms of an agreement between local and state governments. Unlike most other Australian state libraries, the State

Library of South Australia remains part of the Public Library Services, which oversees the statewide public library network. This is a legacy of its origins in the highly influential Institute network.[71] The former was born from the trunk full of books, but the latter evolved with the support of Clark's book boxes. The current corporate structure sees the Director of the State Library reporting to both the Department of Premier and Cabinet and the Libraries Board of South Australia. This structure balances the responsibilities of maintaining South Australia's reference collection with the trusted role of mentoring and supporting a broader state network of lending libraries, providing invaluable services to communities around South Australia, while continually adapting to their changing political, economic and social environments.

This chapter has brought us back to what value means now, and why libraries, these stalwart centuries-old cultural institutions, continue to matter to us in a world very different from the one in which they were established. What does the State Library of South Australia mean to today's public, where do they believe its value lies, and what does this value look like? These are the questions that drive my interest in how cultural value is created, maintained and recorded. This interest grew as I encountered other cultural policy commentators and economics scholars who also viewed the public as an underappreciated source of cultural value.

Chapter 4

How the public values the State Library

These days, it seems every activity requires the completion of a five-minute survey at the end of the experience.

Arts and cultural audiences are accustomed to researchers' eagerness to analyse each stage of their cultural event, from buying a ticket through to talking to friends about it, in the hope of assembling the data that will explain exactly what audiences derive from the experience: to measure 'on a scale of one to 10' their enjoyment or otherwise, their likelihood of returning, and whether the experience constituted value for money. Very few researchers provide the space for audiences to speak for themselves, express in their own terms what a particular experience meant to them, what they loved and enjoyed, as well any disappointment or displeasure. Finding a way to organise such qualitative audience or visitor feedback so that it will make sense and be of interest to funding bodies, policy-makers and administrators is a challenge.

We are told that government funding bodies want the financials and numbers only, 'good numbers', those that tell a good story in a short space. Box office records smashed often make the news and are usually accompanied by economic impact statistics from across the city or the state; web hits are extrapolated to become engagement data. We are all obliged to provide tangible and measurable outcomes to demonstrate value for money to our funding bodies. Sadly, in this context, cultural experience becomes reduced to easily and quickly digestible data, which can be graphed and contrasted with the previous year, projected for next year, or compared with the institution next door. Providing the space to explain how an institution has become valued by members of the public over their lifetimes is beyond the capacity of most arts organisations, especially those who still see their audience or public as more than merely a market.[1] Some of us still consider 'the public' to be fellow members of a shared community. Public engagement with our cultural offering is a sign that the cultural institutions we represent are relevant, are producing experiences that explore topics of interest and are part of an ongoing conversation to inform, inspire and even challenge. My intention is to demonstrate here that the public and how they value the State Library still count, particularly when that value goes beyond economic impact.

As discussed earlier, numbers can mean anything, or nothing. What counts when it comes to the value of culture, however, is the story – the illuminating detail. What happened on the day or night? How was it received by critics and peers? How did it contribute to the development of that stream of creative enterprise? Where is it located in the larger story of social connection and cultural understanding of the institution or the community? How did this experience add to or reflect people's lives? Why did they come, did they enjoy it, and will they come back? How did it change them or their attitudes? Capturing or at least understanding the centrality of the audience's experience to the question of cultural value is what decades of cultural policy research suggests is required for a true and authentic accounting of government investment in culture. It sounds obvious, but, in the age of commercial primacy, perhaps it's not taken as seriously as it should be. How, then, can an organisation confidently and coherently describe what they provide and the value they create for the public?

This is the gap in the story of the State Library of South Australia I wanted to fill. My questions to members of the public were crafted in an open-ended style to encourage conscious reflection and to draw out personal meanings from respondents, offering the chance 'to understand the world as seen by respondents'.[2] I wanted to appreciate the intricacy of the relationships between the institution and its public, and whether this relationship can be maintained and communicated directly, without the mediating effects and additional expense involved in engaging third party consultants, [3] or annual subscriptions[4] to online digital platforms.[5]

The most significant investment I made in this work was time, a commodity often scarce across the education, health and cultural sectors, but an investment certainly worth making. As Walmsley suggested, I needed to spend time 'hanging out' with the visitors to truly understand their experience of the Library, from their perspective. People could complete a survey and hand it in, or spend extra time – where possible – to have a coffee with me. This approach would allow me to connect with them over a semi-structured interview while they were at the Library, without disrupting their experience. After years in the arts and becoming accustomed to searching for answers to fill in fit on acquittal forms or please a minister, I adopted a different approach, one derived from the social sciences: I went into the field to see what I could find, not to target something I was looking for. The responses to the following questions guided my research:

1. Why do you visit the State Library of South Australia?
2. What benefits do you think the State Library of South Australia creates for you and/or the Adelaide community?
3. What is your earliest memory of attending any library?
4. What is your earliest (or best) memory of attending THIS library?
5. What does the State Library of South Australia mean to you now?
6. How does the library support, service or contribute to your main purpose for visiting today?
7. What else would you like to tell us about what the State Library means to you?

I gave respondents as much space and time as they needed and have reproduced here the subjects' survey responses verbatim. I changed nothing in their answers to questions, thereby avoiding translation or any modification of their intent or meaning. I have simply relayed the responses exactly as they were given to me and woven them together to reflect a collective and meaningful reply. The responses ranged from the highly specific and purposeful to the more contemplative and serendipitous, often from the same person, indicating that each person receives more than one kind of 'value' from each visit; it also means there are a great many more responses than individuals who filled out the survey. I grouped similar responses under themes to identify a network of common meaning amongst survey respondents,[6] an approach that helped to create an understanding of what cultural value looks like, and what that value means to the people who have the most to gain from it. These emergent 'value themes' are:

- Inspiration
- Community resource and site value
- Quiet escape and security
- Civic trust and public service
- Social/cultural connection and exchange
- Self-improvement and transformation
- Heritage and continuity
- Quiet escape and security
- Education.

The best way to describe these themes and their value associations is by using the responses to illustrate their meaning, as presented in the following section. Within these themes, I organised responses in clusters of 'value associations', responses that were very similar but expressed differently, demonstrating how each of the themes consisted of different elements. To put it simply, each of these value themes also describes how cultural value is manifested in the Library – what generates it and what it looks like for different people.[7]

This next section weaves together the survey responses to tell a story about what the State Library of South Australia means to the people who use it, visit it and 'really friggin' love the place'.

In other words, what follows is evidence of what cultural value looks like at the State Library of South Australia.

Question 1: Why do you visit the State Library of South Australia?
This question provides an overview of why the public engages with the State Library and what they expect from the experience. Almost all respondents gave their reason or reasons for being there (82 of the total 84 respondents). Collectively, they made 176 statements about what had motivated them to visit the Library. In this way, I was able to identify what they expected from the institution.

The largest number of responses (51) could be grouped under the theme of 'Community resource and site value'. This theme reflects how respondents' visits were motivated by the perceived or expected benefits arising from their engagement with the resources available at the Library, such as the collections, staff and reference books, as well as the benefits derived from their physical or digital connection with the site. The public were prompted to visit the State Library for the environment and facilities ('to recharge my phone', 'quiet place to study', 'business meeting in café', 'research that I cannot do from home'), as well as to access the collections ('special collections', 'exhibitions', 'The Story Wall', 'to read about the early civilisations'). Several respondents visited the State Library for public events (7) and to attend the 'seminars and talks', 'Friends' presentations', while two others had brought visitors to highlight the site as a place of cultural interest. These responses indicate that the public gain value from a diverse range of services, resources and facilities provided by the State Library, which are shared by the community and which require being physically on site.

The second most common motivation for visiting the State Library can be described by the theme 'Education' (42). These responses included both formal studies related to tertiary or school education ('looking for references', 'assignments', 'project discussion' and 'group study'), as well as more informal study purposes ('for research', 'reading', 'to find medical texts'). There were six respondents who visited to gain 'access to books'.

Responses grouped under the theme of 'Inspiration' (21) represented the third most common motivation and reflect more intimate, relational and intrinsic engagements with the Library and convey a sense of familiarity with the institution, indicating previous experiences, a level of prior knowledge and expectation. This is reflected in value comments such as 'It's a beautiful place – and it's a nice quiet working environment', 'I am a volunteer', 'I love it' and 'To explore possibilities'. There were eight respondents who were in the State Library to pursue personal projects, such as family history research, as well as one member of the public who, intriguingly, was there 'To write a novel'.

A significant number of respondents to this question (20) were motivated by a sense of history and an appreciation of the heritage of the site. These responses were grouped together under the theme 'Heritage and continuity'. This category of value includes 10 motivations relating to 'ancestry research', 'family history' and the public event series *Genealogical Gems*. In what was to become a recurring theme across the data, three respondents mentioned the building's historic architectural character, with two respondents visiting specifically to 'show visitors the Mortlock Wing'. The cooperative nature of the relationship between the state and its public is evident in one respondent's motivation, who had visited 'to correct a photo identification at the library', demonstrating a sense of ownership and responsibility to ensure the integrity of information associated with the collections. The historical collections had also attracted three respondents intending to conduct an 'archival search', access 'in-depth local history' and more specifically 'to explore possibilities of finding out more about Mortimer Nolan and the Jesuit missionaries in South Australia'. Another respondent had visited the State Library because they 'like the photo exhibits of old South Australia'.

Responses grouped under the theme of 'Civic trust and public service' reflect the relationship between the public and the members of staff, which is based on the State Library's egalitarian service provision, as well the level of faith and trust the public shows in return for those services. Eighteen respondents indicated how highly they valued this relationship, a value encompassing their appreciation for the ease of accessibility to the facilities and the authenticity of the knowledge upon which they can draw via interactions with the trusted staff. Public events drew five survey respondents to the State Library such as 'Tangent' events, held in partnership with the State Theatre Company, and the 'Hairy Maclary Family Fun Day', which was aimed at families with children. Four respondents nominated free access to services as their motivation to visit because 'the internet is good and free', while two others were drawn to the 'free English classes'. One respondent was prompted by a sense of civic engagement, stating 'I am a volunteer who transcribes'. This again points to the collaborative, mutually beneficial and co-creative nature of the experience at the Library: many give their time and expertise to the care of the collections in return for the benefits they receive, which will be described in the next section. Three respondents also cited the authenticity and integrity of the institution as they were seeking 'information on different subjects', 'advice' and wanted 'to keep up to date'.

Of the remaining three major themes, 10 expressions of value were categorised under 'Quiet escape and security' ('I needed an open meeting place free from excessive disruption or noise' and 'beautiful place – a nice quiet place to study'); eight respondents nominated motivations related to 'Self-improvement and transformation' ('to prepare for IELTS exam' [International English Language Testing System], 'for job hunting' and to 'refresh'), while six respondents provided motivations which were grouped under the theme of 'Social/cultural connection and exchange'; for example, the free language classes ('I went to attending [sic] at one-to-one and free conversation class'); participation in interactive events 'such as 'Edward Abbott's "The English and Australian Cookbook" dinner . . . and discussion'; or a lecture from the Australian social researcher and writer Hugh Mackay.

The most common motivations for the public to visit the State Library were grouped under the theme of 'Community resource and site value'. This theme relates to the Library's infrastructure, environment and facilities; the public events; and the shared resources available for study, and research. Their research was supported by access to the shared archival and reference collections, the availability of free Wi-Fi and computers, as well as the conducive environment created by the historic architecture, the trusted expertise of staff and the integrity of the information they planned to access. Others visited for more subjective and intangible reasons: a personal connection, familiarity with or emotional attachment to the site, or for more civic and institutional purposes, such as volunteering.

Question 2: What benefits do you think the State Library creates for you and/or the Adelaide community?

I wanted to gain insight into what Library users consider to be the value generated by the State Library for individuals, but also what they perceive to be the value for the community in general.[8] This question elicited a broad range of responses, these demonstrating a depth of reflection, empathy for others and understanding of the operations of the State Library. From the 80 respondents to this question, I identified 366 forms of value, with the most common responses grouped under the themes of 'Community resource and site value' (81) and 'Civic trust and public service' (81).

As with Question 1, most respondents to Question 2 identified value in the shared resources and opportunities available within the physical site. They described the State Library as a 'repository', providing 'community access for the story of our state's people and institutions', which offers 'a space to explore every kind of information . . . to study to relax to be entertained'. The value of the collections was ranked highly, with many perceiving benefits in the 'wealth of information and access to old publications and books that cannot be accessed anywhere else', belying the myth that the Library could be replaced by Google. Some suggested that 'The SLSA is more than just a collection of material or the gateway to online information. It holds the collective memory of the people of South Australia', or words to that effect. Others perceived value in benefits beyond the immediate individual experience: 'For me, the resources of the Library are an important social and cultural resource'. Another indicated a connection with institutional value, perceiving the State Library as a 'hub for encouraging people to value the resources and facilities provided by the state government'. The State Library facilities are highly prized for their provision of 'Quiet relaxed atmosphere to study, meet, discuss things', as well as for 'coffee' and the 'kindly staff'. Respondents recognised value in the free access and collective activities, appreciating a 'politically-neutral space for attending various functions, like art exhibitions, which I regularly attend'. Some respondents answered with a degree of passion for both the Library and its community, viewing the Library as 'a shared community experience', which is 'absolutely a necessary part of a civilised society and must be upheld and adequately funded and staffed'. These latter responses offer insight into the direct connection between the respondents' State Library experience and the respondent's expectations of the state government – the custodian, main funding source and provider of library services for the community.

In Question 1, 18 responses were categorised under the major theme of 'Civic trust and public service'. However, for this second question, 81 responses indicated that this major theme was very important to respondents, indicating the strong relational connection between their Library experience and how it contributes to an informed, positive, and civic society. The State Library is considered 'One of the landmarks of this State that embodies our collective identity and underpins our history', which 'helps me learn about our state heritage and our city'. Respondents also perceive transgenerational benefits from the State Library's role as a 'Great archival depository', providing 'access to historical documents', as a 'holding place of SA publications' and 'archive of cultural history' 'for generations to enjoy'. Respondents recognised the role played by staff in creating this institutional value for the public, describing them as 'friendly', 'kind' and 'helpful'. Respondents also appreciate the 'searchable physical publications and documents not always available online', providing access to 'a wealth of information' and creating 'deep understanding in almost all subjects'. The benefits associated with the role the State Library plays in bringing people together were acknowledged in responses such as 'Libraries play a vital role in healthy interactive communities'; that the institution 'makes us feel good about living here and having access to the State Library'; and is 'great way of getting out, doing something new & for us heading into the city'. One respondent expressed their ongoing trust in the State Library having been built up over time, describing it as 'my first port of call to locate all kinds of information', indicating a history of a need satisfied. Another suggested the State Library is a source of 'information that is true (i.e. not fake) and which can be and often is contextualised by professional librarians'. The significant reference to the librarians indicates the active role these team members play as expert mediators and co-creators of the experience for a public seeking trustworthy information in an online world awash with fake news. Trust in the organisation and its services is also seen in the number of respondents (5) who suggested they value the State Library as 'a safe space for everyone', 'a safe and secure environment', in which to 'communicate with our friends and study'. These results indicate the ways by which the State Library provides services and features for the public beyond its official role as an information service provider, in that it offers a secure place for vulnerable, lonely or insecure members of the community. The responses 'safe and secure' and 'safe space' may refer to the presence of security guards, a familiarity with the processes and knowledge of acceptable behaviour acquired over past experiences, or possibly gained from being in the company of other like-minded members of the public. The State Library is also valued for the freedom it provides, which 'allows people to engage in their niche interests and hobbies', by providing 'endless resources and possibilities for learning as an adult'. The State

Library gives members of the public the 'opportunity to learn about the past but also keep abreast of new interests', which 'promotes inquiry & shared story telling', human characteristics which, as described earlier, ensured the survival and success of our species. It also echoes the original mission of the institution, established for 'the cultivation and diffusion of knowledge'.

These responses show that the public gains value from tangible engagement with the site and their interactions with team members, as well as with the collections. One of the most interesting results was the number of responses indicating how some members of the public associate their Library experience with the past, and how that influences their projections of the future. Georgina Born, Professor of Anthropology and Music at University College London, describes these memories or traces of the past as 'retentions', and their counterpart, 'protentions' – respondents' projections or anticipations of the future. Hence, in the context of the Library experience, the past is always re-enacted through 'retentions' of previous events, just as the future is experienced through 'protentions' of possibilities'.[9] This is seen in the 53 responses associated with what the institution represents or symbolises in terms of public memory, legacy and stewardship of the collections. The State Library offers 'a richer frame of reference, widening one's horizon about how we make sense of the world'; it is considered a 'resource for historical and cultural heritage', and 'holds the collective memory of the people of South Australia'. Respondents also associated value in their expressed belief that the Library provided 'Freedom of thought' (25) and 'Expertise and integrity' (24) through their engagements with the librarians, indicating a strong appreciation of the ongoing care of the collections, inspiring a high level of trust, gratitude and respect. Other respondents appreciate that 'there is no limitation to use library' and 'the internet is efficient and unmoderated', suggesting that the open web access available at the State Library may have value for members of the community for whom such civil liberties and free public services may be unusual. Respondents are also aware of the multi-faceted nature of the institution's operations and why it 'collects, preserves, interprets our culture', perceiving benefits associated with providing 'permanent housing of important information for the public'.

The two themes dominating responses to Question 2 – 'Community resource and site value' and 'Civic trust and public service' – demonstrate how the public experiences the institutional value of the Library, which is 'created in the way that [the] organisation relates to the public'.[10] These responses also address how the public interacts with culture, 'as a vehicle to engage with each other and with the world, and to discover their role and identity within it'.[11] The public do not experience the State Library as an episodic or fleeting form of entertainment. Rather, these responses suggest that the institution is part of their lives, informing how they perceive their place in the world, and they believe others feel the same.

Question 3: What is your earliest memory of attending any library?
A significant body of international research describes the effects of early childhood exposure to arts and culture, and how positive early experiences indicate the likelihood of individuals engaging with the sector as an adult. The responses to this question describe this connection between positive early childhood experiences with libraries and the value they now associate with the State Library as adults. This question elicited personal and long-held responses, illuminating the values the respondents associate with the State Library, what they have grown to expect in a library experience, and how their early library experiences are frequently entwined with some of their fondest childhood memories. All but three of the respondents offered their earliest memory of a library experience. These recollections and the value placed on them varied in scale and format, from 'receiving our excitedly anticipated carton of books every month from the Country Lending service of the Library' and 'the school library which seemed so huge and exciting', through to sensory memories – 'the smell of

books, the wonder of taking one home and the amount that were available'. These memories demonstrate how these early experiences inform individuals' ongoing relationships with libraries. Respondents most frequently recalled their sense of wonder on visiting their first library, making 'Inspiration' (73) the dominant theme for this question.

A clear link between when these respondents first learned to read and their earliest memory of a library is evident. Some learned to read at a library 'as a child attending reading group'. One respondent recalled their first visit to a library as a 'four years old – I've held a library card or reader ticket for 50 years'. Another asserted that in '1954 I discovered books. Have been a fan ever since'. Others recalled specific times and locations, such as the 'Glenelg library when I was 8 yrs. I went every week for many, many years. I still go there', and 'going to the Burnside library to borrow from the children's collection and getting the books stamped'. The State Library and the Adelaide Children's Library feature in several responses, such as the 'children's library in the city when I was a schoolboy', 'Mother enrolled me at the Adelaide Children's Library just around the corner on Kintore Ave' and 'going to the old Circulating Library which used to be in the Institute Building'. Some noted a sense of purpose informing their memories, one recalling 'as a child growing up in Melbourne, going to my local library in Camberwell to look up all the books on dinosaurs' and 'when I was about 5 and went to our local library in the city of St Albans, UK, and chose books independently. It seemed to me to be a treasure trove'. Respondents remember library services as a means of overcoming physical or social isolation, while 'being a lonely teenager in a strange town starting work. The local library gave me refuge and worthwhile activity.' The presence of librarians and other staff was recognised in references to 'speaking with friendly teachers and staff'. The lifelong impact of early library exposure is highlighted by the respondent who recalled borrowing 'a book called *Libby, Oscar and Me*. I loved the book and didn't want to give it back. My son is now called Oscar.' Others recalled a sense of belonging and welcome, which inspired regular return visits. 'As a kid in the 1970s in the fantastic children's library. We came most Saturdays for storytelling and reading, borrowing too. All the way through high school too, borrowing fantastic cassettes. What an amazing collection of interesting music!' Many recalled being involved in events or activities, accompanying 'my parents and my cousins who were older to participate in various events' or were inspired by 'hearing Hilda Baillie reading *Winnie the Pooh* at the Tumby Bay Area School library'. One combined a trip to a library with family routine when they 'used to go every Friday night. After the library we would get an ice cream or a donut. It is still one of my fondest childhood memories.' Another recalled 'walking from home to library (1960s) with my library bag on a Saturday . . . with my big brothers. Selecting books on my own (all grown up) and then walking home.' The transnationality of the library experience is also evident in anecdotes of libraries from around the world, such as 'my primary school in Colorado. Loved libraries', 'I went to the state library of China' and the 'local village library in S. India'. One respondent did not have prior library experience before they attended university, while two others suggested their first library experience was in 'the Mortlock'. The diversity of these childhood or early visits to libraries demonstrates the importance of a positive early experience with any library; they set the tone and inform connections with other libraries later in life.

The second most common theme for this question was 'Community resource and site value' (60), where respondents recalled 'reading in the big chair in the children's library' or 'the reading area all the books, floor mat and cushions'. The physical possession and access to books was an important part of these early memories, whereby respondents recalled 'seeing so many books that I hadn't read yet' and 'a lot of books'. Some respondents also had strong recollections of mobile library services, such as 'receiving library books from the city [Adelaide] while living in the country', the 'country lending service . . . about 65 years ago' and 'the box of books that came from the NSW Education Department library in Sydney. It travelled on the train once a month 400 miles to our little one teacher public school. It brought the rest of the world and its wonder and joys to a small village, [which] was only offering an unstimulating and deprived environment'.

I identified 299 statements of value to this question. They featured value associations reflecting the connection between the wonder and joys of discovering a welcoming space specifically for children, which opened a world of 'enchantment' (24), encouraging them to develop their reading skills in connection to school (30), and to engage with their local library for fun or entertainment (30). This response suggests that the public's early library experiences also informed aspects of their personal identity ('Possession and belonging', 31). Visits to the library were part of family activities (54) and provided opportunities to develop personal agency ('Independence and transition', 9), enabling respondents to freely explore, select and borrow books. These were significant milestones, and memories have remained throughout their lives (20), as evident through their recollections of titles, covers, stimulation and smells. The clarity and vivid nature of many of these responses suggest that some positive value associations made in childhood are recalled and reactivated by each visit respondents make to the State Library, linking the public to library experiences which are both temporally and geographically ambiguous – they span place and time. Engaging children with books in libraries and providing a positive experience is more than entertainment and literacy development: encouraging their learning and stimulating readers' imaginations are critical to how children see the world and their place within it.

Respondents may have had their first library experience in regional New South Wales, China, England or the nearby suburb of Glenelg, accompanying their siblings on a weekend outing, hoarding borrowed dinosaur books or reading the fictional tales of *Libby, Oscar and Me*. As intrinsically important and personal as these experiences were to respondents, by signing up for a library card they joined an international community that fosters knowledge. Respondents recall this positive experience and impact on their imagination each time they visit a library for research, inspiration or understanding. Every visit reinforces their memory, reconfirms their understanding of the world and their place within it.

Question 4: What is your earliest (or best) memory of attending THIS library?

Respondents were generous with their recollections of the State Library of South Australia and almost all respondents answered the question (80). I identified almost twice as many statements of value than the previous question (558). This question was designed to determine what distinguishes their State Library visit from other library experiences, to understand where the Library's specific appeal for the public may lie and, therefore, what forms of value underpin the relationship between the public and the institution. What emerged was a picture of the State Library as a dominant cultural force: both a site of creativity and of heritage. The Library plays an active role in the public perception of Adelaide's community identity, as well as representing a connection to past and future generations.

The physical location of the State Library on North Terrace dominates respondents' earliest or favourite recollections, with 141 value statements aligning under the major theme of 'Community resource and site value'. The Mortlock Wing features in many of those first impressions.[12] Respondents 'visited and fell in love with the Mortlock Wing' and the aesthetics of the building, recalling 'seeing the Mortlock Wing' and 'being just so impressed with the wonderfully unique Mortlock Library'. The favourite memory of several respondents was simply 'studying in the Mortlock Wing' or 'when I knew I can study at Wing – Mortlock [sic]', suggesting that they value the space not only for its beauty but also its functional affordances. One respondent recounted their best memory as 'a surprise wedding in the Mortlock'. Another recalled how 'The second we entered it was amazing – the old books, the wood, the lighting . . .' Other elements of the site, both old and new, also resonate with respondents, even though they are no longer operational. This was especially true of the Adelaide Children's Library, which was not technically a subsidiary of the State Library, but was located on the same site. The Adelaide Lending Library was the parent organisation of the Children's Library but likewise no longer occupies the site. However, respondents' childhood associations with the physical space informs their memories and perceptions of the State Library today – they see no distinction between the two organisations. For example, 'we used to visit the State Library when it was still a borrowing library with the children's section downstairs' and 'came most Saturdays for storytelling and reading, borrowing too', 'a whole library geared to my age-group and interests – treasure trove!', 'borrowing the kids' books' and 'magical old books with nondescript covers'. As with the previous question, these responses indicate the extent to which memories of a well-curated library space, established specifically for children, informs the experience of those children when they become adults; they also demonstrate that members of the public are somewhat ambivalent or plain unaware about the Library's management or administrative structures. They care primarily for the presence of a *library* within those buildings on that site. Their relationship is with the location, which provides a point of continuity from their earlier experience to the present day.

Other respondents recalled being part of a shared or community experience, such as 'studying in the Hub as people played the piano', 'a wonderful tour and orientation given by Stamos, showcasing the resources available', or 'bringing a group of about 20 pensioners who had never been in their lives and seeing their surprise at the range of exhibits and displays of information on offer because they had expected only books'. As in the previous questions, family members figure in their memories. These recollections offer glimpses of family life and precious childhood moments, of when they 'tagged along with Mum (she had some stuff to do)', or 'spending the day with my Mum at this library', or 'went with my Dad, held his hand. Was in a grown-up world of wonder. Felt safe. Just wanted to stay (about aged 7 I think).' Others associate their best memory with finding their family within the collections, describing 'coming to do family history research as a young adult', how it was 'so exciting to find a special reference. Perhaps a newspaper photograph of my Dad', and the exhilaration of 'a eureka moment finding my great-grandparents' records'.

The State Library also appears as a resource and site of transition for new arrivals to Adelaide. Respondents recalled how they 'became a borrower when I first came to Adelaide more than 40 years ago', had 'just moved to Adelaide to live here' and the Library 'helped me assimilate into the South Australian culture and history'. For some, the State Library provides a pathway through the dislocation of moving, of finding comfort in new surroundings; it becomes part of a routine in a new environment for those who 'came here and I like this place. Then, I start to visit this library every day.' The English language classes feature in several recollections. One respondent described attending a 'one-to-one conversation session, and the teacher help me to correcting my resume, this was priceless help for me'.

These responses show that the public place a high value on not just the buildings, events, books and services associated with the environment and facilities (140), but include references to what the State Library enabled them to do – the impact it made at different and often confronting stages in their lives. This suggests a curious mix of intrinsic and instrumental forms of value, underpinned by the institutional value generated by service provision, trust and stewardship. These memories and their corresponding value associations (retentions and protentions – 24) span generations of families and connect respondents to the State Library over different periods of its development as a physical location and public institution. The respondents' comments suggest that the Library and the public have evolved in tandem with community attitudes while still retaining a connection; the Library remains a constant in their lives, representing, in some instances, a deeply personal set of value associations ('Family and childhood' – 52). The second most dominant value association reflects the sense of enchantment (60) experienced during respondents' first encounter with the State Library, intimating that the association does not diminish with age, but remains clear in respondents' memories, sustained by their ongoing connection with the State Library over their lifetimes, with the result that 'every time I go it's the "best time"'.

Question 5: What does the State Library mean to you now?

The previous questions established the forms of value that the public have come to associate with the State Library, as well as the previous experiences that inform their current perceptions of value. Question 5 was designed to gain insight into what that value represents to the public in symbolic and intrinsic terms, rather than instrumental or purpose-driven associations. I was surprised that this question generated the highest number of value articulations (518), with the majority aligned with the major theme of 'Inspiration' (87). This was followed by a relatively even spread of responses across the themes, 'Heritage and continuity' (80), 'Community resource and site value' (77), 'Social/cultural connection and exchange' (75), 'Education' (70) and 'Civic trust and public service' (70). These results indicate a strong mix of values, generated by the various uses afforded by the spaces, sites and collections, as well the 'temporal ambiguity' of the experience; that is, respondents perceive value in the Library well beyond their own life time and purpose.

Respondents place great symbolic value on the buildings and the environment created for the public, with one stating that 'it's a very important institution that signifies the essential goodness in society, upholding and defending the right to learn, and the value of knowledge being freely accessible, as a cornerstone of a progressive society'. Several respondents were passionate in their belief that the State Library was 'unique' and an 'irreplaceable institution, so valuable a resource for so many reasons'. The buildings and services represent 'an important, valued, deeply entrenched part of the psyche of our community and an integral, significant part of our city'. These comments suggest that members of the public believe the State Library is connected to Adelaide's civic identity; others wrote that the State Library is 'an iconic landmark, an essential and vital service for our state', a 'symbolic hub of culture and civilisation' and 'the repository of everything meaningful'. However, one respondent felt it no longer lived up to their memories and was 'a sad shadow of its former self. It seems to be the worst of all state libraries in the country, moving backwards, uninspired and uninspiring. I would very much like it to return to its former glory – active, fun, exciting, experimental', when once again it will become a 'resource and also a source of pride'. Some valued the egalitarian – free – access to the services and resources, suggesting that the State Library is 'a space for all, provides service for everyone', noting that it is 'a champion institution of free, dependable information and digital sustainability', as well as remaining 'somewhere I can find the most obscure books I need!'. The attraction and benefits of the physical site is demonstrated by one respondent who 'live[s] in the country and it is a 3-hour drive to get there, but we are so fortunate to have such a wonderful asset'.

The responses that aligned with the theme of 'Inspiration' reflect the public's deeply personal connection and the formative role the State Library plays in their individual identity (52), such as those who claimed that 'it means many things to me', how it represents a '2nd house', 'a place to feel free in' and an 'honest friend'. The aspirational quality of responses associated with possession and belonging (44) are reflected in statements that the Library is 'a place where I can be a better me', 'I just love it', that it is 'one of [the] good places where I have good quality experiences' and remains 'a place where I want to go'. One respondent suggested that 'my transcribing work there keeps me alive! I'll be 91 in three weeks', whereas another considers that 'it's a place to meet with others and have a study group, or simply study by myself'. Others were inspired by being able to pursue knowledge or information for personal projects or niche interests (26), suggesting they place a high value on access to specific facilities (110), 'especially the jewel of the Mortlock Library, I've attended talks there but have also spent many hours in the Somerville Reading Room going through old TV Week magazines to find particular articles'.

The responses aligned with the theme of 'Heritage and continuity' show strong value associations with the history of the buildings and collections as a cultural place maker (39), and how their relationship with the State Library informs their image of the state of South Australia. The State Library is seen as 'a State treasure', 'a treasure trove – please keep it free and accessible!', 'I would be very upset not to have this wonderful place to go to'. Respondents appreciate the State Library's 'unique role in being the custodian for all printed word [sic] in our state', providing 'access to South Australiana, family history', and ensuring the 'preservation of historical documents, out of print books and archival material', 'and access to old publications and books'. Respondents suggest that the archival collections are highly valued, and that their potential value is also recognised. The State Library is perceived as 'a link to our past and our future', symbolising 'history, continuity' and that it is 'good to know that it is here'. 'The State Library of South Australia is an iconic landmark, an essential and vital service for our state' and continues to 'provide valuable support and collaborative partnership with Public Libraries in SA to provide our communities with the best library service possible'. The rich complexity of these comments is best reflected in two simple responses: 'it is part of who we are!' and it 'gives answer to my thirst for knowledge'. These two statements fulfil the promise made at the State Library's inception in August 1834, regarding the cultivation and diffusion of useful knowledge throughout South Australia. The civic retentions and protentions (32) demonstrate how the public believes the State Library engenders both personal and collective identity, impacting on respondents' self-perceptions and their aspirations for the future. This aspirational form of value connects individuals to the community, family members and events through history, and into the future. It demonstrates their hopes and expectations that the Library and its collections, as well as the values they engender and the benefits they currently provide, will be available for others in the future.

Question 6: How does the State Library support, service or contribute to your main purpose for visiting today?

This question returns the respondents' focus from the symbolic to the practical. It was designed to identify how they engaged with staff or with the resources, and how those points of engagement create a sense of value. The responses reflect the basics of service provision: from noting their use of items of furniture – a desk to sit at – to web access to the accessibility of collections. The responses also illustrate the respondents' recognition of the expertise and integrity of librarians and other members of staff. This confirms the role of the various Library staff in cultural value activation, indicating how they inform and influence the quality of the public experience. I found this confirmation really heartening and assume that all individuals working with the public in cultural institutions will also. As demonstrated by the question relating to earliest library experiences, these interactions between visitors and members of Library staff improve the likelihood of the public associating value with their library experience and therefore their probability of returning.

Yet again, the theme of 'Community resource/site value' was the most popular (103), underpinning all other forms of value associated with the public experience. The tangible support provided by the State Library is demonstrated by 'providing a free public space to sit indoors', which is a 'great flexible space and facilities', an 'open space for study', 'a wonderful place to work, and it always is'. Respondents depend on the State Library for their research as they 'get everything I need there', 'it has the information I need' and 'the necessary references I need for my research. If not, it helps me get them.' Others feel supported by being able to 'recharge phone', as well as the availability of 'computer access', and 'fast Wi-Fi, [which] is very supportive for my study and research'. 'The reliable Wi-Fi makes my presence in the Library possible – without it, I could not spend whole days working'. Some respondents suggest a range of ways in which the State Library supports their experience: 'My work here today depends on the Library's support and services. It does [this] by supplying a place I can come work by supplying desks, internet, chairs and security.'

Access to the collections also features strongly, with one respondent indicating a personal connection with the institution and its resources. They describe how the State Library 'completely supports my research but also my personal interest of looking at books, e[s]pecially old books and visiting the Mortlock Library for interest and to see old publications that I was involved in creating in previous occupations and workplaces'. The value associated with the State Library environment and facilities has a transformative effect on respondents' sense of wellbeing, noting they 'feel safe, and I know I have time to finish what I need to get done', or 'I like to come here, because I found [sic] myself in a good mood'. For respondents not engaged in specific research, the public programs and exhibitions feature as a source of support, allowing a deeper engagement with a new topic or collection area. The provision of these educational opportunities 'often draws attention to something new or looks at something old in a new way', such as 'the exhibition of political cartoons – fun, thought-provoking and a good retrospective of the current year'. Another saw a range of social and community benefits offered by exhibitions, such as the collaboration between the South Australian National Football League (SANFL) and the State Library: 'SANFL is the oldest football association in Australia (older than Victorian equivalent). It is the nation's indigenous sport. It touches people across the community and bridges the city/country divide.' Another respondent sees the State Library as a supportive social outlet for their family: their 'children spend most of their time at home. Feel lonely. I try to get them to attend some activities. Value: kids feel happiness and act [sic] with parents.' These responses demonstrate that a community cannot be divided into niche segments of sports fans and library users. People have more than one interest. The State Library can cater to the passions and needs of people who may not identify as regular library users.

The second most dominant theme for this question was 'Civic trust and public service' (78). Of all the major themes, this theme best encapsulates the reciprocal nature of the relationship between the institution and members of the public and relates to responses that recognise the level of authenticity and trust in the Library. Indicating an appreciation of the State Library's duty of care and responsibility to serve and support the public, these responses are closely aligned with Holden's 'Institutional value'. They demonstrate a high level of awareness of the role played by the Library as a public service, as well as the longitudinal value represented by the collections and expertise of the professional staff. A high number of respondents (22) associate the support delivered by the State Library with the integrity and expertise of the staff and how they are 'making extraordinary papers from SA's past available for research. Cataloguing and digitising these so they are "findable"'. One respondent acknowledged those taking part in the behind-the-scenes conservation and preservation work, commenting that their support is 'wonderful', while another appreciates 'the nice people here', who they find to be 'always pro-fessional and helpful. Their dedication to serving the public shines through.' This statement includes the staff who work behind the scenes to acquire, catalogue and maintain the resources, not merely those at the reference desk. The 'experienced people are worth their weight in gold' and are able to support the public because they are 'knowledgeable and willing to help' when 'showing the public how to find particular information. And how to use the various resources', providing 'assistance when I needed clarity of resource location and help to load the microfilm'. The teams working to support the public are considered 'expert and helpful' and 'facilitate access to records from "deep storage"', or 'help navigate the catalogue, or help work the electronic equipment'. The value of this professional facilitation relates again to the State Library's original vision and ongoing function, supporting the public by 'making its materials accessible to the public', as stated in the Library's original mission. As these value associations demonstrate, the public perceives value in more than merely the immediate customer service provided by the librarians; they are also aware of the work that goes into collection management and digitisation, and the expertise involved with the public events and exhibitions, all of which depend on the quality of the site and its facilities.

These responses suggest that the State Library's institutional value is realised through a combination of information provision and collection management, set within familiar and safe surroundings and serviced and equipped for free public access, all of which are supported by trained, knowledgeable and trustworthy professional teams.

Question 7: What else would you like to tell us about what the State Library means to you?

This final question was the most open-ended and deliberately vague, providing an opportunity for additional comments about the value and meaning of the State Library. Not all responded – 59 of the 84 respondents. That said, this chance to reflect on their experiences and relationship with the State Library elicited some of the most detailed and personal insights into how individuals' relationships with the institution impact on their lives. These responses also reveal the significant symbolic role of the State Library in the North Terrace Cultural Precinct as the perceived keeper of the state's collective memory.

The significance of the State Library's location on North Terrace is reflected by the dominance of the theme 'Community resource/ site value' (72). Unlike previous questions, here this theme was only slightly more prominent than the institutional values represented by 'Civic trust and public service' (71), which was closely followed by 'Inspiration' (67), the category that reflects intrinsic and subjective cultural experience. The heartfelt and wide-ranging statements reproduced below best represent the cultural value of the State Library: it is both personal and collective. The following statements also present the interdependence of cultural value and the services and experiences provided by the institution. One cannot exist without the other.

Members of the public consider the State Library a 'great place to be', with 'an excellent mix of old and new'. The State Library is unparalleled: 'there's nowhere else that has such a great collection of items and the expertise to help people access and use them', upholding its principles of democratic access as 'an area for citizens from all walks of life to share the learning space together'. The State Library is also significant, even for those who 'do not visit often, I like knowing it is there and that it probably always will be', anticipating both immediate community benefits and a potential future need. Respondents claim to 'love that it's there', recognising the benefits the State Library represents for future generations, stating they 'value its sense of continuity as a place of learning, a safe place for free exchange of ideas beyond political, religious or ideological boundaries. It's also a place that preserves our history and makes it available'. Echoing the aspirations of the original South Australian Literary Association, some respondents assert that 'it should serve as a cultural anchor, somewhere that can be treasured through [the] generations'. The State Library's symbolic and legacy value is also indicated by descriptions of it as 'a showcase of our State, it's heritage and its future'. Some respondents see it as a living connection to the past: 'I treasure the story that our forebears, setting out to found a new colony on the other side of the world, brought a trunk full of books with which to found a Library! What a foundation'. Responses such as these demonstrate how some members of the public experience several different timeframes simultaneously when they visit the

State Library. These comments also highlight the almost mythic status of South Australian colonial history for some members of the public. The perception of how the state was settled, and the realities of colonial settlement, may not match the idealism and aspirational quality of these responses. However, these responses represent a line of continuity and between the colonial past and the present, as well as the persistent symbolic significance of the 'trunk full of books', which adds value to the State Library today and informs respondents' sense of community identity.

Identity and belonging feature prominently in responses to this question, offering the clearest insight into the subjective nature of respondents' relationships with the State Library. They feel deeply about the institution, as expressed through replies relating to the provision of 'access to my local historical records, of the people I know and places and events I love'. Others say they 'just love [it] and would spend a lot more time there if I could' or simply 'I really friggin love it'. Several respondents also expressed how much they value the Library staff, describing them as 'amazing and not adequately acknowledged by the people in charge of the state'; 'I would like to add my appreciation of the staff. I have made many friends over the years and especially appreciate their knowledge and advice'; 'If it was to suffer cuts in personnel or resources I would be devastated.' The interpersonal nature of these statements reflects how the respondents' ongoing relationship with the institution is facilitated and reinforced by their contact with members of staff.

The significance of the State Library for new arrivals to Adelaide is also shown in statements highlighting the opportunities provided for improving their understanding of local language, culture and customs. The institution is a site where 'I can make a close connection with Australian native people to learn their culture and specific accent'. In one of the most illustrative responses, 'the State Library of South Australia give me a sense of blongness [sic] makes me a part of Australia'. This response articulates the value and influence an independent, free, supportive and welcoming environment can have on an individual's sense of self and community, especially when challenged by language or cultural differences. These sentiments are reinforced by respondents who recognise the State Library as 'an area for citizens from all walks of life to share the learning space together', underpinning the theme of 'Social/cultural connection and exchange'. Some respondents visit the Library for the language classes, which also offer additional learning opportunities for other participants, as we will see in several of the interviews in the next chapter.

The transgenerational value of the State Library experience is also evident in responses describing meaningful family associations, such as 'I encourage my grandchild to attend the exhibitions with me which he enjoys, as he is also a great reader'. Another respondent suggests they 'would love to see more days/sessions where authors are celebrated and children can listen to shared stories'.

Summary

Survey respondents believe that 'it is very important to have public institutions like the Library'; 'Personally, I think it is a wonderful institution that needs to be valued'; the State Library is 'simply a vital part of Adelaide's cultural fabric'. The following graph combining all responses to all the questions shows the many ways in which the public values the State Library. They range from service provision and the enjoyment that comes from sharing resources and space, through to the intellectual and inspirational opportunities, and sense of connection with the state's history, community and future users.

Respondents gain a sense of personal and cultural identity through the historical, cultural and democratic associations embodied by the Library, represented by 'Community resource and site value' (585). This theme encompasses the shared and free access to the collections (digital and analogue), the professional teams, and the physical structures occupying the site on North Terrace. Respondents also seek and 'find themselves' in the State Library, represented by the theme 'Inspiration' (439), which

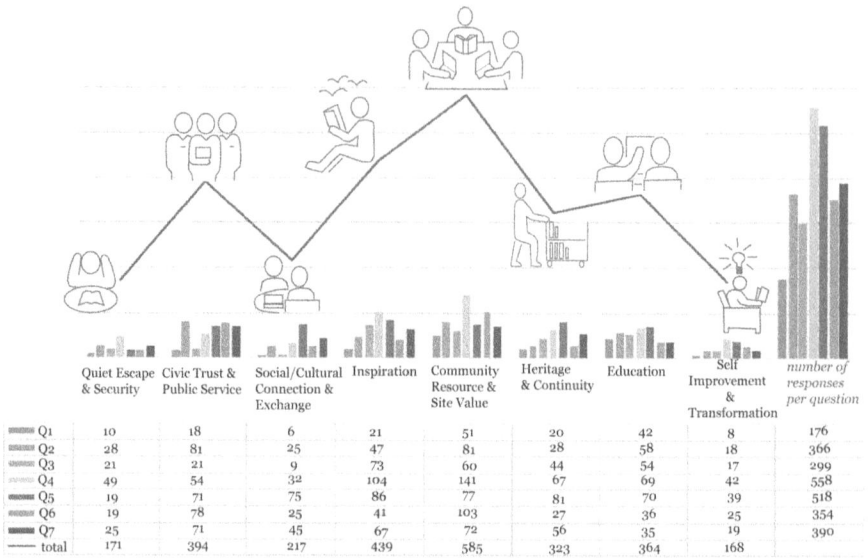

	Quiet Escape & Security	Civic Trust & Public Service	Social/Cultural Connection & Exchange	Inspiration	Community Resource & Site Value	Heritage & Continuity	Education	Self Improvement & Transformation	number of responses per question
Q1	10	18	6	21	51	20	42	8	176
Q2	28	81	25	47	81	28	58	18	366
Q3	21	21	9	73	60	44	54	17	299
Q4	49	54	32	104	141	67	69	42	558
Q5	19	71	75	86	77	81	70	39	518
Q6	19	78	25	41	103	27	36	25	354
Q7	25	71	45	67	72	56	35	19	390
total	171	394	217	439	585	323	364	168	

Overview: Major themes for public articulations of value

includes the accumulation of personal benefits derived from family research projects, as well as familiarity as they transition through formal education (364) or move towards claiming a place amongst of the Australian community. The State Library is a valuable source of authentic information, a free institution fostering 'Civic trust and public service' (394), exemplified for respondents by the librarians and other staff they encounter, including visitor services and security teams, as well as the librarians and preservation teams behind the scenes. The public understands their essential work and appreciates how they contribute to their experience, even though they may never directly engage with them. The survey responses demonstrate the co-creative nature of the cultural value realised through their engagement with the State Library and extends to encompass their experiences of the North Terrace Precinct and beyond their own lifetimes, exemplified by the theme 'Heritage and continuity' (323), connecting respondents to past and future generations, creating their sense of community identity and confirming their place in the world today.

The following combined list of value associations for all questions shows what this process looks like in action; how cultural value is made manifest in the State Library; and what is most valuable for the public.

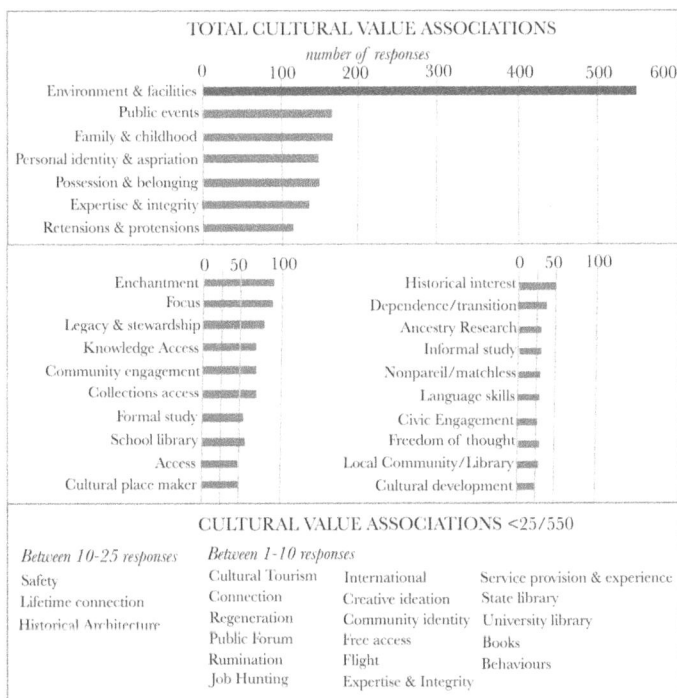

TOTAL CULTURAL VALUE ASSOCIATIONS

number of responses

	0	100	200	300	400	500	600
Environment & facilities							
Public events							
Family & childhood							
Personal identity & aspriation							
Possession & belonging							
Expertise & integrity							
Retensions & protensions							

	0	50	100			0	50	100
Enchantment				Historical interest				
Focus				Dependence/transition				
Legacy & stewardship				Ancestry Research				
Knowledge Access				Informal study				
Community engagement				Nonpareil/matchless				
Collections access				Language skills				
Formal study				Civic Engagement				
School library				Freedom of thought				
Access				Local Community/Library				
Cultural place maker				Cultural development				

CULTURAL VALUE ASSOCIATIONS <25/550

Between 10-25 responses	Between 1-10 responses		
Safety	Cultural Tourism	International	Service provision & experience
Lifetime connection	Connection	Creative ideation	State library
Historical Architecture	Regeneration	Community identity	University library
	Public Forum	Free access	Books
	Rumination	Flight	Behaviours
	Job Hunting	Expertise & Integrity	

Overview: Number of responses aligned against value associations

The survey respondents are in no doubt about the value of the State Library of South Australia, with the public associating value with the sharing of the spaces and resources, even though these are experienced individually and differently at various times in their lives. This complex network of relationships is comprised of engagements with the physical library site, engagements that have occurred over a number of previous experiences and across the collections. The visiting public, and the professionals and volunteers with whom they interact, together create an experience where individuals gain a sense of belonging, develop a sense of ownership and find answers to their 'thirst for knowledge'. On an individual level, this experience informs their appreciation and understanding of the value of the Library, as well as its public value for the community – potentially over generations. The State Library is recognised as 'a source of civic pride' and 'an essential part of "my" South Australia'. These responses show that 'the invisible work of culture formation' is not only alive and well at the State Library, but is understood, valued and activated by the public.[13]

To gain a greater understanding of how individuals experience and value the State Library, survey respondents at the Library were also invited to participate in short interviews. This approach provided me with the opportunity to personalise the questions and tease out stories through conversation. These interviews can be seen as narratives of value and are based on Walmsley's findings from his investigation into the 'deep hanging out' approach, explained earlier, whereby engaging directly with the public during their cultural experience provides clear insights into how they value it and why. These profiles shed additional light on the survey data and reflect the complex layers of the Library experience and the cultural value it activates for both individual users and the broader community, especially in the context of the North Terrace Cultural Precinct.

Chapter 5

Narratives of value,
in the words of the public

Listen carefully at the Library, and you can hear whispered conversations and supressed giggles, hiding behind a self-conscious hand. People hunch over books, laptops and notes, trying to help, to hide the secret, share the joke, or maintain some semblance of privacy. A stifled cough, a clattering chair or shattering ring tone, with an embarrassed 'sorry'. The furtive turning of a page . . .

Although members of the public are often heard in the Library, the chance to listen to their stories is less common. I devised a simple plan to ask members of the public what they valued about the Library. I wanted to talk to the people I saw amongst the stacks, study areas and in the panelled alcoves of the Mortlock Wing. The students, the researchers, the regular visitors or perhaps someone visiting for the first time. Those engaging with the Library as *a library* – a source of information, a public institution, a physical cultural site. Of all the places in Adelaide where people can research or read these days – home, university, school, cafes – what drew them into the city, to North Terrace and into the Library?

In previous roles I had gathered evidence of people's experiences, usually through surveys, visitor books and old-fashioned conversations. However, these techniques are now considered too subjective and time-consuming and have been superseded by digital tools. The survey and interview methods I used here may indeed appear pre-digital and time-intensive, but the detail and high quality of the responses demonstrates that they were worth pursuing. Offering people encouragement and allowing them free rein to talk about their experiences in their own words rather than presenting them with prescribed options or boxes to tick can be difficult. Yet this is what I set out to do, and achieved, via a simple invitation to join me for coffee. These interviews were important, as they allowed me to explore people's experiences of the Library in greater depth than the surveys of the previous chapter; the interviews promoted trust and companionability, encouraging a greater transparency, empathy and depth of discussion.[1]

This chapter presents 14 interviews with members of the State Library public, 13 of which were selected randomly and conducted over a coffee across two days at the Library.[2] I used a set of open-ended semi-structured questions to allow for a natural flow of conversation. The one interview that was not randomly selected was with Associate Professor Natalie Harkin from Flinders University. Natalie is a nationally recognised scholar, artist and poet, whose creative work with the Unbound Collective explores Adelaide's colonial heritage from the Indigenous perspective. The North Terrace Cultural Precinct carries challenging associations for the local Indigenous communities. This legacy, as well as policies regarding access to collections, means that many Indigenous South Australians have a conflicted relationship with the State Library. Their voices were conspicuous by their absence. Through Natalie's interview, we can understand how the unresolved historical legacies of colonial contact between settlers and the Indigenous people of the Adelaide Plains continue to inform how some members of our community perceive the State Library – as keepers of colonial archives. Rather than avoiding the past and perpetuating the silence associated with the treatment of Indigenous people and their archival records, the interview with Natalie suggests a more open and authentic future path for both the Library and the public, facilitating truth-telling about Adelaide's shared past and what new approaches to managing a colonial archive can mean for the future.

While the following interviews represent only a small sample of the value generated by the public through their engagement with the Library, the generous insights and heart-warming nature of many of their narratives demonstrate that not all forms of value can be captured on a survey form or spreadsheet. News of the pending death of libraries has been proven to be false. Bursting with life and creativity, the State Library of South Australia is the wellspring of future innovators, an evolving welcoming space, and a solace to the disenchanted.

LUKE: 'When you enter a space like this you see the possibilities'
Luke recently returned to Australia after several years teaching English at universities in Japan and South Korea. He was on a 'fact-finding mission' and yet to decide whether he would return to live in his hometown of Brisbane or make the move to Adelaide. Luke had arrived in the city only 90 minutes before the interview took place. The Library was the first site he wished to see as part of his decision-making process. The institution played a role in his decision of whether he would make Adelaide his home.

Luke described himself as 'very much a bookworm', having 'always loved libraries'. He engaged with 'the one in Brisbane quite a bit' during his studies as a linguistics major. 'I really love journals. I love reading, anything related to language learning and teaching, so I wanted to see how extensive your collection was here.'

He commented on the limited amount of natural light in the building but was looking forward to seeing the Mortlock Wing. He also expressed an interest in visiting the Art Gallery of South Australia. Luke spoke of enjoying public events, demonstrating his willingness to engage with a range of cultural opportunities. When asked about the kind of interactions that were important to him, his response indicated the significance of visitor services teams in cultural institutions, as well as the value he placed on opportunities for community engagement:

> *I guess [interactions] with other people, the friendly staff, very dedicated and available, which I've found has been the case today. I did ask a couple of questions and they were really helpful. That's probably the main thing. Events with guest*

speakers are really important too – authors, researchers, musicians or whatever, just to make it a bit more of a focal space for more people, so I'd like to see more of that.

As both a teacher and researcher himself, Luke considered my presence at the Library a positive sign, reaffirming the importance of directly engaging with the public. At the time, I had not considered my presence would signify anything of relevance:

The fact that you guys are here and you're obviously taking it very serious[ly], about the role of the library in the community and you want to see improvement. It's a really encouraging sign . . . the whole concept of libraries as the hub of the community . . . I visited the Brisbane State Library many times over the course of the years and I've never been asked to do an interview, and I think that says it all.

Libraries in general and, since his visit, the State Library of South Australia in particular, offered Luke a range of personal and professional support services that he not only appreciates for his own benefit, but which he also encourages others to use. He is aware of the different functions and purposes afforded by a reference library, as opposed to a lending library. He had already devised strategies for how to make the best use of the available library facilities in the city, depending on what needs would arise. For Luke, the site value and the services provided by various types of institutions serve different ends. This became clear when asked if he shares his experiences of libraries with others:

I'm an English teacher by trade and I'll bring my students, of course, to visit a place like this all the time. It would be great if there were borrowing facilities as well, but there aren't usually with State Libraries, I understand that. But I can also recommend to students the lending library in the mall . . . That would be a good first step, then we could come across here for research . . . so this would be a very good place for them to do their research.

Luke's responses indicate a level of planning and forethought prior to his visit. He was not simply considering what was available; he was envisioning how he would make use of the facilities, should Adelaide become his new home. His encounters with the State Library team members that morning had contributed to his favourable first impression of the city and the likelihood of his living here. His experiences in the Library were positive and, where they may have fallen short (borrowing and natural light), he actively devised alternatives to meet his needs. A significant part of his forward planning involved thinking how he would communicate the Library's value to others, particularly his students. If he moved to Adelaide, he would become an advocate for the value of the city's library facilities in general, but specifically for the facilities and opportunities provided by the State Library.

Luke's lifelong belief in the vital role of libraries in the community became apparent when he was asked about the importance of libraries to his life. Using his previous experiences in other libraries as a basis, he presumed that the State Library was crucially important to the life of this city:

> *Oh, really crucial. I'm very much a bookworm. I've always loved libraries. I think the actual space itself, the fact that it's on this really prestigious street in the middle of town, that's got to act like a focal point. Just, yeah, for me, the diversity of knowledge here that is available, that's always a huge stimulus for me and it always brings me back . . . because I was born on a farm and it was very . . . not much in the way of books . . . Yeah, so when you enter a space like this you see the possibilities.*

Luke is clearly drawn to libraries and knew of the Mortlock Wing prior to his arrival in Adelaide, suggesting that it was 'one of the most beautiful reading rooms in the world'. However, the story he would tell his students or others about the State Library would highlight the people he encountered, those who had made him feel welcome and comfortable in the space:

> *Well, just the friendliness, it's notable, not just here but on the streets of Adelaide too, everyone is really, well, they have time to respond to questions, they don't rush you. It also seems as though there's not a lot of people waiting for help, so for a larger population centre that's usually a problem – they don't usually have enough time to devote to each person. There's always someone else waiting in line. So I feel here that's not the case. They can really devote themselves to each person.*

Luke's responses are informed by his travel and lifelong love of learning and books. His experiences overseas add weight to the significance of his responses, in that his interest in the State Library may reflect his previous experience of moving to new cities: he may have taken a similar approach to getting to know the cities he had lived in while in Japan and South Korea.

Luke was struck by the friendliness, patience and level of attention granted by the visitor services team to a newcomer to the State Library. This personalised level of service, as well as the suitability of the city's library services, supported and informed his decision-making process regarding his potential move to Adelaide: he perceived the State Library as suitable for his needs. He recognised the State Library as a community information resource, a hub of cultural activity, 'notable' for its friendliness and the professionalism of the team members he encountered.

The impression the State Library made on Luke complemented his overall impression of Adelaide, influencing his decision on whether he would move South Australia. Although I am unaware of whether he relocated to South Australia, calculating the economic impact of a single young professional male moving to the state to set up a small business would be an interesting exercise.

MICHELLE: 'Libraries . . . are very important to me'

Michelle is new to Adelaide, having moved from Ohio (US) to be with her partner. Her new mother-in-law had suggested she 'come check it out'. During her first visit she brought her own book and quietly read. On her second visit – the day of this interview – the

State Library offered a quiet and secure place where she could sit and write Christmas cards. At the time of our interview, Michelle was not studying or researching any specific topic. She was exploring her new city during a time of transition and personal dislocation, engaging with a recommended and familiar space in which she was becoming comfortable and more confident amongst the Adelaide public.

When asked what kind of experiences or interactions at the Library were important to her, she responded that 'just being in a space that is designated for reading and writing helps me to focus'. Michelle's responses closely align with the theme of 'Quiet escape and security', whereby she feels safe and relaxed in a library space, enabling her to reconnect with familiar and valued experiences from her past, reliving them in her present reality and new surroundings. This experience also allows Michelle to reconnect and communicate with people who are important to her – through Christmas cards – despite being removed by distance. The disruption associated with moving continents and subsequent conflicts of personal identity are allayed by the familiarity of a library space. The State Library acts as a conduit, connecting her to her support network overseas as she navigates her new life and relationship. This sense of connection and familiarity across time and space was also noted in the survey data, particularly in relation to new arrivals and international students.

Like Luke, the comfort and familiarity Michelle now experiences in the State Library is the result of previous experiences in various libraries over the course of her lifetime. When questioned about the importance of the State Library to her life, as well as the cultural life of Adelaide, she mentioned her lifelong connection with libraries and a love of books, particularly when experiencing tight economic circumstances or a liminal stage of personal transition:

> I can't really speak to this library, as I haven't spent a lot of time here. But libraries in general are very important to me. You know, all throughout high school I went to the main branch library downtown, to take out books, do research projects and

*to borrow books if I couldn't afford to buy books myself . . .
Yeah, or it's great too if you are reading something by a new
author, someone you haven't heard of before and you don't
really want to invest in a book of theirs.*

Like Luke, Michelle also sees the State Library as a gateway into
the cultural life and history of Adelaide, a gateway accessed
by interacting with a staff member. She initially visited to see
the much-celebrated Mortlock Wing and was invited on a tour
through the buildings 'by a lady down at the front', most likely a
volunteer guide:

*She was very excited to give me a tour, so she showed me
around the whole place. They were having a sort of special
exhibition of toys from the past upstairs, which was really
cool. Then she left me in the Mortlock Wing and I had a look
around at the different displays.*

Michelle was clearly stimulated and excited by that first visit and
enjoyed the guided tour, discovering far more than the anticipated
quiet and secure place to read. Her sense of discovery and growing
confidence was palpable. When asked about the single story or
anecdote she would share about the State Library with others, her
response positioned her as an advocate of the State Library, and
what it offers those interested in the history of Adelaide:

*That Mortlock Wing is so gorgeous, that they should go look at
it and check out the displays on the ground floor of it because
that is where you can see the history of Adelaide and it's kind
of cool to see. There's one photograph of the CBD, I don't know
when it is [taken], but I think it is several decades ago, and you
can see how spare it is.*

Michelle was a young woman exploring a new relationship in a
new country and was far removed from all that was familiar to her.
Her responses demonstrate the institution's capacity to act as a
point of geographical and cultural orientation for newcomers to
Adelaide, achieving this with a level of comfort and security they

recognise from previous experiences in libraries in different parts of the world. The security and comfort she experienced in the State Library allowed her to focus, be sure of herself and consolidate her resilience to support her transition to what may be a new way of life. The volunteer guide was critical in delivering that sense of engagement, security and welcome. The impact of this role on newcomers, either embracing their new city or still finding their feet, is difficult to appreciate in quantifiable terms, but easy to understand as part of a personal narrative of self-discovery and adventure.

PAMELA: 'I seem to be one of those funny breeds that likes to see people face to face'

Pamela worked in the State Library as a volunteer with the English Language Improvement Service, known as ELIS. Her role was to help new arrivals from non-English-speaking backgrounds to improve their English language skills. The State Library offers this program free of charge, providing educational materials and conversation classes facilitated by trained volunteer tutors. Pamela's perception of the value she provides for the ELIS participants and to the State Library reflects the value of volunteers to the community. This perception is also in line with the Volunteering Australia's National Standards' definition of volunteering as 'Time willingly given for the common good and without financial gain'. Volunteering is considered a 'critical part of Australian society . . . Volunteers can provide the time, skills, expertise and points of view that enable an organisation to pursue programs and activities that benefit the community.'[3] ELIS is a modern-day reflection of the self-improvement and mutual support model that underpinned the formation of the State Library. However, Pamela sees the value of this service as delivering not only improved language skills but pathways to cultural understanding:

> *Migrants who want to settle here and participate in our culture in a much more meaningful way for them find it easier to integrate because many of them arrive with not an awful lot of idea about Australia.*

Pamela found that many new migrants had been exposed to American culture through mainstream Hollywood movies before they arrived in Australia and she hoped to impart a genuine sense of Australian culture to participants, even though she occasionally found it a challenge:

> *As we have people from all countries of the world and they speak all different languages, they all have different food that they eat and the different clothes that they wear and things like that. They always want to know 'oh what's your favourite Australian food?' . . . Lebanese food is my favourite food, so I try to let them know that it's not a homogenous society, but it's also a really exciting thing to learn about because we are a multicultural society. We're not homogenous and what you will do in your home is not what I will do.*

Pamela is an ELIS Desk Tutor, seeing people on an ad hoc basis for 30 minutes. A socially confident and outgoing person, she enjoys helping people, in a role 'that's all about communication and I really like that, and you get to talk to people from all over the world'. She sees many of the participants on a regular basis, confirming the importance of positive experiences, promoting return visitation, and the value of social interactions and connections made through the service. Those attending the service are encouraged to arrive with an enquiry to ensure that the conversation is practical as well as educational, with topics ranging from employment to immigration issues. Pamela's description of the service implied a bespoke, personalised approach to knowledge transfer, fostering a high level of cultural exchange:

> *It can be very interesting because you are talking to people from many different countries. For example, we had a guy from Iran . . . he'd come out every three months to be with his family here . . . And he'd talk to me all about his family in Iran and his daughter who is a doctor. He came here to practise his English and talk about their New Year, which is the twenty-first*

of March and what they did and the carpets they'd put on their
wall . . . so that's a very exciting part of things.

Pamela shared other examples of conversations she'd had with participants in the ELIS program, demonstrating the richness of the social and cultural transfer that takes place in the State Library, as well as the serendipitous nature of these interactions. When addressing participants' queries, all volunteer desk tutors adjust their responses to improve the participants' language skills. These personalised interactions and tailored conversations, based on specific enquiries, foster social and cultural understanding between participants and volunteers and within the broader community by sharing with others. Pamela embodies these instrumental benefits of the language classes, benefits that include the creation of social capital and community cohesion through knowledge exchange, as well as interpersonal connection through the pursuit of language improvement. These connections create benefits associated with positive impressions of Adelaide and Australia.

Pamela finds the diversity of people and their queries both exciting and interesting. She gauges her success by means of the immediate feedback of participants and is rewarded by their level of enthusiasm. She has found that ELIS participants are often isolated. The classes provide opportunities for connection and social interaction with their tutors, with the sharing of personal or professional topics for discussion in lieu of trusted friends or family members:

I had a young guy who came to see me this afternoon. I saw
him three weeks ago and he's been back to China . . . he had a
disappointing experience applying for Melbourne University
to do a degree and he needed to talk about that . . . he needed
an outlet and I felt constrained. If I was talking to him pri-
vately, I would have been a little bit more forthright . . . but . . .
as a volunteer, I've got a little bit more 'public face'.

Pamela is mindful of her responsibilities as a representative of the State Library, simultaneously remaining sensitive to the well-being of participants. When asked about the benefits generated by the State Library for the South Australian community, Pamela's response draws attention to the integrated nature of library service delivery, as well as the cross-institutional approach she engaged as a tutor:

> *The provision of free newspapers is really good because they have an absolutely fabulous collection of everyday newspapers. I try to direct [participants] there to learn about Australian culture, particularly the weekend papers. They always have very good cultural magazines which are absolutely fantastic to point them to, to help them with their reading . . . reading is the best thing they can do to help them with their talking.*

Utilising the Library's collections in this way demonstrates the diversity of value that one service can provide for the public. The newspaper is a trace for the future archive while also becoming a teaching and learning tool for the present ELIS Program, which has a limited budget for teaching and learning resources. This use of shared resources is strikingly similar to the way in which the Society for the Diffusion of Useful Knowledge and mutual support groups operated, in that they shared cheap and readily available printed material with others who could not afford to buy their own. This approach also demonstrates how resourceful many volunteers in libraries and other cultural organisations need to be to maintain services on a shoestring budget. The informality and conversational approach to learning and engagement belies the transformative impact these classes can have on the lives of the participants, who overcome specific challenges while improving their language skills in an engaging, nurturing and accessible environment. In improving language skills, participants become part of the Library community and increase their chances of integrating into Australian society.

Pamela confirms what may be implied from several of the interviews with international visitors and survey respondents; namely, that many new arrivals lack confidence and comfort in their new surroundings. Their lack of proficiency in speaking English exacerbates social isolation and personal dislocation at a time when they may need contact and support:

> They will come, very lacking in confidence, but they will sit there and speak for thirty minutes. It's then getting them to stop and listen, to have that two-way conversation with people and be able to listen and answer questions. That's really the basis of it. They think it's their speaking, but it's the listening and responding part of it they need the practice with.

Through the development of networks between students and tutors, ELIS participants improve their capacity to engage with others, overcoming their lack of confidence, isolation and dislocation. The impacts Pamela alludes to are supported by the findings of the of the United Nations State of the World's Volunteerism Report (2011) that found:

> There is mounting evidence that volunteer engagement promotes the civic values and social cohesion which mitigate violent conflict at all stages and that it even fosters reconciliation in post-conflict situations. By contributing to building trust, volunteer action diminishes the tensions that give rise to conflict and can also contribute to conflict resolution. It can also create common purpose in the aftermath of war. Indeed, people bound together through active participation and cooperation at local level are in a better position to resolve differences in non-confrontational ways.[4]

Part of the Library's contribution to the civic harmony and social cohesion of the state, Pamela's volunteering work provides opportunities for new arrivals to build trust in local institutions and cooperation with each other. Talking to Pamela about her motivations for volunteering at the State Library, I could see why she relates so well to the participants, having earlier experienced a sense of isolation herself:

> *I don't have a group of people who I find are really supportive and who, um, understand me. So I guess, particularly coming to the library after I did my degree, that was my way of overcoming that, and reading the newspapers so it sort of became social . . . I used to feel that I'd been out and at least socialising with people and things like that. So it's a bit of a different relationship.*

The State Library offered Pamela the opportunity to socialise and interact with others at a time when she, like the new arrivals she assists, was feeling alone and dislocated from the community. She identifies with the new arrivals as 'Others', not quite belonging in the 'social norms in this society'. This admission is also inspiring, in that she also is not merely aiding others transitioning to a new community, but in the process, is also gaining the support *she* requires, demonstrating the exchange value and reciprocal nature of volunteering. When asked what experiences she most values about the State Library, she offered a personal insight, one particularly relevant during and since the COVID-19 pandemic lockdowns:

> *I could actually go for days not talking to anybody . . . it's really important to me that I do this sort of work so I do actually have some social interaction with people. As I'm getting older it's really important to talk, because if you're not talking consistently to people, your voice muscles get tired . . . it's not easy for me to have ongoing conversations with people. I find when I do, my voice muscles get tired . . . I'm worried that I'm going to lose that ability . . . so that's another aspect of being able to socialise with people is being able to physically talk to people so your voice box keeps healthy.*

The ELIS program may not be considered the main function of the State Library, but is a vital public service, one that contributes to the common good in myriad ways rather than delivering direct and measurable economic outcomes for the state. With the new arrivals feeling welcomed into our society and semi-retired people like Pamela being able to socialise and maintain connections, everyone in our community could be seen as beneficiaries. We all enjoy a stable way of life and appreciate an identity that focuses on a fair go and equal opportunity amongst all citizens and visitors. We can speculate that such instrumental benefits, delivered by a volunteer labour force, may be partly the result of free services like the ELIS program at the State Library.

When asked about her 'best experience' at the State Library, Pamela suggested a recent afternoon function hosted for the State Library volunteers in appreciation for their services:

> They had a fantastic contemporary ensemble playing with a female singer and a cellist, rhythm guitarist and a drummer . . . I really enjoyed listening to that music. That to me was really good. Also, when I started volunteering here I put my name down to be a tour guide . . . and I did the tour and that was really fascinating, looking at the way they were digitally archiving things and the newspapers going to microfiche and the book binding place and those sorts of things. So, you saw underneath the bottom of the library and that was really fascinating to do here. That was a great time for me.

When asked how important the Library is to her life and the cultural life of Adelaide, Pamela suggested that 'we probably won't know until it's not here anymore'. She was aware of the funding cuts to the State Library's budget and their impact on both staffing levels and resources:

> Having been here and seen what's happened to the library over the last year or so it makes you really think about how important these places are to people and what a valuable resource . . . and also a little bit sad about how underused they are by people.

Pamela considers that the convenience of digital technologies impacts on levels of social interaction, which she so clearly values:

> Our technology is encouraging people to sit at their computer

and not go out and see another human being and I hate that.
I'm home and unless I go out, I don't see another human being.
I seem to be one of those funny breeds that likes to see people
face to face.

When asked for the story or anecdote she would share with someone about the Library, Pamela would tell people that the State Library is:

A great place to come if you are in need of intellectual stim-
ulation . . . You feel like you've been out for the day [which]
is not recognised about the place and appreciated. It can be a
very stimulating place, and you feel like you've been out in the
world. That's what I like coming here for.

Pamela's most valuable contribution to the Library community and by extension to Adelaide may be the genuine pleasure she brings to her delivery of the visitor experience and the relationships she generates with the ELIS participants. The Library is more than a source of personal enjoyment and social connection for Pamela. She also appreciates all facets of the Library's activities and promotes them to visitors. Her empathy with visitors, and her enthusiasm for sharing her experiences with others, could be considered an exchange of goods of the same value, benefiting all the parties involved and consolidating the institutional value of the State Library.

SOPHIA: 'Nobody ask for your visa'

Before visiting the State Library to participate in the free ELIS classes, Sophia had been living in Adelaide for two years. She visited the Library for a specific purpose and, like Michelle and others, she found more than she expected.

Originally from Spain, Sophia moved to Adelaide for her husband's work commitments with a Spanish company which had relocated members of its team to South Australia. She wanted to work during her time in Australia but to obtain a working visa, she was required to achieve a high level of proficiency in English:

I began to come for the English classes . . . I come for this, it's
fantastic. . . . I used to come monthly or perhaps twice a month
but this month I want to come every day because I am going
to take the IELTS in two Saturdays so I want to come . . . to
receive English classes.

A mother of two young boys and a lawyer by training, Sophia is
drawn to the State Library for peace and quiet while she studies
for the IELTS: 'I go to concentrate and there is a person who is
working, seeing if there is any problem, if somebody is speaking
and this morning it was fantastic. I could work so very, very good.'

Like Michelle, the State Library also offered Sophia welcome,
comfort and familiarity in a new country, reinforcing her sense
of identity and purpose. She had visited at least one other public
library in South Australia, but found it did not suit her needs:

I went yesterday to Westlake [sic] Library and it was horrible
because I didn't know there were libraries with activities for
children. So I arrive . . . very worried for my exam and at 10
o'clock, all the children singing in the library [rueful laughter]
oh I can't believe it. It's fantastic, I love that activity but it's
just that I didn't know that here in Adelaide the libraries . . .
because in Spain, it's . . . a library means silent [sic] which is
what I need now.

Due to her circumstances at home, a quiet library space was vital
to Sophia as she prepared for her exam:

I can do at home, but at home I now have my sons, [they] are
on holidays, and it's like, all the day, 'Mum, blah, the food!'
[laughter]. So I wake up, I leave the food, I go to the library and
I don't want to know anything [hear anything from her sons].

Sophia demonstrates again how important the English classes
provided by the State Library are for new arrivals to Australia and
how they function as a gateway to Adelaide community and cultural life. The volunteer teachers such as Pamela play a vital role,
providing assistance, as well as creating a sense of welcome:

The first time I came, the teacher, the English teacher was so friendly and welcoming. She understand [sic] me so well and she helped me a lot with the pronunciation, like you can't say that. It was like 'Oh my God', she was doing this for nothing like the volunteering work and for me it is so important. That was, I can't believe it, that you know here in this building it is so beautiful and so big and . . . in the centre of Adelaide. To come take English classes here . . . nobody ask for your visa and [laughter] . . . the condition[s] for foreigners in Australia are so hard and sometime[s] you feel like illegal person . . . 'I have 507 visa! I have 507 visa!' It's like . . . not for nothing but when you arrive at a place where nobody asks you nothing . . . [HR: You can just come and be yourself?] Yes, relax.

Sophia's responses exemplify the pressures faced by new arrivals, pressures that most residents may never experience. Her visa status, and how it determines her position in the community, looms large in her daily life and she values the openness and welcoming reception of the staff and volunteers at the State Library. Her visa status, or where she comes from, does not define her. She does not need to prove her eligibility and can use the space for her purposes. No one questioned her right to do so. While the value of this accessibility is likely taken for granted by many amongst the Library's public, it is notably precious to people from other countries, where similar services and facilities may be limited or restricted. These democratic values are another link to the State Library's ongoing contribution to the community and to the principles of universal access to education and information that influenced its founding.

The 'access value' that visitors and new arrivals gain by engaging with locals is strong in both the survey responses and interview subjects. The State Library creates value for the public through its formal information delivery services. However, for some respondents, the serendipitous interpersonal interactions between the visitor service teams (paid and volunteer) and the public are just as, if not more, significant. The responses and interviews highlight that the capacity of volunteers and team members to demonstrate empathy and respond to the needs of new arrivals is critical to the co-creation of cultural value. This is an important contribution to the creation of institutional value, which we touched on earlier: the volunteers and visitor service professionals are representatives of the Library, which symbolises (as a government institution) the way people understand their relationship with the state. If they feel welcome and respected by the State Library, they feel part of the broader community.

The language classes enabled Sophia to focus on her exams without the distraction of her young family. These classes also made her aware of other opportunities offered by the Library. She has since encouraged others within her group of friends to visit, to simply enjoy the space and 'pass the time'. She has become an ambassador:

> *I am telling my Spanish friends the other day, 'please come to the library, is fantastic place, one of the best in Adelaide'. You know, not all the people have the same circumstances and necessities . . . I want to study . . . the friends I have, most of the wives came for two years and . . . it's like they pass the time, they don't do anything . . . so they come here to enjoy the time. But I want to be here because I want to study, because I want to work, so for me it is very important to have a place where I come to study.*

Sophia's compulsion to study reflects her background as a lawyer, as well as her relationships with libraries and other cultural institutions from her past, all of which inform her subjective experiences in South Australia. When asked how important the State Library is to her and perhaps to the cultural life of Adelaide, her response reflected the ongoing nature of her education. Finding locations and spaces to support this pursuit, which in turn supports her personal identity:

> *Is very important because I really don't like so much the art gallery or the painting, or [those] kind of cultural activities. But*

> *I have always loved to study, so I don't know, it is part of the culture [where] I feel better. I have always been surrounded by books. I studied law [laughter] so I have to study a lot so . . . when I finish I say 'I'm never going to get a book [again] in my life. I'm fed up.' But some years, yes, I study again, because you are used to do[ing it] and you know you can never stop to learn . . . Yes, it is part of me.*

Perhaps the greatest value activated by her experiences at the State Library, though, will be within her own family, by providing a powerful example to her children of the value of self-improvement and transformation. Sophia wanted to share the space with her sons, providing them with their own entry point to both Adelaide and the library experience:

> *So there was a group of students and one of them said 'Oh it's like . . . Harry Potter! [laughter] Oh it's like the library in Harry Potter! Well is true! [laughter]. Is like, [sic] is beautiful too, that part of the library and so . . . last Monday I came with my son because I wanted that he could see the library of Harry Potter but was closed on Monday so is our bad luck . . . the youngest will be on holidays so next week they will come with me . . . the silence is a problem for them but I have seen this part [HR: the Hub?], this is perfect for them with the Wi-Fi and I will be studying upstairs.*

Sophia's positive experiences of the State Library will inform her children's levels of engagement and socialisation with other Library users and the Adelaide urban community. Through their visits, her sons will have the opportunity to learn what to expect and how to be behave in the shared and enchanting atmosphere of the 'Harry Potter' (Mortlock) Library. The Hub space, designed as a more social and interactive community space, is an environment where the benefits of the Library's facilities can be experienced without the need to temper boisterous behaviour. Sophia, the studious parent, and her children are accepted at the State Library as equal citizens and are made welcome. No one asked to see their visa.

The anonymity and welcome she and her family received from the staff must have been refreshing, with the State Library providing them with environments to suit their needs and respective stages of life, regardless of where they come from. The institution reinforced Sophia's personal identity and her capacity to engage with her new community. As important as this is, perhaps of equal value is the formative role the institution played in her sons' relationship with Adelaide, and in turn, with every library throughout their lives. I wonder how they look back on their time in Adelaide. What do they say about the State Library of South Australia now that they have probably returned to Spain?

ALEX: 'It's something we can proudly show off'

It is not merely lonely children who are enchanted by the State Library's 'Harry Potter' associations. Alex is visiting the State Library to prepare for his return to the workforce. The State Library provides both an escape and an enjoyable ambience as he revises and updates his knowledge of the contemporary world of finance.

> I came into the State Library because I like a nice quiet place to study. Sometimes the university is ok, but sometimes you just feel like a change. I find that the Mortlock Wing is just the perfect place to just sit down and study because it's just, well, it feels like Hogwarts. It's just a fantastic environment to study in.

Alex's response demonstrates several elements of the educational and transformational values offered by the State Library. Once more, we can see a common thread linking today's users to the institution's nineteenth-century origin in the mutual improvement and self-education movements. Alex obtained his tertiary qualifications several years ago and hopes to improve his job prospects:

> I'm not working at the moment, so I'm a former student in finance . . . I'm in the process of revisiting some stuff because I'm thinking about doing some further professional qualifications maybe at some stage . . . just going over some old

textbooks and things. Getting back into the swing of things because it's been a while since I actually had hard core sat and studied.

Alex visited the State Library 'at least once a week'. He has engaged with libraries since he was a child, with his comments illustrating how the quality of those first library experiences contributes to how he values the State Library as an adult. His earliest experience was:

Probably a school visit to Tea Tree Gully Library, the public library out there. It's all been rebuilt since then . . . It's moved across to bigger, newer premises. But I was in there the other day and I thought 'yeah, this is familiar'. But it was when I was in the toy library that I went 'whoa, that's bringing back memories' because I forgot you can even borrow toys from the library.

I asked about how he interacts with other members of the public during his visits to the State Library. His answer provides an interesting insight into the collaborative nature of institutional value: the collective awareness, site-specific expectations and behaviours between patrons. These elements vary, depending on which space in the Library you visit:

Certainly, there is the Mortlock Wing and you've got different areas of the library. If I'm in there, the interactions of value with people are just if they keep quiet [laughter]. I don't mind the slamming of a book or a cough every now and again, but if you're going to walk around in there and talk and take photos and stuff, just be discreet about it and that's what I value in there. But, in the other part I don't mind if someone comes in and sits down and has a chat with you . . . you know if I was studying for an exam, I would go to the Mortlock. If I was studying for, you know, just having a read, doing a crossword or whatever, I would go into the other part.

Alex describes the unspoken, unwritten rules amongst patrons, the accepted codes of public conduct not enforced by members of staff, but by the public themselves. He displays a degree of ownership of and belonging to the State Library – in common with other survey respondents: they are not only co-creators of the experience, but 'co-custodians' of the space, self-moderating their behaviours and transmitting that expectation to others. Rather than being silenced by the stereotypical stern librarian, members of the public have internalised the role of moderator, becoming self-appointed guardians of the experience for others because they value it so much themselves. They voluntarily maintain and preserve what they believe is valuable. It's an intriguing group dynamic. A sense of community emerges from Alex's observations, and demonstrates a personal connection with both the site and the professional staff with whom he interacts regularly. Security officers, particularly those at the cloakroom, are often the first people with whom visitors to the State Library interact:

> *People here are really great because they're there if you need them. On a couple of occasions, I've spoken to people on the front desk and the first port of call for me is when I'm dropping my backpack off up [there], you know, I'm talking to the security guys. They're really friendly . . . I don't know whether that's part of their job specifically, but they certainly go above and beyond in terms of how friendly they are. They're more like a concierge service really, you know, drop off your bags . . . they're all really friendly . . . I value that.*

Private security staff are usually engaged by cultural institutions through external companies, although their public presence means they function as representatives of the institution. They are regular, friendly faces and often put themselves in the line of physical and verbal threats to protect the collections, as well as visitors. Like the volunteers, they contribute to the creation of cultural value by providing a reassuring human presence and points of interaction in the Library, even though technically they do not work for the institution.

Alex's experience of welcome and comfort in the space contributes to his satisfaction with the Library. When asked to share his best experience at the State Library, he suggested it was:

> *[W]hen I found out that the Institute Building was part of the Library . . . I was stoked with that. You can go through there and you've got galleries up here and I knew that, but I thought you had to go out and around and everything to see what was in there. But now, from time to time I'll leave that way specifically so I can see what's going on in there, because you know, they've had a virtual reality thing. They've had something on rockets . . . I would never have thought to go out of my way to find that, but given it was there, you know, fantastic. So I'd wander around there and spend twenty minutes, half an hour reading stuff, learning about Woomera, and what goes on with rockets. It was a pleasant and exciting thing.*

The State Library enables Alex to extend and refresh his professional knowledge. In doing so, he is also able to explore other topics that spark his curiosity. His serendipitous discoveries of exhibitions in the Institute Building demonstrate the unforeseen aspects of cultural experience: value is also activated through unanticipated encounters and personal interactions between people and objects, which are unplanned and surprising. Yet they extend an individual's understanding or intellect, resulting in the emergence of a new interest, passion or professional pursuit. This very subjective and coincidental phenomenon offers a perspective on the latent nature of cultural value and the unexpected way it may be activated. Aspects of cultural experience such as these are usually absent from the cultural value debate, making Alex's narrative of surprise and discovery a valuable contribution.[5] He described how these surprise encounters assist him to overcome boredom and keep his visits fresh – and are a direct consequence of the State Library's location:

> *[It's] all part of the fun of coming in here. You never know. It's not just coming in to study. People are different. Things going*

on will be different and where it's situated as well. If you get bored with the study, which happens, just go along to the art gallery or the museum, you know? It's right next door.

Some representatives of an institution may view feedback suggesting that the visitors to their institution are there because they are 'bored' as a negative. However, Alex's random explorations of the State Library, as well as the Art Gallery of South Australia and the South Australian Museum, demonstrate some fundamental aspects of human agency and curiosity, as well as the networked nature of the State Library experience for the public – it is their entry point to their experiences of the North Terrace Cultural Precinct. The separation of institutional boundaries doesn't really figure in his mind. Alex's studies are driven by his professional goals and ambitions, yet he is more than a potential employee or economic unit. As an adult member of the community, he contributes to the maintenance of these spaces and displays a sense of proprietorship. By engaging with the North Terrace Cultural Precinct for the purpose of accessing information, as well as participating in serendipitous boredom-reducing cultural experiences, Alex is exercising his free will as an active, thinking citizen, exploring the intellectual life of the community. He is part of the open civic forum of cultural experience and a participant in knowledge generation and exchange:

I think the location of the State Library couldn't be better. Because it's certainly, in terms of stature . . . it doesn't detract in any way from this area at all. It certainly adds to it and by having the museum and the art gallery and university right next to it, even Government House just there. You don't go in there, but it all creates a synergy and an area . . . it is a cultural hub and it's very important to South Australia to maintain that because it's become a feature of Adelaide and of South Australia, and no doubt Australia. It's something we can proudly show off – 'Look we've got a library, we've got a museum, we've got this and this and this'.

Alex is also aware of the precinct's potential as a tourism draw-card, not so much as a driver of economic impact, but as a source of state pride. It is 'something we can proudly show off' and it contributes to the state's identity. As new institutions develop along North Terrace, he also sees that cultural value increasing:

> *And in broader terms along North Terrace, you've got the new RAH down there and there's a few others, SAHMRI and things. That's all adding to the scope, you know, it makes me proud to be South Australian.*

Alex's responses reflect what Georgina Born describes as 'retentions' and 'protentions': the ability of some members of the public to see value in the cultural experience today, such as that provided by the State Library, but also what it could provide in the future.[6] When asked to describe the importance of the State Library to his life as well as to the cultural life of Adelaide, Alex became quite animated, expressing his belief in the transformational value and potential of not only the State Library but of the North Terrace Cultural Precinct, describing it as a singular entity:

> *[I]t's something people should be proud of, as South Australians, to have that, you know? It's not 'oh, it's a library' or 'oh it's a museum' or whatever. It's a precinct that we can say 'South Australians come here to make themselves smarter'. That's got to be a great thing. An education precinct, that's got to be . . . It's great.*

Alex's relationship with the State Library and the North Terrace Precinct highlights the potential for inter-connectivity between institutions and their visitors: policy and planning decisions for the precinct must consider these relationships across the cultural precinct. There is a risk the public may lose their sense of connection, welcome, ease of access and ownership, if the public's perception of the civic value of the cultural precinct is ignored.

Alex recognised the diversity of needs and levels of interest in the Library in the wider community, a recognition generally lacking in policy and advocacy conversations relating to the role and value of the arts and cultural sector. When asked whether he shares his experiences at the State Library with others, Alex describes how he selects his target audience:

> Some people are going to appreciate it more than others. If you're talking to an avid reader about some experience you've had in the Library, they're going to take away from that a lot more than somebody who, for instance, doesn't place as high a priority on learning and education. So yeah, if I go to the Library, I share it around. It's not something that I go 'Oh, I'm a book nerd because I sit there and read in the Library'. No, it's an important thing, and me telling other people might inspire them to come along as well.

As with a cricket match or a talk on rocket science, not every member of the public is going to want or be able to attend. As explained earlier, institutions and cultural events like festivals are compelled by the pressures of the prevailing market mantra of constant growth to continually strive to improve attendances and thereby increase the return on government investment, a problematic and unsustainable expectation.[7] Alex provides an alternative view of how to nurture cultural value. The most passionate supporters of and greatest advocates for the State Library and all the North Terrace cultural institutions are their existing audiences, those who maintain the productive ambience of the spaces and who share their experiences through their networks of fellow students and potential users to promote the institution and the benefits they confer. This 'word of mouth' promotion demonstrates the incremental generation of cultural value, fostered by the reciprocal trust and ongoing relationships between the public and State Library team members. This is a clear illustration of Holden's concept of institutional value. It is a relationship based on trust in the institution and the public's experience of connection and community, such as Alex encountered. When asked for a story he would share about the Library – apart from his delight of the Mortlock Wing and appreciation of the resources and enjoyment of the exhibitions – he spoke with the fervour of a committed supporter who:

> . . . can't stop singing the praises of the security guys because like I said they're not (I'm doing air quotes here for the recording) [laughter]. They're not meant to be what they are, in terms of what their actual role is. But they're very important to adding to the overall vibe of the place. I think that when the Mortlock Wing opened, and the renovations that have been done here, you know, that's great, that's really cool. I think the facilities here are world class . . . It is a State Library and it is something that we can be proud of.

As a returning student of finance, Alex is also aware of the complex and precarious nature of the institution's relationship with government, alluding to the efficiency dividends all cultural institutions along North Terrace have regularly faced in recent decades. He goes to the heart of the challenges perpetuating the cultural value debates:

> I know it's difficult sometimes when you have to quantify, and I understand too, from a government perspective, sometimes it's difficult to justify their budgets towards something like this [the Library], but if you can hand them the stories and qualitatively value it, rather than quantitatively, then it starts . . . it just hits home how important it is to the culture of South Australia.

Alex nurtures not merely a fondness for, but a functional and productive relationship with the State Library of South Australia. He is also well positioned as a citizen to appreciate the many ways by which the Library contributes to the reputation, identity, culture, education and economy of South Australia. Any policy decisions regarding the future of the North Terrace cultural institutions will affect him and all those like him who are usually invisible to policy-makers. With a thorough understanding of the economic imperatives driving the policy decisions impacting on the State Library's budget, he can understand and articulate the challenges as coherently as he does his passion and appreciation for the site. He also acknowledges the need to balance the quantitative data informing policy decisions by including qualitative 'stories' to convey what the State Library means to the public. Alex recognises the need identified by both economists and cultural value scholars in Australia and overseas – the necessity for a balanced approach to reporting cultural value.

JAMIE: 'You get a feeling for a place by going to a place like this'

Not all patrons of the Library come to research or read. Jamie was visiting from Sydney for the cricket. When asked why he also decided to visit the State Library, he explained that it was near the cricket ground. When further prompted, he commented that he was visiting because 'Well, it's also . . . an iconic establishment on North Terrace'.

Jamie visits galleries or state libraries when travelling in different cities. He finds cultural institutions to be rewarding experiences, providing insights into how communities see themselves:

> Oh, you learn about the history of the place or the . . . pride which people take with their local cultural . . . entities, whatever they are, be it sport or opera or whatever. You get a feeling for a place by going to a place like this very efficiently . . . clearly they preserve certain values and it's really . . . I mean you can go and admire a few old buildings down in Port Adelaide and it gives you the same feeling. But you get . . . it's much more efficient to come here and take everything that can be learnt, perhaps. Potentially, everything that can be learnt.

Jamie recognises the State Library as a cultural heritage site, as well as an archive of knowledge and teaching resources. In his view, the site is significant for what it represents – South Australia's values and historical associations. His use of the term 'efficient' when describing a visit to the Library as a means of 'getting a feeling for a place' indicates that he prefers to make the most of his time by accessing concise learning or cultural experiences. He had time to spare but did not want to waste it, so was seeking quick and effective experiences, ones that could be enjoyed during the lunch breaks at the cricket. Jamie is a return visitor, counting two or three previous visits over the last 20 years. He believed that he 'can see that South Australia ... values a place like this because it's been well maintained or well thought through as a place to attract people'. In his view, the presentation of the Library reflects how it is valued by South Australians. At the same time, it represents the state to visitors, like a business card or corporate logo. Its architectural beauty, the time-efficient experiences on offer and the reliability of service combine to play a symbolic role in the promotion of the South Australian identity. From a marketing perspective, the State Library contributes to the State's 'brand' values.

Jamie does not make any overt comparisons between the State Library of New South Wales and the State Library of South Australia; rather, he conveys the expectation that what he can experience in his home state he will be able to access in others. He describes 'Our State Library on Macquarie Street, it's a major cultural centre. There's always an art exhibit or an historical exhibit. Or both.' Jamie's comment is further indication of the transnational theme, which emerged in the survey data and earlier interviews, whereby the public's familiarity and comfort with the State Library is influenced by their previous experiences of other libraries. However, Jamie also recognises the evolving nature of information access and the developing roles played by library institutions in communities. When discussing the Mortlock Wing, he observes that its use may change over time to reflect the changing expectations demanded of institutions and the ongoing responsibility to maximise the potential of the space:

> One day those books will be taken down from the shelves and
> something else put in its place. That wouldn't be a tragedy,
> because I think if it's seen as a centre of information about

history and culture obviously there's the opportunity of all other aspects of human knowledge to be accessed here. As long as it's a well-resourced access point for all that ... whether or not the books are on the shelves, it doesn't matter, in my opinion in this information age of the internet.

Jamie is interested in the developments in the field information access and technology, recognising the State Library's role in facilitating and promoting good online practices, particularly for young people:

It probably gets taught in schools now, but kids need to be taught how to access the internet, certainly to be critical of what's there. It does require a lifetime of experience, I find, to be sure, you know, reasonably sure that you are ... getting the best out of it.

Although Jamie believes that libraries will continue their role as facilitators of online information access for schoolchildren, he also values more traditional experiences and interactions. He has strong opinions about the role of libraries in communities, based on the educational or enlightening potential of information and 'entertainment':

I have internet access and a quiet place at home ... But if I go to the library it's probably to get a book or a DVD. I don't approve of libraries having DVD collections because I think it is the wrong emphasis. It's a source of entertainment. Mind, I've said that I came here to be entertained, at least mildly intellec-tually stimulated ... but when I see DVD sets of TV series and some of them are pretty inane, I think 'hmmm, I'd rather not see my rates going towards that'.

Echoing the early colonial debates on the purpose and function of a public library in South Australia, these sentiments question the nature of the content to be offered, who should pay for it and, consequently, who will have access.

Jamie demonstrates a depth of insight (even while occasionally contradicting himself) into the future of libraries, particularly the changing roles of librarians. Like Alex, he is aware of the economic challenges all library staff face in the current policy environment, joking about the extremes to which libraries may be forced to go to quantify their return on government investment:

> *Librarians I dare say have cause to be anxious . . . they probably have to justify themselves annually in terms of membership, number of borrowing card holders, number of counts of people as they enter through the door and all that sort of stuff, so relevance is obviously important. You know, they could put on strippers I suppose and boost their numbers [laughter] but obviously they won't be doing that . . . Where do you draw the line? To me, offering DVDs is just a step too far, but for others, you know, it might be that the line is somewhere else.*

Jamie cuts to the heart of the issue of equating higher visitor numbers with success, the misinterpreted authority of quantitative data collection devoid of qualitative context. 'Strippers' may well increase the numbers through the door, but obviously their presence doesn't support the goals, mission or values of the institution. It was a joke, but each time I read it, I find it harder to laugh along. Like Alex, Jamie recognises the reporting incongruities expected of cultural organisations when justifying public expenditure, while maintaining their mission, values and relevance. Alex's and Jamie's responses indicate that members of the public have a sophisticated understanding of the complexity surrounding cultural value and how it affects institutions such as the State Library.

As a repeat visitor to Adelaide, and a regular user of the State Library of New South Wales, Jamie provides an important perspective on the role of the State Library in the context of the North Terrace Cultural Precinct; that is, how the institutions like the Library, Gallery and Museum reflect the priorities of the Adelaide community, South Australian values, and how they may develop in the future. This perspective, which has been expressed by several survey respondents and other interview subjects, appears to reflect a unified experience of the North Terrace Cultural Precinct in the minds of both South Australians and visitors to our city, rather than separate experiences of multiple institutions. And with each interview it became more difficult to separate them.

CARLO: 'Very valuable, very helpful and very meaningful for me
Carlo had been in Adelaide for two years and was completing his Master of Education at the University of Adelaide. Originally from China, he spent several years working professionally in Italy, adopting a European name to ease his former colleagues' pronunciation difficulties. Carlo is an articulate interview subject, offering detailed descriptions of the significance of his experiences at the State Library. He presented a complex network of values and meaning gained through his Library experiences, which impact his studies, his personal relationships and sense of belonging in South Australia.

Carlo is a regular visitor to the State Library's ELIS classes, attending 'every day or every other day'. By establishing a rapport with some of the volunteers facilitating the program, Carlo developed a strong affinity with the institution, such that he feels a sense of belonging and inclusion.

> I come here for one reason; to refine my English. So, because I know there are two volunteer programs, which one [should I attend]? One of them is the group conversation which I attended several times. The other one is the desk tutor, so I can make an appointment which is about 30 minutes long so I can have face to face conversation with the volunteers, either discussing my assignments or my writing or simply just practising my conversation skills and I feel that that is really, really helpful.

Carlo is aware of and impressed by the benefits these classes offer to all international students new to South Australia and for whom English is a second language. The location of University of Adelaide and University of South Australia campuses along North Terrace means that their international student cohort has convenient access to the classes held at the State Library. This proximity enables Carlo to visit the Library between his lectures and tutorials, a situation that suggests that these universities benefit from the free services delivered by the Library, which not only improve students' immediate outcomes through improved communication skills, but also their familiarity with Australian customs and culture. Ultimately, these language classes will improve their chances of academic success and future employment. Before COVID-19, the ELIS classes were promoted through word-of-mouth amongst Adelaide's international student cohort, with Carlo hearing of these opportunities though another Chinese friend, who attached a high degree of 'importance to refining his English'. Given his already-proficient level of English as a second language, Carlo confessed to feeling frustrated by the limitations of the group conversation classes aimed at people with a limited command of English. He appreciated the opportunity the classes presented, but was after more of a challenge himself:

> *To be honest I felt group conversation was very easy for me . . . it was very good to know that they provide these kinds of programs for international students or for anyone who doesn't speak English as their first language. So I really appreciate this, what they have arranged for us, because this is free of charge and it runs every week from Monday to Friday, so both in the morning and in the afternoon.*

He described how often social and cultural isolation was experienced by international students and how the Library helped him to overcome this. When asked what interactions or experiences at the Library were most important to him, Carlo was clear that it was the opportunity to interact with the volunteers and engage in conversation with an Australian person as a means of improving his language skills:

> *The one-to-one conversation. Because that is exactly what I need. I really feel that it is one of the most amazing things at this library because as an international student I feel it is my*

responsibility to always refine my English and sometimes it is very hard for me to find a lot of opportunities to do that. If you don't really know lots of local friends . . . you don't really have the opportunities to do that. You can't simply walk on the street and stop a stranger and say 'please practise English with me' [laughter] . . . so you need to find a place with people who are willing to do that with me. I feel very fortunate to have finally found a place like the library. And also, because the location is really convenient, very centrally located and not very far from where I live.

The experience he describes is akin to a cultural introduction, an open forum where Carlo and his peers may learn behaviours and social mores to ease their transition into the Adelaide community while also improving his employment prospects. This was confirmed when I asked him to nominate his best experience at the State Library:

I feel that I've already established a kind of connection with some volunteers that I talk with very frequently. They share part of my life, I feel . . . I need some suggestions, some advice, some information or just some perspective from some local people about the university I will potentially go to or the degree I will do . . . It's not just about the language classes. I know I now feel that kind of personal connection, also the emotion . . . because all of them are all very well qualified people. They are. A lot of them were teachers when they were young, so that is the reason why I feel that the advice from them is very valuable, very helpful and very meaningful for me.

The interactions between the public and the service delivery teams have an impact beyond their official roles or purpose; they randomly support newcomers such as Carlo, Sophia and Michelle with their transition into the Adelaide community and culture at a time when they have few others to turn to or trust. These interactions build trust and confidence for people pursuing their aspirations in new surroundings. Carlo describes how he can always visit the

Library and 'have a chat with them' if he has some 'difficulties in doing anything, or if there is something very confusing'. Another example indicates not only his deep understanding of Australian cultural practices, but also the diversity of public service delivered by the Library via the conversation classes:

> *Yesterday I asked about the way people celebrate Christmas here, because this is about a cultural issue. We have Spring Festival in China this is the occasion on which there is a family reunion and I have heard that people celebrate Christmas also by family reunion here . . . I didn't really know that it's appropriate to join one of my local friends at the family celebrations of this festive season, because we . . . in China, if you try to celebrate Spring Festival with friends, sometimes it is not culturally very appropriate because . . . it is exclusively for family reunion . . . it is not a perfect time for people to share with their friends. I received an invitation from one of my friends here to say he is very willing to share part of his Christmas holiday with me, but I didn't really know if it was culturally appropriate . . . because sometimes it can be just out of kindness or out of politeness, so I do not really know if he really means that. I just wanted to confirm this, so I came here and I asked one of the volunteers and they said it was ok.*

Several interview subjects acknowledged that the advice provided by the State Library on local customs and behaviours, as well as the opportunity to engage with the Library community, contributed to their sense of welcome and confidence. While their experience of the State Library creates a positive impression of the city generally, these value perceptions – critically for this case study – illustrates how the State Library builds trust, community identity and social cohesion for many members of the public. This is evidence of Holden's description of institutional value:

> *In their interactions with the public, cultural organisations are in a position to increase – or indeed decrease – such things as our trust in each other, our idea of whether we live in a fair*

and equitable society, our mutual conviviality and civility, and a
whole host of other public goods. So the way in which our insti-
tutions go about their business is important. Institutional value
should therefore be counted as part of the contribution of cul-
ture to producing a democratic and well-functioning society.[8]

Although there may be other avenues available for such advice, some new arrivals to Adelaide prefer to come to the State Library for such personal services. These opportunities, delivered by local and trusted experts, supported international students in their transition from diverse social and cultural backgrounds to the South Australian community. This interpersonal exchange and cultural transfer impact directly on the quality of Carlo's experience of life in Adelaide and represent an extension of the traditional role of the State Library – that of information provision – to being an active agent in the creation and reinforcement of social cohesion and cultural value:

It's not just about conversation, they are helping you with very
valuable advice and information . . . On culture and local life . . .
everything! . . . I feel very relaxed and also very secure because
now I know very clearly that whenever I have a problem I can
come here [laughter].

Impressed by the quality and helpfulness of the Library's services, Carlo has become an advocate for the State Library amongst his peers. However, like Alex, he also acknowledges that the experience is not for everyone:

I also recommend this library for some of my classmates so
some of them came here. [However] every person is in dif-
ferent circumstances so I can't expect all people to do the
same, simply because I like coming here. But I do try my best
to recommend this place to other people.

Carlo also volunteers at the Adelaide Airport, which adds to his appreciation and respect for the volunteers at the State Library. In his volunteer role he is 'very happy to see people doing the same thing. Always strangers helping strangers. I really appreciate that.'

Carlo's English language skills enabled him to complete a Master's degree at the University of Adelaide. However, he intends to pursue further post-graduate study and become a teacher. He plans to maintain his connection with the Library through the conversation classes to ensure that he meets the high level of language skills this next career step requires:

> *My next degree I will probably do at Flinders . . . in terms of language ability, it will be very demanding because in order to be a teacher you need to have good language skills so that is the reason why I will continue coming here.*

Like Alex, who intended to encourage his students to use the Library, Carlo will continue to embed the benefits of his experiences at the State Library in the community by passing on the language skills he has gained to his students. When asked for a story or anecdote about the Library he would share, he suggests the value of the conversation classes, and the convenient physical location of the State Library. His response brings into focus the value he co-creates through his interactions with the volunteers, as well as his subjective appreciation of the collective experience on site:

> *I want to mention, it is very important, the environment here is excellent. The vibes are excellent for reading. Sometimes you know I always bring a book here because . . . when I am waiting for my time slot, I just do some reading . . . I feel that everybody around me is doing the same thing, so it is easier for me to focus on my reading or my other things . . . Yes, very good environment plus very nice people, nice and helpful people. It is a perfect combination.*

Carlo gains security, confidence, advice and focus at the Library, which not only benefit his studies – his main purpose for living in Adelaide – but also his plans for the future. However, his responses also indicate a deep appreciation of his direct interactions with other people and the opportunity to share a space, a place that serves more intrinsic social needs for connection, cultural exchange, and the building of trust between members of the community. Carlo's level of dependence on the State Library is commensurate with how he gives back to the institution, as an advocate for the language classes in the international student community. The State Library has helped him to form friendships and find a place where he, and others like him, will be welcomed, supported, and eventually feel they belong.

KATE AND GRANT: 'The heart of everything that goes on'

Kate and Grant are work colleagues from Flinders University visiting the State Library for a meeting. The State Library cafe provides a convenient venue to meet with other colleagues, who are based at the SA Museum. According to Kate, the cafe:

> . . . sits between the museum, gallery and science centre and it's generally free of screaming children and loud tourists. It's a more professional space and a bit more respectful in a way, I think. You can actually have formal meetings without disruption.

Kate works part-time at the SA Museum Science Centre and is completing a doctorate at Flinders University. She regularly visits the Library's cafe because 'people leave the place tidy'. She believes this shows a relationship between the State Library and the public that is more respectful than that between 'a lot of other public spaces'. Grant agrees, viewing the quiet atmosphere at the State Library as more conducive for a meeting than other public spaces in Adelaide:

> You know, just the fact that it's a library really does draw a different mentality from the crowd. Everybody knows that you've got to be quiet in the library and that it's a space to think. Whereas the museum cafe is 'bring your family along – we're here for ice-cream and drink'. It's a whole different environment.

Their observations about the behavioural requirements between institutions also illustrate how the public plays an active role in jointly creating the experience at the State Library: through a tacit knowledge of the need to be quiet and respectful of other members of the public. Kate explains that 'it's not necessarily an anti-fun tone or anything like that. It's just a different space. But it's still flexible. I've attended events here that have been very much fun spaces and different vibe altogether.'

As the survey responses also show, Kate and Grant are aware of distinct public preferences for each cultural institution, depending on the visitors' needs or purposes at different stages of life. When asked to describe their best experiences at the State Library, Grant admits that he rarely, if ever, visits the State Library with the intention 'to use it as a library', using the university library and Google Scholar to access information. However, he was aware of the opportunities the Library afforded his family:

> I've never had to come in here to find a book, which is odd. But we did come through for the Dream Big Festival that they had earlier this year . . . North Terrace was all lit up with activities for kids and the Library had opened its doors . . . they had an art project going on and . . . they had a little toy exhibition at the Library and that was really nice. Just to walk through the Library. You're not here for any research or other purpose. It was off the cuff. It's like 'Oh yeah, the Library's here, it's good'. You know, we didn't stop and do anything here, but it was nice to go 'oh yeah, the Library's here. We must come back one day and have a good look around.'

Even though he does not use it himself, Grant appreciates the potential offered by the Library and recognises the latent value it represents as part of the cultural infrastructure of the city. He is 'really happy that there is a State Library here' and if he 'lived closer to the Library then I'd be here more often'. This is known as 'option value' – it's there for when he needs it. 'Option value' is an economics term and can be described as 'a willingness to pay for retaining an option to use an area or facility that would be difficult or impossible to replace and for which no close substitute is available'.[9] This term has been applied to how members of the public who do not currently use a library still perceive its value and significance to the community, because they believe it will always be there when they need it:

> While non-users do not experience the benefits enjoyed by library users . . . non-users receive significant benefits from public library services and often value them as much as users. Elements of this value stem from the option, existence and legacy values that public libraries confer. Although an individual may not use or ever visit a library, the knowledge that it will be indefinitely accessible creates what is known as 'option value'.[10]

Similarly, Kate is not a current user of the State Library collections. She suggested that her best experience of the institution took place at an exhibition at the Flinders City Gallery, which was at the time located within the State Library:

> It was a taxidermy art installation kind of thing. They had Joe Bain from the museum come out and explain how he got into it and what being a taxidermist involves . . . They drew a small crowd but everyone was really interested in the subject and we got to ask really good questions and it was a sort of intimate space. Really cool use of the facilities. I hadn't really known that that gallery was there, so it was a really cool way to sort of be introduced to it.

The State Library not only has the potential to share staff resources and expertise, but as shown by Kate's participation, the institution is able to attract members of the public (non-Library users) who may not have been aware that such events and exhibition spaces were available at the Library. Her response indicates the potential for audience development and other collaborative opportunities between or across the North Terrace cultural institutions, a situation relevant to ongoing discussions about the Lot Fourteen site.[11] Given the value placed by many survey and interview respondents on their experience of the North Terrace Cultural Precinct and their perception of community identity tied to the area, it would appear that there is a significant level of public interest in the future of Lot Fourteen.

Kate identified the public as the primary beneficiaries of collaborations between institutions. This was evident during a space industry conference held in 2018 in Adelaide:

> *I work in the Discovery Centre for the museum and, when we had the Planet Conference on, the space exploration conference, people would come up to me and ask, 'what space themed activities do we have on in Adelaide?' And I'd say, actually, the whole cultural precinct has got the space theme, so I did actually tell them about what was going on in the Library and we had the fliers and I explained 'you start at this end and you work your way through'. I have told people about what's going on here and what I've seen.*

That team members across the North Terrace Cultural precinct are willing to cross-promote events of other institutions builds on the public's trust in all institutions. This aligns with Holden's descriptions of institutional value, underpinning the public's perception of and their relationship with government. As the cross-promotion of one institution by another, it also contradicts the principles of economic philosophy regarding competition between institutions. Grant and Kate show how the public's point of entry to the State Library may occur through another institution, but the experience builds familiarity with its potential, which informs an intention to visit with the family at some point in the future. Grant also demonstrates the symbolic value of the Library when asked about its importance to Adelaide:

> *Culturally for Adelaide, I think it's really important. I look at the library, the museum and the art gallery . . . [Laughter] It's a triumvirate! There's the three of them, the three points of*

education and its fantastic that they're right next to each other and they're easy to find. So, I imagine there is a lot of local history locked away in this place . . . stuff that people wouldn't imagine was here until they had a very specific question . . . people have actually found information on the property they own, so they can go back and find old land hold texts and documents and who used to live in this old cottage . . . Very personal journeys, you know? I don't think you would just walk in here and go 'I want to learn something about Adelaide'. You need a really specific question to chase up and I just take it for granted that that sort of thing is kept here safe.

Even as a non-user, Grant values the continuity of the Library's role in preserving archives and providing access to South Australian cultural heritage on behalf of the public until their interest or need arises. The significance of this undefined future demand constitutes an option value for Grant. Kate also reiterates the importance of local and family history preservation and the option value present within the State Library collections and services:

I've got a family history in South Australia and, more so, my partner had a rural family history in South Australia and they've had family property and those kinds of things . . . you take it for granted that all that information is always going to be there and most of it isn't digitised and that's where the internet fails [laughter] and you need to have a physical library to store this stuff.

The physical integrity and future access to documentary materials is important to Kate. However, like many of the interview subjects, she also values the location of public events and where the collections are housed and made accessible.

The cultural precinct we have here along North Terrace is unlike any other capital city in Australia. The fact that we have the library, the museum and the art gallery all in one row . . . There're so many events that are run in collaboration and it's all synchronised. Like the Dream Big festival was a good one. The space exploration was a good one. Fringe, same deal and it's awesome and if any one of those institutions for whatever reason was valued less, it wouldn't work as well and there'd be this sort of disconnect if one of them was moved somewhere else or something like that. That's really important.

Kate's experience working with the public in the South Australian Museum provides her with insights into the collection management challenges faced by cultural institutions. Grant and Kate both appreciate the role and limitations of digitisation programs, as well as the irreplaceability of original physical artefacts – their intrinsic and historical worth. When the conversation automatically turned to online accessibility, they begin to talk over each other. Kate highlights the scale of effort required to digitise South Australia's cultural collections and their value to future generations of researchers:

You'll never catch up, it's never going to catch up, it's never going to get the backlog, and the museum's in exactly the same way, in terms of how they catalogue everything . . . The work is never done, and likewise the material will always have value. It's never going to lose value. You're never going to say 'no-one' is ever going to want to know about this person because all their living relatives are dead. Someone is going to want to know about that person and that person's history.

The state collections are of value not merely for those seeking access to them today, online or in person, but also for those accessing them in the future. The collections' latent value is realised when the enquiry is made, the item retrieved and the potential it represents activated through the interaction with an unknown member of the public, at an unknown point in time.[12] Kate also perceives the past and future usefulness of the unique collections in informing new cultural productions – such as academic research, or creative works – a perception that resonates with many survey respondents. She recognises the Library collection's potential to create new knowledge to be shared via many forms across the community:

> Even if you yourself don't want to do the research, a lot of people have interests in things. Like historical fiction. I'm a huge Colin Thiele fan so there's books like Fire and Stone, which is the story of Coober Pedy. There's [sic] books like . . . the story of the Barossa and the role the German settlement had on South Australia, and all of the facts that he got to write that book would have come from the State Library. The families that set up the Barossa, how they would have got there, how they would have divided up their land, how big the settlements were at those time periods. That actually came from here and there's no other way you're going to find that out. People don't keep personal records like that.

Although they appreciate the benefits the State Library provides for the community, Kate and Grant also believe that the Library is underutilised, suggesting that many in Adelaide are not aware of its presence on North Terrace.

> They've never had to come here and use it for anything, that it's had absolutely no impact on their life whatsoever. They can't even imagine the site where the building is, let alone the actual face of the Library itself . . . I find it fascinating, they could just barely remember the museum, because they were there once at school, but the rest of it is invisible. So, this is sort of one of the best kept secrets in the State for the people who live here. It's really underutilised, I think, and unrecognised.

When asked for one story or anecdote she would share about the State Library, Kate describes the archival collections and how people will be able to access these in future. She also raises what she considers to be the responsibility of the public to support the Library, to reinforce its identity and relevance in the community over time:

> I think the one thing that people need to appreciate is that the information is always going to be here, but as members of the

State or even just the city of Adelaide, they really should be a little bit more active in their interest . . . I don't know a lot of people who knew that it was here. They know the string of buildings that look like old buildings, but no one really distinguishes between where the Museum ends, and the Library begins. It's the same for the Art Gallery . . . it all blurs into one. But that's a pro and a con of having a cultural precinct – it flows, and perhaps a bit too well [laughter].

Informed by her experience at the SA Museum, Kate suggests that the public may not actually know which institutions constitute the North Terrace Cultural Precinct, unless they are regular visitors to one or all of them. Her statement contrasts with Jamie, visiting from Sydney, who was well aware of 'the iconic' status of the State Library and its prestigious location on North Terrace, believing that its location reflected how the people of Adelaide value their cultural institutions. However, according to Kate and Grant, the local community are unaware of the cultural riches on their doorstep. Kate suggests the responsibility for this divergence of value recognition lies with the public themselves, suggesting they are neglecting their civic responsibilities for their public spaces and institutions. She expects members of the community, as voters and taxpayers, to have a vested and active interest in the policy leadership shown by government in the stewardship and maintenance of state institutions and the collections in their care. If the voters and taxpayers do not hold policy-makers to account over the maintenance and development of cultural institutions, it is unlikely they will be considered a policy priority. She has a point. The legacy hard won by previous generations, who lobbied and paid for the establishment of South Australia's cultural institutions as donors or taxpayers, could be lost if today's community fails to preserve them. As addressed in previous chapters, a functional democracy depends on an informed public. However, as observed by Grant and Carlo, neither the Library nor its companion cultural institutions are accessed regularly by everyone all the time. Many take no notice at all until the option value is under threat.

Grant describes how he would be more likely to turn to his local library for a book. However, if he had serious archival research, he would 'home in and come to the Motherlode, straight away', once again referring to the option value and recognised expertise of the State Library, declaring:

It stands taller. It's a bit more grown up and serious than the other libraries. You know, the other libraries, you've got your kids there, you've got some readers, grab a novel. That sort of stuff. But this one, it does seem, it suits the combination with the Museum, really well. This is an archive, it's not somewhere for people to just pour through at random.

Like Sophia, Grant appreciates the atmosphere of the State Library as more conducive to serious archival research or focused study. The visitor support teams are critical; without them, he observes, 'you'd have no idea which way to turn. You'd need people to steer you in the right direction. It wouldn't function without them.' Kate also recognises the value of the public library network, which originated in the Institute Building in the late nineteenth century:

The State Library is effectively the same as the Science Centre. It's where all the important stuff is and while the Museum has a gallery out the front, all of South Australia is filled with tiny town libraries, and it's the same thing. It's all part of the same thing, all part of the information repository in some way.

The cultural precinct and individual institutions play an integral role in the personal and social identity of South Australians and the community's intellectual development. Grant and Kate, who exemplify the option value of the State Library, describe how their perceived value of the organisation relates to a potential or future use, in addition to being an immediate resource. The State Library plays a critical role in the preservation and accessibility of South Australia's cultural heritage, as a custodian and trusted institution, one that impacts on the creative and academic sectors of the state. Informed and experienced advocates like Kate and Grant may not be making use of the research or archive collections right now. However, both possess a deep appreciation of the latent value of the State Library's collections, its foundational connection to the history of South Australia and the expertise of its current stewards. They treasure the richness of opportunity presented by the Library, believing it is the responsibility of all South Australians to take an interest in safeguarding its present and future. Such forward-thinking, enthusiastic and informed advocates for the State Library are indeed invaluable.

EDWARD: 'For me is being part of Australian or international culture'
Edward recently arrived in Australia from Iran. Like several of our interview subjects, he was using the State Library for instrumental gains: as a gateway to future employment and to improve his English language skills. However, the services provided by the Library had far deeper, transformative ramifications for a new arrival, connecting him to both Australian and international culture and community:

> *I'm here to improve my language skills because I am looking for a job and want to stay here and this is very useful to me. I want to attend . . . all available class and program like this [sic], along with this convenient environment to reading and surfing web because there is internet access and table and desk, everything is set up to do something like this and is very useful for me.*

Edward visits the Library every day for the group conversation classes and to access material related to his professional background – information and technology. However, when asked what is important to him on these visits, he identified the personal interactions he had experienced:

> *Oh, first of all, lovely person, lovely staff is very helpful and are very interest to help people and everybody who come here [sic]. After that I love this library because I can find . . . my professionally related books.*

Edward did not share his visa status as Sophia had, but his determination to enter the workforce and improve his English skills implies that he aspires to become an active citizen, contributing to the South Australian community. The State Library provides the tools and advice to help him to achieve this. His appreciation was obvious, particularly when contrasted with his experience of libraries and information access in Iran:

> I can find a lot of books and lectures about my profession and very interest[ing] things . . . everything is free to use. Because in our country you should pay partially or monthly to use the library. Internet access is very low or limited. Everything here is free and useful.

The free and open access to the State Library is a highly significant aspect of the institution for many international respondents. This highlights the subjective nature of cultural value: it varies depending on the visitor's background and experience. For Edward, the lack of free library services in Iran renders the State Library even more valuable, particularly for the support and guidance it provides at this challenging time in his life.

Edward is self-conscious of his English language skills. He has written over 50 job applications and made numerous revisions to his resumé. The web access at the library allowed him to research resumé formats appropriate for the Australian job market and found they were very different from those he was used to:

> I found out [the] root cause about what's happened. I found resumé type and format and content is very different in Australia. After that I found content is very important along with Aussie-type of wording.

Edward discussed some of the challenges faced by new arrivals when grappling with the differences between formal English and the Australian vernacular. He engaged with the peer-to-peer conversation classes at the State Library to navigate these challenges. He described this experience as 'one of the lovely things here is peer-to-peer person who helped me to review and correct my resumé and cover letter. Very lovely and helpful. Is very important to me.' With the support of the volunteers, Edward was able to navigate the practical issues of formatting and wording while engaging with the more formal elements of English language instruction. I asked him about the impact this guidance had on his confidence and job prospects and potential future in Australia. Through the conversations with volunteers at the State Library, Edward was able to address his frustration and confusion about his lack of success in the job market:

> *Before I come here, I think of Australia, as a developed country . . . has job vacancies in my field. . . . I very confident [sic] with my experience and my history but after I arrive here and searching for job, I feel it's a bit tricky and you should have the very strong and wide network of people and professional person to help find a job. Maybe it's a main part of job searching, is the network here.*

The State Library provides Edward with opportunities to not only improve his language skills, but to gain local insights about how to break into the job market. He obtains much-needed direction and practical guidance during a destabilising liminal point in his life. A site of personal and professional transition for many of the interview subjects and survey respondents, the institution offers a supportive and pragmatic entry point through which to connect to potential futures.

When I asked whether he shared his experiences at the Library with others, he gave an example of how the Library provided opportunities for social engagement and community service, but was also a means to reconnect with his past:

> *I suggest to my . . . friends who have lived here for more than seven years and never come here at all. I suggest to bring their childs [sic] to play with the useful things, because I play with the Lego parts when I was a child and it's very . . . Sometimes I go there and play, it seems a little [nervous laughter] . . . Is*

very lovely to make something with Lego parts . . . life . . . is different. Some things are very different . . . I sad [sic] because I can't bring with myself my Lego [sic]. My Lego. I left behind . . . I love this area because childrens [sic] play with everything creative and it's very . . . this much I share with my friends, and my neighbour and they come here and use for everything.

Like Michelle and Sophia, Edward engages with a version of his past self, to a time in his life when he was not confronting the challenges to his confidence and lifestyle, where he could do something literally and tangibly constructive to assist his current transformation. Edward activates memories of his childhood and recent past by playing with Lego at the State Library, an activity that overcomes his loneliness by reconnecting him through imaginative links to friends and family in Iran, those who are now the custodians of his Lego. Edward's attachment to Lego is more than a means of engaging with his past. Recent research suggests that playing with Lego assists with problem-solving and reflection, fostering a transference of intellectual problem-solving capabilities into the 'real world'.[13] The Lego may have been placed in the Hub to occupy children like Sophia's sons. However, it also holds an appeal – which may not have been predicted – for adults such as Edward undergoing a personal transition and looking to connect with a new way of life and people in his new community. Edward visits the State Library to address the challenges associated with his moving to a new country and constructing a new life for himself, one Lego block at a time. This was made clear when I asked how important the Library is to his life and the cultural life of Adelaide:

It's very important for me. First of all, because of programs and facilities are here. But important things for me is [sic] being part of Australian or international culture . . . I can make conversation with people who are natively Australian or come from another country and they share their experience and for living together. Is very important I think, it's very valuable part

of my life to be here and to use these facilities . . . It's growing
my network too and it could be useful, very useful to find a job.

The faith and trust Edward places in the State Library exemplifies
the reciprocal nature of 'Civic trust and public service' – the public
places its trust in the integrity and expertise of institutions to
deliver service to members of the public. His experiences reflect
the institution's original associations with mutual improvement
and self-education. Underpinning educational movements such
as the Society for the Diffusion of Useful Knowledge and the
Mechanics Institutes was access to shared information, designed
to both ensure an informed electorate and support the dissemination of knowledge throughout communities.

Whether Edward gained employment in his chosen field and
was able to stay in Australia is unknown. However, like Carlo,
the understanding of Australia that he gained through the State
Library was reciprocated: he shared stories of life in Iran with his
fellow participants, exemplifying the theme of 'Social/cultural
connection and exchange'. His interview highlights key political,
social and cultural differences between life in South Australia and
his homeland, such as the limitations placed on access to library
and information services in Iran. Edward's testimony also demonstrates the varied personal support the Library provides to new
arrivals, such as access to familiar objects like Lego, or assistance
with digital-formatting issues. When asked to describe what he
would share with others about the State Library, he made very
clear his sense of satisfaction and engagement with the institution. He also recounts the wave of physical sensations and intrinsic
personal resonances that affected him when he first visited the
State Library:

The old-fashioned library is very, very interesting for me
because [it's] about civilisation or architecture . . . I never seen
before library like this [HR: the Mortlock Wing?] Yes, full of
books, very old books in different size, books like this, you
know? And I'm 'what is it?' because I want to touch it [laughter]

and everywhere atmosphere is very interesting for me. Is the snapshot that I come here for first time, and it's very wonderful for me.

Edward's experiences at the State Library connect him to the history and heritage of Adelaide while consolidating his personal identity and resilience as he confronts the challenges of life in a new country. Much of what he gained is intangible and deeply personal. However, the latent potential which the State Library is assisting him to activate may have measurable instrumental benefits for himself, his community and South Australia, at some time in the future. But at this liminal moment in his life, the State Library's support is personally reassuring, comforting and truly invaluable.

JOHN: 'You can just have some peace and quiet'

John was one of the older interview subjects. From our preliminary conversation, he indicated that he was homeless. His brief interview showed how this cohort of visitors to the Library engages with its services and the role it plays in their lives.

When I asked John why he came to the Library, he replied that he was 'already in town. I had lunch at the uni and I have a barbeque to go to this afternoon'. He visited the Library 'pretty much every day' and came mostly for the free Wi-Fi. His first memory of visiting a library was as a child, with his 'mother dragging me around and her getting lots of books'. John insisted that as a child the books were not for him, indicating a sense of exclusion or lack of interest associated with his parents' use of the library. There is no sense of this first memory being an enjoyable experience, though it does indicate a degree of familiarity.

John's taciturn nature made him a challenging interview subject. However, he was quite definite about the kinds of experiences and interactions at the State Library that were important to him. For John, the Library is: 'Somewhere safe, where if it's too hot you can come in or if it's too cold you can come in, and you can just have some peace and quiet to do some reading or whatever'.

John values his time in the Library and may not have regular access to reading materials beyond the institution. Most telling is his appreciation of the physical shelter from extreme weather and the personal safety the site affords. In 2021 almost 7500 people were classified as homeless in South Australia.[14] Over three-quarters of these were in boarding houses or shelters, with men representing two-thirds of people sleeping rough or taking shelter in improvised dwellings. The State Library offers everyone safety and shelter during the day, as well as a positive, or at least harmless, means of occupying themselves. John did not explain what he was accessing when using the Library's Wi-Fi. He prioritises safety and shelter, while also addressing his immediate physical and psychological needs. His responses emphasise the value of basic human services for some members of the public, which again illustrates the variable nature of the value of the Library: for some members of the public, shelter from Adelaide's sweltering heat may be taken for granted; for those with nowhere else to go, it is much more highly prized.

One of the visitor services team at the State Library told me that John was one of a group who regularly visit the State Library together, rarely coming alone. When I asked if he shared his experiences at the Library with others, however, John returned to his earlier brevity, insisting that 'no, it's just a personal time for me'. He was shy, appearing conflicted between a willingness to participate and a reluctance to give too much away about himself and his companions, as demonstrated when I asked how important the Library was to him and the cultural life of Adelaide:

> I mean for me it's very important that I come here every day, otherwise I don't know what I would do. It seems for the cultural life of Adelaide, I don't know about the culture, but it seems important for Adelaide that lots of people come here. I see other people here every day.

His experiences and observations highlight the diverse range of motivations and needs attracting people to the State Library. John may visit the Library every day for peace and quiet, but he recognises familiar faces, be they students, researchers, or other regular visitors. This community of random strangers offers the opportunity for some interview subjects to interact and engage with each other. However, John values the security, peace and quiet above the chance to socialise.

The story about the State Library that John did share with others indicates an inspiring and potentially transformational dimension to his visits. Although he was reluctant to provide any-thing too revelatory or personally detailed, John was happy to describe an object on display in the Mortlock Wing, which had been on loan from the South Australian Museum since 2004 to signify the historical links between the institutions: 'I went on a tour here and . . . you can get really good photos and there was an eagle (HR: Oh that's right, it's in the case isn't it?) Yeah'.

There was nothing more he was prepared to share. By way of thanks, I gave him an additional coffee voucher. He'd asked for another, for his friend.

JOSEPH: 'We all know each other, and we know a different culture'
While some international university students visit the State Library primarily for the language classes, Joseph was there for the peace and quiet, which allowed him to focus on his research: 'So today I come in just to search my medical articles, to complete my research at university . . . this place is very quiet, I think, and it's given me a good room to search. I am liking this place.'

Joseph, who had lived in Adelaide for one year, is from Saudi Arabia and is studying a medical science degree at the University of South Australia (UniSA). The experiences and interactions that are important to him in the Library revolve around the range of avail-able resources and the people who facilitate his access to them:

> The most important thing is when I just find easy way to find these books upstairs, when I want to search article and all the staff here are very kindly and friendly, where they are dealing with us. Sometimes we had meeting here with other people. Sometimes with students, my university, sometime

from the community, people coming here from the community.
Sometimes they have I think different discussion upstairs.

Like several of my interview subjects, Joseph values the State Library as a neutral public meeting space. He shares his experiences as part of the ELIS program, describing the sense of community that has developed amongst participants. However, when asked about his best experience of the Library, he focused on access to resources, as well as the interpersonal interactions with Library staff:

The best experience I'd say is the easy access to information here, so this library helped me to find articles in easy way. When I ask something of staff about a specific book, they help me and can find it and after that I just sat to research. It's easy to get information, than [sic] to stay in my home.

Unlike other subjects, Joseph does not mention the free Wi-Fi or the internet. As a student of the University of South Australia, he would have online access to digital library resources from home or elsewhere. However, his response indicates that the State Library provides more than the information services. The State Library's physical books and the research support provided by the teams represent an additional benefit not found through the university. He has also become an advocate for the institution:

I invite my friend here, in this library, [to] show him how I get to ... research articles. And sometimes we came [sic] here to have a discussion and we find this place is good place for have our discussion ... we see other people, they start to talk and start discussion and some people start to look at the laptop, search something. Yes, it's made me feel better than home.

His response reveals the care he takes in judging the appropriateness or otherwise of engaging with other members of the public, either in a conversation or a joint search on their laptops. Like Alex, Kate and Grant, he greatly appreciates the quiet space and focus provided by the Library, and he understands that others may also. However, he also acknowledges that this does not preclude the possibility that others may also wish to engage in 'discussion', which makes coming to the State Library 'better than home'. This observation and his conscious self-restraint demonstrate how the institution encourages appropriate behaviours, illustrating one of the key elements of institutional value. Joseph's level of empathy for other users and their potential research needs reflect his own, demonstrating the co-creative nature of the library experience and the public's custodial role in its preservation.

When I asked how important the Library was to his life and that of the community, Joseph nominated the social and educational elements of his experiences:

> In [the] past you have difficulty if you want some information, to get at specially, if you start to research or write an assignment at university, so it was difficult to access or get some information . . . but these days Library make it easy for all the people to access any information they want. Also, I like the English class discussion here . . . we all know each other, and we know a different culture and that makes sense for each person to get to know anything he wants.

Joseph demonstrates the reciprocal nature and benefits of cross-cultural exchange, also identified in the surveys and by other interview subjects such as Carlo, Edward, Michelle, Pamela and Maria. Finding themselves isolated and dislocated, new arrivals to Adelaide come to the Library as the first step towards reinforcing their confidence while creating a new home. Gaining reassurance from connecting to a community of peers, they also experience shared empathy with others in similar circumstances.

When I asked for a story about the State Library he would share with others, Joseph's response reflects the complex network of values common amongst all respondents. He also expresses his gratitude and an overwhelming sense of satisfaction with all the institution offers:

> I will tell maybe that this place may be the one, the best place in Adelaide. I visit here because it give me . . . a good way to

> *relax, that [is] far from stress or from the home, something like*
> *that . . . also they give available resources here so we can find*
> *easy way, so, I like this library.*

Joseph's positive impression of the State Library has the potential to influence more of his friends, family and community when
he returns to Saudi Arabia. His experience and advocacy illustrate how the State Library exemplifies and activates institutional
value and, by extension, promotes the proliferation of democratic
values and behaviours by supporting social connection, know-
ledge-sharing and cultural exchange amongst visitors. All of these
elements inform Joseph's image of South Australia and add to the
cultural value of the Library.

> *I hope that . . . in my country, open like this library, especially*
> *in my city because we don't have like this library accessible*
> *[sic]. [HR: What sort of libraries do you have in Saudi?] It's like*
> *private libraries, not like public, you know? So you have to*
> *become a member, you have to pay that and you know, not all*
> *the people can pay . . . but I like here [sic], all the people can*
> *come here and get anything that they want and I like that.*

Joseph is deeply appreciative of the opportunities for social interaction, cultural exchange and learning provided by the State
Library. His description of the experience as a 'good way' and the
State Library as being 'Far from stresses' also resonates with the
major value theme of 'Inspiration', with its personal and imaginative connotations. Joseph's awareness of others and his empathy
for the importance of appropriate behaviours and ideal use of the
spaces indicate a degree of ownership and belonging. He contributes to the unspoken collective stewardship that ensures all can
enjoy and experience the space as he does. I wonder whether he
will miss such collaborative and open opportunities when his time
in South Australia comes to an end, and whether the experience
of connection will resurface when he returns to a country without
many of the freedoms he so clearly enjoyed in South Australia.

I thanked Joseph for his time and contribution. His courtesy, warmth and respect for all in the Library, including for me, is worth preserving: 'It's been my pleasure and I hope my information is valid for you'.

I assured him it was, thanked him and wished him well.

JACK: 'I am your average user here, but at the same time, obviously I'm not'

Jack visits the State Library daily and, like John, is one of Adelaide's homeless. He is intelligent and had a lot to share. Jack's interview became a wide-ranging exploration of his use of the State Library and his appreciation for the social and intellectual opportunities it presented, as well the deep sense of connection and assurance it provides.

It was clear his research at the Library was more than a way of filling in time. Jack visits the State Library for the free Wi-Fi, which enables him to undertake research to support his computing work, to 'answer emails, look up things, like how to fix people's computers and also, as you can probably guess, in the human rights area. Big fan of human rights.' He is interested in mental health issues and the associated medical research. Most of his use relates to fulfilling other people's information needs. When I asked him to describe these needs, he said 'People request things of me in emails and I look it up'. His research also addressed outstanding questions he had about his own medical treatment and similar issues encountered by friends and associates. Jack's engagement with the Library demonstrates how a significant group within the community gains access to information that, with no fixed address, they may otherwise not be able to acquire.

When describing his first memory of visiting a library, Jack spoke of a staff member who had a background in medical research for the universities. He also recalled other members of the public he'd met and had spoken to in recent years. One was a medical student, whom he had encouraged to think creatively in his research and practice, the aim being to propose new approaches to treatment.

He described with pride that on graduation the student gave an award-winning talk about medicine and new ideas.

When asked what kinds of experiences and interactions in this library were important to him, Jack described how the Wi-Fi allowed him to correspond with senior figures in international medical associations. He showed me copies of these letters and emails. He was concentrating his research on issues relating to prescription psychiatric medications, particularly those with adverse side effects. In providing a neutral and accessible avenue through which he could explore his personal medical history, the State Library was supporting his attempts to gain a greater understanding of the treatment he had received for mental illnesses. He in turn supported others with similar personal research needs, an activity that fosters his personal confidence and sense of social connection:

> I am your average user here, but at the same time obviously I'm not . . . it is these interactions that are important to me. The email gives me the ability to contact journalists . . . the chief medical writer for Rupert Murdoch's News Limited in Australia and she reckons I've saved her five years of research. Now I've got that in one of my emails.

Jack's research and online engagement demonstrates how the public values the State Library for more than free access to the internet and a safe indoor meeting space. He values *what the access enables*, such as: communication with people around the world; the reinforcement provided by the acknowledgements of experts and journalists; and the ability to remain an active citizen within a democracy despite impoverished circumstances. Jack's response also shows how the State Library continues its original mission to cultivate and diffuse useful knowledge, via the provision of free IT services. This objective of the South Australian Literary and Scientific Association, formed in 1834, is appreciated by many amongst the public of Adelaide today, especially by the more isolated or vulnerable members of the community.

When asked how important the Library is to his life and the cultural life of Adelaide, Jack focused not on the city's cultural life, but on community life. He discussed his passion for social justice and 'things that kill people when they shouldn't . . . the increased deaths are preventable and shouldn't be happening'. He also gave an example of cancer research he had pursued after a friend's wife was diagnosed with breast cancer. (His frustration with an imperfect medical system was as palpable as his desire to help others.) Jack was able to access the latest medical publications through the State Library's Wi-Fi, searching up-to-date peer-reviewed publications to identify information about treatment options for his friend. Like the vital language classes for new arrivals, the institution provides him with a secure familiar site and the facilities essential for maintaining his skills and helping others at no personal cost. The benefits to the community are well worth the public investment. The institution, especially open spaces like the Hub on the ground floor, provides Jack with a valuable sense of social connection, shelter and intellectual engagement at a point in his life where he is isolated and marginalised by society. Jack may not be a recognised health practitioner and may also have been overstating the impact of his research; however, for members of the public who cannot afford to access medical specialists, Jack represents a conduit to (presumably) authentic and trustworthy research materials via the State Library. His responses highlight an under-reported aspect of the State Library: the provision of an outlet for marginalised groups to research, connect and communicate. I can imagine how comforting this may be during already dark times.

Jack was a considerate interview subject and was clearly trying to help, often reflecting on his own interest in research. When I asked for one story about the State Library and why people should come here, he illustrated the interconnected and subjective nature of the experience at the Library: 'Just have a look – there's the free Wi-Fi, and a relatively nice environment. When it's quite hot, there's air conditioning in here. They're reasonably friendly.'

Jack visits the State Library every day, primarily to help others. He shares what he finds with those in need, to support and help friends as they too navigate their way through difficult times. He finds purpose, comfort and company in the State Library, pursuing his enquiries within a secure and welcoming environment. This allows him to feel as though he is keeping abreast with current research and maintaining his research and computer skills. Perhaps, one day, these skills may assist in leading him back to satisfying employment and a more secure way of life.

SHELAGH: 'You get to have everything'

Shelagh completed Year 12 studies only a few weeks before my interview and was awaiting confirmation of her university placement. She visited the State Library whenever she had 'some time to kill'. Shelagh was using the Library to explore an author and topic that had nothing to do with the 'nightmarish subjects' of her recent science and maths exams, but everything to do with personal interests and her ongoing education.

> *Right now, I'm reading Crime and Punishment ... by Dostoyevsky. I finished the first chapter, like, last time I came here so I'm going to read one more chapter then go home ... I hear it's quite philosophical, like it's, you know, it's about morality and stuff. I'm interested in philosophy, but the writings of Nietzsche and stuff, they're kind of like inaccessible to me. I mean, I understand it, but it takes a lot of effort.*

Shelagh is delighted by the learning possibilities offered by the State Library, which allows her to explore subjects beyond her structured goal-oriented formal education. She recognises the value of broad literary reading in improving her understanding of issues such as ethics and morality, even though she did not have a specific requirement for such knowledge in her current life moment. Her window of opportunity – the brief time between high school and university, between childhood innocence and adult responsibilities – offered a chance to broaden her imaginative horizons. By nurturing her imagination, she is supporting her own learning in a way she cannot yet appreciate. The value of Shelagh's experience at the Library is currently unknowable.

Shelagh is caught in a very instrumentalist view of knowledge acquisition, whereby education is aimed strictly at job prospects rather than broad understanding and theoretical options. I suggested to her that reading a diverse range of material, especially with such challenging topics as philosophy, can sometimes help self-directed learners to develop a focus and improve their understanding. Shelagh replied that she was 'hoping to do that by reading other stuff'. She chose to travel to the State Library to find such materials, as opposed to using her local library near her home in Glenelg:

> There are libraries close to my home but the thing about them is that a lot of the books I want to read, they're not actually there. They have to come from somewhere else and you have to wait for them. Yeah, I kind of don't like that [laughter] so I come here. I like that all the books are here all the time [laughter].

When I asked what sort of experience she values in the Library, she confirmed that she also recognised the importance of the different spaces available to the public, each with its own designated purpose or function:

> It's really quiet. It's quite big so there's quiet zones. Yeah, I like that. That's it pretty much. Like you can't borrow stuff because it's a reference library. Some people would consider that a drawback, but I like it because you get to have everything. It's fairly well lit. I like the vibe here.

Shelagh's references to the lighting and 'the vibe' indicate a recognition of the site value and shared facilities of the Library, which enabled the level of focus, comfort and security noted by many of the interview subjects. She had also visited her local library or the library at Flinders University to study for her exams, implying that these other library spaces have pre-established associations with studying for a particular purpose. She described how she would 'see all the other people there studying so much, and you think "yeah, I must not get distracted"'. The State Library, however, symbolises a more open and imaginative space. A subjective freedom of thought. An air of magic for someone of the Harry Potter generation. Shelagh granted herself permission to explore creative and literary interests, during a time in her life when she is able to entertain an unstructured and non-instrumental sense of pleasure away from home and her future university commitments.

Appreciative as she was about the State Library, Shelagh did not share her delight with others, perhaps indicating a level of social isolation and disconnection, not uncommon amongst introverted teenagers. Her reticence may also point to the limitations of relying on word-of-mouth or social media recommendations in some cultural contexts: 'I didn't think people actually come here. I shouldn't cloud your judgement, but I don't know anyone who comes here to study for leisure like I do.'

She thought it was 'nice' when I assured her that there were many others like her, such as Michelle and Carlo, enjoying the State Library facilities in pursuit of personal research projects. With this reassurance, she describes other elements of her experience that were important to her, displaying an intense appreciation of the tactility of the reference collection on the open shelves, and the pleasures of serendipitous discovery:

> *You can endlessly browse ... I just like the physicality of books. It sounds [laughter] abstract and stupid but I was just walking through the shelves and I saw this – it's not a picture book – it's like an art book on Soviet art and I never realised I was interested in that book.*

Shelagh had not considered that her reading of Dostoyevsky may have sparked an interest in other aspects of Russian cultural history, exclaiming 'Maybe that's why I picked up that book!'

The pleasures and benefits of browsing a physical library collection are recognised internationally, particularly by students.

According to the *Washington Post*, this sentiment was articulated by students of Yale University who protested against the proposed removal of books from the campus library:

> *The potential that libraries represent for students is the ability to go to a random shelf, pick up a random book and realize that there's this whole new world that exists', said Felipe Pires, a junior from Brazil majoring in computer science. 'That's not how the Web works – that's not how hyperlinks work.*[15]

Such serendipitous intrinsic experiences are devoid of instrumental purpose but are fundamental to imaginative engagement. Reading for pleasure, just because you can. This lies at the core of both the early and enduring challenges faced by the State Library, as Jamie alluded to earlier: should the state and by extension taxpayers, fund reading for pleasure? Shelagh demonstrates a growing sensitivity, tied to the spread of neoliberalism, that any pursuit that does not have a quantifiable outcome or benefit cannot be considered valuable and is therefore designated (even self-described) as frivolous and wasteful. She has internalised this concept, expressed through her self-deprecatory comments about her 'study for leisure' and a simple love of books, a concept that lies at the heart of the debates around cultural value. The devaluation of the subjective leisurely library experience is symptomatic of commercially oriented approaches to managing and understanding cultural experiences and the inability or incapacity of some to appreciate a pursuit that is not part of a pre-planned logical outcomes-driven process. It is a pursuit at odds with a commercial perspective that excludes any activity as unpredictable and aimless as picking up a book out of curiosity, without expecting some sort of quantifiable benefit. The information between the covers may just be interesting, hilariously anachronistic or finally address a question long held. The outcome or value of the interaction is unpredictable, not because it is intangible but because it is the result of a chance encounter between the dormant value of a book in the Library and a random member of the public, with no agenda and no guidelines. Shelagh's decision to spend time idly browsing the open stacks is an investment removed from time, place and expectation. The outcomes are similarly divorced from location, temporal context and obligation. The value she activates through her leisurely reading is inspirational, contemplative and potentially transformative in that moment. It may even have instrumental benefits down the track. In that moment though, Shelagh's experience is the intrinsic value of the Library made manifest, exemplifying the public's subjectivity and value co-creation at the heart of Walmsley's 'Neo-institutional value'.

The outcomes-driven mindset that Shelagh displays (and may actually be rebelling against) is not isolated to South Australia, or even the present moment. This reductive mindset is a symptom of the governing economic rationalist paradigm of the early twenty-first century. The economist Richard Denniss describes how:

> *Democracy, like child-rearing, requires more than economics or political philosophy . . . All democracies struggle to decide how much to spend on museums and art galleries compared to science and technology. But where neoliberalism encourages different elements of our society to see themselves as rivals for scarce public funds, a cohesive society would ask itself how much more economic growth would be needed before it could fund great arts and science programs at the same time.*[16]

Aside from Shelagh's intrinsic enjoyment of the moment, the cultural value or benefit of her experience is currently latent and unknowable, and this does not mean its potential does not exist. I can only speculate that her knowledge and understanding of Dostoyevsky, and the ethical insights gained through her literary and philosophical explorations at the State Library, may one day inform her future decisions. Nevertheless, outcomes-driven policy environments and their attendant funding arrangements provide little scope for appreciating such a pursuit with no set agenda or predictable purpose; instead, they convert participation, immersion or engagement with a cultural activity into a transaction, where the cost of time, money or energy should return some sort of commensurate benefit or instrumental reward. Opening a book offers potential and possibility, or perhaps nothing at all. It could be a few minutes' diversion exploring something of interest that may never be encountered again. Or it could be life-changing. The outcome of Shelagh's actions and their value are unknown, not because they are intangible but because it is an activation of latent value generated by her unique imagination and cognitive capacity at that point in her life. As Ben Walmsley describes, her ungoverned use and appreciation of the Library is 'an acknowledgement of the power of personal experience and narrative'.[17] It is also a clear picture of the cultural value of the Library and its potential to inspire our community.

Shelagh's Library experience demonstrates other surprising and sophisticated insights into how younger members of the public may engage with the institution, in that she displays a complex understanding of information and cultural transfer in the twenty-first century. The Library offers her unprescribed options, not a narrow, pre-determined set of strategic answers:

> The thing about the internet is it's too specific. It's too personalised. It kind of forces you to be in your own head, right? It kind of caters everything you see based on what you like, right? On the internet you're surrounded by people who think like you. Exactly like you. But the Library, you can just come across something spontaneously, something that you didn't like very much, then you'll be intrigued and look at it. So yeah, I like that.

Shelagh may be the most powerful young woman in Adelaide, and her experience with the State Library is facilitating her growth from a high school student to an active member of the South Australian public. She knows she needs to know more and has turned to the State Library rather than the internet to guide her. She may not pursue her philosophical interest beyond *Crime and Punishment*, but this experience, at this pivotal and transformative time in her life, is likely to influence her next decisions or life choices. The role of cultural institutions like the State Library is to offer this neutral helping hand. The authenticity of the available expertise must be beyond doubt and the team members' belief in the public good unquestionable, because we don't know who the future leaders will be, how they will respond to the decisions they will face and how these decisions will form the world in which we will all live and die.

While Shelagh's love of browsing the bookshelves in the Library may not affect any of her professional decisions in the future, there is a chance that it will influence the greatest power she is guaranteed to wield: when she votes for the first time, and every time after that, assessing for herself the moral stance and judgement of our future leaders. That is where and when our culture's worth can be judged: its role is not to stand up and be accountable in the same terms used to measure industry, or to be judged against the checks, balances, or election strategies of policy-makers. Culture's job is to measure us, to explore and shine the light of assessment and judgement on who we are, our relationships with the world and our values as a society. Disputing culture's value is as useful and demonstrative as blaming the mirror for our own reflection. We are responsible for what it presents because we are the objects of culture's collective study, the raw material for an inquisitive and randomly cumulative process of creating and communicating understanding that has informed, entertained and shaped our species for millennia. Shelagh is merely continuing this process, identifying an avenue for exploring her current curiosity, to think, to dream and store information for future use, the object or application of which is unknown. Culture, as represented in institutions like the State Library, really has no appreciable objective value. Its value is latent and representative, much like money: entirely symbolic and unrevealed, until its value is realised when activated by a person. I'd add that the value of culture (and cash for that matter) is also subjective and not fixed: ten dollars to one person in one context and time has a different meaning and value for someone in another. Cultural collections, ideas and institutions await activation and engagement, requiring people like Shelagh to embrace them and give them life, explore their possibilities as they fill in time or follow a pathway to their personal transformation, the value of which is unknowable, though its potential can mean everything.

The final question to Shelagh was for the story or anecdote she would share with others about her relationship and experiences with the Library:

> *I haven't been coming here for so long. But maybe twenty years down the line I will be, like, super-wise and I can say 'I came here every week!' so that would be my story [laughter]. It just hasn't happened yet . . .*

Shelagh reflects the hope, faith and intangible goals to which we, public servants in the cultural sector, all aspire: we want to make a positive difference to people's lives. It is what we hope to achieve when we engage school students, welcome a stranger to the space and share the stories, collections, and knowledge we curate. Shelagh also demonstrates what may be the most challenging obstacle in identifying the value of the State Library: not even those gaining the greatest benefit are aware of what that value may be, or may never be, until the need arises, the memory is stirred and the trace of a story reminds an older woman of the summer she spent reading *Crime and Punishment* in the State Library – with everything it revealed returning to her. How it inspired her to believe that decades into the future it would make her 'super-wise'. If this is the value and meaning one young woman can attain from just one or two books, imagine the latent value of an entire collection for every young person in the state.

NATALIE HARKIN: 'There's a right of reply'

As the survey responses and interviews have shown, time plays a critical role in the relationship between an institution and its public. With each visit, memories of previous visits with family rise to the surface; recollections of excitement, discovery or resolve are triggered with each encounter of a familiar scent or sensation. Many described how this layering of experience contributes to their personal and community identity, informing their relationship with the state and the State Library. These experiences create a sense of familiarity and expectation, of trust and security. The Library becomes a place of memory and memory-keeping for individuals and the state.

Some members of the public though have more complex, conflicted and, indeed traumatic, memories associated with the State Library. Their experiences relate to inaccessible and uncomfortable chapters in South Australia's colonial and recent past, relationships that contradict or dispute the popular mythologies of history. This naturally impacts on how they value the institution. To ignore the State Library's role as a keeper of colonial archives would be remiss, a role that, for most of its existence, perpetuated false narratives and maintained what are today considered unacceptable collection practices. Until recently, through misrepresentation, past discriminatory practices or the blind eye of neglect, South Australia's cultural institutions have not been democratic sites, accessible and welcoming to all members of the community. However, culture has a habit of revealing what politics and economics attempt to avoid. More than a habit, it is culture's role to reveal and explore uncomfortable truths.

I met Associate Professor Natalie Harkin from Flinders University to discuss the relationships between the State Library and Adelaide's Indigenous communities. Natalie is a Narungga woman, born and raised in South Australia, on Kaurna country:

> We are from the Chester, Cullen, Yates, and Owens families. My Nana identified with her community at Point Pearce Mission Station. It's where she called home. But we've got history right across South Australia, because of how we were forcibly moved and relocated by the state . . . this includes family being removed from Albany in Western Australia, so we have Noongar heritage as well. I have a three-mission history, from Poonindie to Raukkan/Point McLeay and then to Point Pearce, where my Nana was born and where her family are buried. It is a typical history of movement in South Australia.

Natalie is an award-winning poet and a member of the Unbound Collective, a collaboration of Aboriginal women academics, researchers and artists working in Indigenous Studies and Creative Arts at Flinders University. Natalie and her collaborators, Associate Professor Ali Gumillya Baker (Mirning), Professor Simone Ulalka Tur (Yankunytjatjara) and Dr Faye Rosas Blanche (Yidniji/Mbarbarm) employ creative arts practices across their teaching and research. This research centres on decolonisation as a means for activating justice and social transformation. This is not a static transitory experience or critique, with Natalie describing their work as decolonising with intent for action: 'We create and collaborate on so many fronts, and I contribute largely through poetry and theorising the colonial archive, ideas of blood memory and haunting. This is our collective activism and I love it.' Drawing on filmic, performance and transgenerational storytelling, the Unbound collaborations are deeply personal and communal and reveal forgotten and neglected corners of South Australian history with a gentle, but relentless, interrogation. Natalie's poetry is beautiful and delicate, well researched and forceful, disclosing layers of personal and social history, which have lain unexamined by both the public and the keepers of the state collections for decades. Natalie's research examines the role of the state archives in keeping alive colonial myths and popular histories, those that render invisible the trauma and intergenerational ramifications of the South Australian colonial experience for Indigenous members of our community. She explains:

> My research has been with privately held and state-based colonial archives, particularly the Aborigines Protection Board and Children's Welfare Department records. I've also had access to many of the state's Aboriginal Domestic Service files, which are so detailed and extensive. The vastness feels like an anomaly because our women's labour stories are seen as minor, or invisible, or not part of the larger narrative of South Australia's labour history.

Many of these records are held in the State Aboriginal Records archives, although some were also made accessible through the State Library when the State Records Office of South Australia was located in the Library buildings. Natalie began this research on her family's archives as a doctoral project, subsequently discovering a history of women in her family who were controlled and indentured to domestic service. During her research, she came to understand the full scale of the statewide practice – throughout most of the twentieth century – whereby many young Aboriginal girls and women were removed from their families as part of the state's assimilation policy agenda and placed with white families and businesses as housemaids, cleaners and servants. Isolated from family, country and culture, these women and girls often worked for no wages or with limited control over their earnings. The State Records of South Australia became Natalie's source material, along with memory stories from women within her community. It was in the State Records that she uncovered a story far greater than her own family:

> There are mountains of state files documenting our Aboriginal women's labour story . . . It was a big industry, and our women were described as the market solution to the Aboriginal problem. The targeting of young girls for removal and training for a domestic service workforce was a significant and clearly orchestrated assimilation measure by the state government. Tragically, they often had no say regarding their placements. They endured so much.

During her research in the collections, stored or accessed through the State Records or the State Library, Natalie became aware not just of the scale of the removal process, but the extent of the documentary evidence recording it. She describes these collections as 'surveillance files': basically, a concentrated record of collecting, cataloguing and classifying information that renders Aboriginal people as a resource commodity, often objectified or stripped of identity and agency. Not stories often told about South Australia, they contradict both the accepted history of the state and the social values of a utopian democracy informed by progressive idealists. That the stories of her family and community are unknown, Natalie suggests, is attributable to the state of the collections, which are unprocessed and therefore unknowable and inaccessible, their value dormant and ignored, like a significant portion of the cultural collections of this state. She explains:

> *These repositories that keep records on our families are vast, across multiple institutions and sites. We don't entirely know what is held in these collections, because so many records are not yet logged or organised in a way that's transparent to the wider public and certainly to the Aboriginal community. It's a big bugbear and passion of mine. These incomplete and one-sided 'official' colonial records are used to generate and perpetuate big ideas and public discourse about history and who we are. These codified processes are very invisible and silent, yet seething. And we also have what we carry with us, our blood memory, our embodied histories and own evidence passed down as what we know to be true.*

Given the combined legacy of lack of research and resources allocated to the key cultural institutions holding Aboriginal record collections, the number of Adelaide families and businesses that benefited from the state's scheme to place Aboriginal women and girls into domestic servitude is also unknown. Like a dark family secret, the discomfort of the community has continued to grow over decades of silence, which normalised the violence and erased community memory through neglect of the evidence. This neglect of historical evidence and the ramifications for many in the South Australian community form the basis of Natalie's connection to the State Library of South Australia and her engagement with the collections. She began with the records of her grandmother, Pauline Chester:

> *I started my PhD with her records, but that was very personal, and I didn't want the PhD to just be about her life. I wanted to*

> *flip the gaze, take the spotlight away from our bodies, and put it firmly back on the State. That colonial policy orchestration story is epic, and so much bigger than just my family.*

As she realised that her Nanna's life and experiences of removal and indenture were not extraordinary, Natalie's family story became like a case study to illustrate a broader issue or concept: they were shockingly typical, and 'representative of something much bigger': 'She wasn't anyone in particular who was targeted. It was just that she was born Aboriginal at a particular time in history. And it happened to all our families. It was just representative of a time in history.'

Genealogy is one of the main reasons why people visit the State Library of South Australia, undertaking their research in person or online from across the world to locate their relatives. This process of investigating the traces of their ancestors informs their identity. Searches through the shipping lists and registry and land records have the potential to reveal another branch to add to the family tree, or confirmation of heritage or some recognition or connection with the past. The results of Natalie's research have been published and exhibited around Australia. Many have had the opportunity to experience her creative response to her discoveries – to release her grandmother's voice from the archive and reinstate dignity, identity and agency:

> *What I wanted to do was flip the records and do something creative to honour her voice. There were a lot of handwritten letters by my Nana, and her mother Grace Chester, my great grandmother. I wanted to do something with these letters . . . take them from the violence of the colonial archive and weave them into something beautiful.*

Natalie made an artwork that recontextualises the reductive effects of the reports of her ancestors' experiences, creating a vessel from copies of their correspondence that offers testimony to her family's love, grace and enduring connection:

I wove a Ngarrindjeri basket from those letters. And then I did a lot of other creative work with archives . . . The basket has been installed with poetry, as well as filmed, and that film has been projected in several exhibitions, including onto walls of key institutions. It's been used in teaching. It's been a really beautiful tool to teach with, also with the poetry. You can see key words and statements tucked to the outside of the basket, woven to tell a different story to the one represented in the archives. That was my intention.

A lack of resources for the appropriate care of archival collections is not the only issue impeding records access. The most important grouping of Aboriginal Records in South Australia, held in State Records, is known as GRG 52/1, which are the correspondence files of the Aborigines Department. State Records is now administered by the South Australian Attorney-General's department. People wishing to access their family records must first request access through the Department of Aboriginal Affairs and Reconciliation, which may or may not be granted by the Attorney-General:

While I've had access to so many Aboriginal domestic service stories from the State's archives, I also know there are many other record groups that I haven't had access to. Also, every record request we make must first be vetted by the Attorney-General's department, under legal and professional privilege, and our records can be redacted or determinations made stating 'Access Denied' – these are of course the records on our families that we most want to get our hands on! It's appalling because the state's Aboriginal Records are the only record group in South Australia that has to be vetted in this particular way. This is our personal history, and we can't appeal what is decided for us.

Although I had surveyed and interviewed dozens of members of the public about their relationship with the State Library, this was the first time I'd been made aware that some members of the Adelaide community have limited access to records about their family. The racism and discrimination underlying these administrative structures was uncomfortably obvious and displays a distrust for some members of the South Australian community. Natalie's experiences at the Library were significantly influenced by the permission processes imposed by the Attorney-General's department on the State Records during 2014–16, when they were co-located on the State Library site. I asked Natalie what she thought was the rationale behind the restrictions to accessing records. I wondered how something so discriminatory could be allowed within a 'public institution':

> *From my perspective, the rationale is that the state is bunkering down to protect itself from litigation. We had a successful case in our community with our late Ngarrindjeri elder, Uncle Bruce Trevorrow, who was forcibly and illegally removed from his family, and he could prove that with evidence from the State's Aboriginal Records. Cameron Raynes also wrote a book called The Last Protector from Wakefield Press, an incredibly revealing book. And that was when the records were open. He could trace the story of children that were forcibly and illegally removed from families under Penhall, who was the last Protector in South Australia. These illegal acts were revealed by tracing the story from these GRG 52/1 files. Uncle Bruce Trevorrow actually won his case against the government, and was the first Aboriginal person in Australia to do so. After his records were made public, the Attorney-General at the time put a blanket ban on GRG 52/1, where everything had to be vetted through his office. I think that was the time when everything just shut down. The state is protecting itself. So that's the rationale.*

Natalie's research highlights this legacy of colonialism in many public institutions like the State Library: how long-held fears, discrimination and prejudice against the Indigenous community have been enforced through outdated legislation and allowed to continue. This discrimination was then reinforced through institutional practices or neglect that still prevent access to past records.

Natalie also described the range of archival collections that document the decades of resistance by Indigenous Elders and their advocacy for improving the condition of their community in South Australia. Attesting to the energy, commitment and determination to achieve recognition and human rights, these archives are a critical element of the recent social history and identity of South Australia. Natalie comments:

> *I was gifted an activist history archive by Uncle Lewis O'Brien, our very senior and esteemed Kaurna elder who's in his 90s, and a non-Aboriginal historian, the late Betty Fisher, who's quite an iconic woman in South Australia as an activist, feminist, conservationist and amateur historian . . . Uncle Lewis grew up with Auntie Gladys Elphick who's a senior Ngadjuri, Kaurna, Narungga woman. Auntie Glad established the Council of Aboriginal Women of South Australia in 1966 with a group of Aboriginal women who worked tirelessly over many years to tackle racism and inequality head on. They established Aboriginal community-controlled organisations in areas of legal rights, health, education, childcare and welfare rights, and the legacy of these organisations is present still today. These incredible women were so strategic, and worked closely with politicians, including Premier Don Dunstan, and with the Aborigines Advancement League, who were largely part of the white Adelaide establishment, but doing what they could and using their networks to work with and advance Aboriginal people in our state.*

With permission from Uncle Lewis, Betty Fisher and members of the community, the State Library is providing Natalie with access to the Gladys Elphick Collection as part of her research.[18] This collection includes a number of important oral histories, already recorded and digitised, although there is much further work to do before their value can be realised. Natalie's work could be seen as an opportunity for the State Library to address not only long-standing collection issues, but also to examine approaches for improving the ways in which the institution engages with the Indigenous community:

> *I've been able to go and have a look at what's there, and, you know, it's a bit of a mess – nothing is in order, and the content isn't transparent to our community. Some of the material is really critical and it's important that Aboriginal people interested in the collection can access and engage with it. But that's not possible at this point. We're only now just going through a process of sorting, and the library has been so supportive.*

Institutional transition is a long and slow process. By their nature, collecting institutions exist to preserve and reflect their community's identity and values. Indigenous culture is part of our community's history and cultural heritage, not separate from it. Natalie has noticed important first steps towards positive change in the treatment of Indigenous records and collections, change that reflects the character and commitment of the institution's leadership team:

> *This iteration of management in the library is amazing. Geoff and his team are really wanting to do something quite different and transformative and, as I see it, relinquish some of the long held institutional power, colonial authority and secrecy. These cultural institutions represent sites of knowledge production and collective memory that can easily perpetuate racialised and gendered violence through public discourse and representations based on colonial fantasies and imaginings of Aboriginality, history and events – this is all from the position of the coloniser who determined what was in and out. On the other hand, these collections are incredible and exciting and hold the key to parts of lives that have been blocked or suppressed. It's a paradox. Some collections are an enigma. Historically, Library staff haven't known or fully understood what they've got, and this is partly due to inadequate resourcing, staff expertise, leadership, and political will. Our communities have a right to both access and respond to what*

is held about us. But finally, I think the tides are slowly turning our way.

And it's not only in South Australia. The International Council of Archives Expert Matters Indigenous Group (ICAEMIG) held its inaugural summit in Adelaide on 25 October 2019. This organisation advocates for Indigenous self-representation as a human rights issue, particularly in relation to accessing archives and libraries:

Colonial archival programs served often as textual armouries prioritising evidence of colonial settlement and creating categories of identity and knowledge to privilege and preserve settler narratives and leave Indigenous heritage on the unacknowledged frontiers of public memory. Across the global colonial encounter, dispossession occurred in the public archive as it occurred on the land.[19]

The summit in Adelaide ratified and released the Tandanya-Adelaide Declaration, a commitment by the International Council of Archives to recognise the responsibilities of archives and cultural institutions to 'reimagine' their role in the creation and preservation of social memory by incorporating indigenous knowledge systems, authority, interpretations and meanings into their principles and practices:

To challenge colonial ideologies in the archival setting is an endeavour of generations, like the colonial program itself. The result will be a new model of public archives as an ethical space of encounter, respect, negotiation and collaboration without the dominance or judgement of distant or enveloping authority.[20]

This world-leading document was endorsed by the Directors of the State Library and State Records of South Australia. To fulfil their commitment, the State Library is working with Indigenous communities to repatriate collection items that may have been acquired under questionable circumstances. The Library and State

Records have collaborated to establish an Aboriginal Reference Group, whose purpose is to:

> *Provide feedback and advice on activities, services and policy relating to Aboriginal people and culture to the State Library and State Records. Members will also have the opportunity to advocate for Aboriginal people and communities, ensure State Records and the State Library's activities reflect Aboriginal experiences and help the organisations to engage and partner with Aboriginal communities to deliver services and programs.[21]*

Natalie is one of the inaugural members of the Aboriginal Reference Group, supporting the two institutions to develop and implement protocols and responses to the Tandanya-Adelaide Declaration. Institutional changes such as these not only increase the cultural value of their collections, but they are also essential if institutions are to remain relevant in the cultural life of their communities.

Natalie has encountered libraries and collections since childhood and admits to becoming nostalgic when considering her earliest experiences:

> *I grew up in Salisbury North and thought the Salisbury library was fantastic there. I gravitated to libraries at school, as well . . . it was where a lot of social stuff happened, the teaching and learning, school projects, and all those books! I didn't grow up with many books in the house, but thanks to my Mum, going to the library became almost a weekly trip because it was next to our local Parabanks shopping centre. We'd borrow books and I'd just devour them. It was a constant . . . a place that I remember really fondly.*

In common with many survey respondents and interview subjects, Natalie's positive childhood experiences influenced her perception of libraries as an adult. These experiences may have contributed to her fascination with and research into archival practices and informed her creative practice as a poet and artist. She shared a more recent experience – an opportunity to revisit the Salisbury Library for the first time since she was a teenager, this time as a guest speaker of the Salisbury Writers' Festival:

> *I didn't realise how important that library was to me when I was younger, until I went back just a couple of years ago for the Salisbury Writers' Festival. It was like I had just stepped back in time. I'm a very nostalgic, sentimental person, and it was a wave of all these memories crashing to me . . . wonderful memories, I just loved being there in that old familiar space. My brother came with me to the festival and it triggered lots of stories for us. I actually spoke about these stories when I presented, because it really affected me.*

Natalie's subjective emotional response to her visit to the Salisbury Library reflects the personal value associations described by many survey respondents when reminiscing about their early encounters with libraries. Today the State Library elicits a similar range of realisations and recognitions related to personal identity, inspiration and enchantment, with many of these associated with the physical space, which are enlivened and reinforced with each visit. This relationship is unconstrained by time, spanning generations and, in Natalie's case, traces the arc of her personal development from a student borrowing books to a published author, whose books now sit on the same shelves she used to scan as a child. The early benefits she gained at the Salisbury Library may be similarly realised by the current generation of children in Salisbury, a community she remains fond of:

> *I think it's just the effect of stepping into something that has an emotional attachment, or to your childhood memories . . . the affective dimensions of a place or a smell or a site can trigger you, and make you realise its importance and impact when growing up and, you know, all of this . . . Community is where you build it wherever you are, and the Northern suburbs was my home, my family, my education, my first job, my life, where I grew up, and where all my rites of passage occurred.*

Natalie does not recall her first visit to the State Library of South Australia. As a student she made the most of the university libraries, which, like the Salisbury Library, were egalitarian and welcoming spaces. She did not feel the same about the State Library:

> *They're public sites, and they're meant to overcome class barriers, and all of that. I think . . . the institutions on North Terrace still feel exclusive and are possibly difficult sites for some people to navigate. Because it is also part of that whole cultural precinct, which sends a very strong message about what colonial South Australia was and still is . . .*

As a researcher, writer and teacher, Natalie has worked in Aboriginal student support and Indigenous studies centres across all three universities in South Australia since 1996. Her teaching and research took her deep into the colonial history of Adelaide. This included the role played by the precinct along North Terrace in the early settlement of the city and how this history is perceived and misrepresented to maintain the popular mythologies of early Adelaide. Public perceptions of the North Terrace Cultural Precinct significantly informed the experience of the State Library for many survey respondents and interview subjects. They expressed pride in the character of the heritage buildings and identified a sense of history tied to settlement, describing how this relationship with the past informs their sense of place and community identity. The area also serves a similar function as a site of memory-keeping and colonial contact for the Indigenous community of Adelaide, but the relationship is of an entirely different nature.

Natalie's current work as part of the Indigenous Studies program at Flinders University is 'very much about decolonising that whole precinct and . . . revealing those other narratives that aren't represented on North Terrace'. Natalie has visited, and worked with, other state libraries in Australia and has seen how colonial contact with Indigenous people has been openly addressed and approached from a truth-telling basis, one that involved Indigenous communities and work towards reconciling their institutional past with respect, determination and honesty. She described the exciting literary, visual arts and digital programs run by the State Library of Queensland, involving contemporary artists such as Fiona Foley, whose public art installations depict sites of genocide and massacre, along with government-sanctioned violence. Vernon Ah Kee, another artist involved, reconnected Indigenous collections in state institutions with today's communities, re-establishing traditional custodial and interpretive practices:

> *I was fortunate to be up there to see Vernon's Transforming Tindale exhibition, and saw how the [Queensland] library facilitated community voices to engage with, critique and respond to the Tindale collection. His community's archives were kept in the South Australian Museum, thanks to Norman Tindale and others from the Board of Anthropological Research. They led numerous expeditions, collecting social, cultural and physical material and data from communities all over Australia. Vernon was able to access the SA Museum collections, take archives and genealogies back to Palm Island, and record his community's and Elders' responses to the archives in digital documentaries, which were then exhibited. He also drew larger-than-life portraits of his family, [which] Tindale photographed, to return the identity, names, and agency of his family and community members. So there's that right of reply, as well as the learning. To have those living-memory kind of archives is so important, and the Queensland Library was phenomenal in working with their local Aboriginal communities and with the SA Museum to develop teaching resources and an entire public program around the research-based exhibition. I think they're doing great work.*

There is no shortage of ideas and energy available to activate the cultural value of the archives and collections of the State Library in South Australia; however, as part of the larger decolonisation project underway across the globe, there is now an added layer of institutional responsibility to reconnect the Indigenous community with the documents and items related to their past. In fulfilling the mission of the Tandanya-Adelaide Declaration, the State Library and State Records of South Australia are activating the latent cultural value of their collections, reconnecting their collections with the people for whom they have meaning. As keepers of the documentary records of the past, cultural institutions exist to bear witness, collecting evidence of the present to be re-created as history in the future. This role is recognised and valued by a large proportion of the survey respondents from the State Library. If the truth about the past is to be preserved and revealed, known and accepted across all communities, the care of collections must be prioritised to enable their access and to allow their value to be activated. The proposed Centre for First Nations Cultures – Tarrkarri – at Lot Fourteen at the eastern end of North Terrace, offers an opportunity to draw together the collections from across the cultural precinct for the first time. Natalie sees this as critical to the success of any real cultural or institutional change with the capacity to not only reveal the alternative narratives of the past, but to reinstate a visible Indigenous presence and authentic voice on North Terrace, along the banks of Karrawirraparri. In reality, that presence never left. Natalie and I spoke of the potential for the site to be an engine room for authentic South Australian narratives, genuine inclusion and democratic opportunities. This proposed cultural centre represents an exciting opportunity to bolster the cultural value of the state's collections. Together with the implementation of the Tandanya-Adelaide Declaration, the centre would showcase for the first time an inclusive balanced history, obviating some of the post-colonial legacy represented by colonial-era cultural institutions like the State Library.

I asked Natalie to describe her best memories of the State Library. She highlighted again the importance of leadership and trust in developing relationships between an institution and its public: a recognition of roles, needs and responsibilities, as well as a willingness to listen and change:

> *It was very refreshing to meet Geoff Strempel, because his commitment to doing something different in relation to the Library's Indigenous collections and community engagement is followed up with action. He's championing the Tandanya Declaration, activating the decolonisation of the archives in a way that isn't tokenistic – it's a heart commitment. I think he recognises that he's in a position to do something, otherwise he represents just another institution perpetuating all of those North Terrace settler-colonial myths and fantasies. It's not easy, but it feels like there is finally a bit of momentum for positive transformative change – I really believe that.*

The trusting relationship between the executive leadership of the State Library and the public can also been seen in Natalie's work with the Unbound Collective, which she says is her 'other best memory'. The group performed in 2015 as part of Tarnanthi, the annual Indigenous arts festival organised by the Art Gallery of South Australia. The performers used projections of videos with music, song and poetry to engage with the physical and spiritual sites of the Library and Museum, producing a beautifully delicate and unforgettably powerful new discourse with the North Terrace Cultural Precinct, on their terms. As Natalie explained:

> *We were basically repatriating love to our ancestors ... It wasn't about the broader white community so much. It was really about us and our families and communities. I'm not a performance artist but engaging in that 'Sovereign Act' felt completely right and comfortable, because I was with my Unbound sisters Simone, Ali and Faye ... Projecting our films and poetry to the outside of the Library and SA Museum and witnessed by hundreds of people. It was so affirming for us ... it felt like we left an ephemeral trace, and we now walk through that colonial space feeling different to before. I remember we projected the words 'she could not find herself in any of your*

*books' on the State Library, which was a direct reference to
Ali's mum's reflection of going to the Library. This is sadly true
for so many of that generation.*

*The cultural precinct buildings that we were projecting
onto are violent sites. We knew we were projecting onto the
outside of the museum, where our ancestors' remains were
held, our old people were still in that building. We projected
onto the Armory Building and the Police Barracks, where
Aboriginal people were publicly hung, and where the troopers
went out to colonise and basically claim country in those very
early days. We projected onto the mortuary, where Aboriginal
bodies were taken, often directly from the hospital, and where
bones were defleshed and then moved to the South Australian
Museum as objects and artifacts. That's what they did in this
little room at the Armory Building. We know where it is. And
the general public walk past these places every day, with no
idea. [We wanted] to do something powerful and loving, so we
got strategic, applied for arts grants, and left that ephemeral
trace through our performative work, to speak back to those
sites, and the violent histories they represent. That's the best
memory I have at the State Library.*

Relationships built on trust are a critical element of institutional
value. The performance by the Unbound Collective and the work
undertaken by the State Library and State Records Aboriginal
Advisory Group in overseeing the implementation of the Tandanya
Declaration are demonstrations of trust in the public held by the
current leadership of the State Library. The ongoing restriction
of access to records by the Attorney-General's department is evidence of the imbalanced relationship between the state and the
Indigenous community. To deny access is to deny trust. Without
this trust, there can be no truth-telling nor the transformational
change for which the public now advocates. The beauty of the
Unbound Collective's performance and the State Library's tangible
steps towards change are immeasurable, visible and demonstrable
manifestations of cultural value. As Natalie explains:

For us it's all about relationality, and I think change comes about through building relationships beyond the symbolic. Good leadership requires vision, creativity and action through community relationships built over time. And it's probably the first time that we've got to this point, which is amazing. So that's what I'm hopeful and excited by, and I'm ok with being part of the long game if it means getting it right. Our mob know policy, process, and patience like no one else. And there is so much work to do.

As an Indigenous artist and scholar, Natalie has an informed and balanced perspective on the potential represented by cultural institutions like the State Library of South Australia, as well as the challenges they face. Like many of the survey respondents and interview subjects, the character of her relationship with the institution has changed over the years, as have the ways in which she has engaged with it, from perceiving its elitism and the violence of its physical site, through to now working alongside the executive team to transform its practices. Her current research is investigating living legacy archive models, which address the misrepresentations of the colonial past in cultural institutions and initiate more community-led research, archival management practices and interpretation of Indigenous collections:

I dream of a time where our archives are properly catalogued, described, transparent, and accessible. Where we have the right people safeguarding that work and being like brokers between the institution and the community. Sometimes the institutions need to continue to hold our archives, because of the storage facilities and there may be no other places for them. But the question of community engagement, access and transparency is paramount, especially how communities can lead the way in how collections are utilised, and with potential to benefit and educate the rest of the world. As our Elders are passing, it becomes even more important to have their stories recorded and inserted in the wider narrative of our history, our today, and our future. These are our stories. They must be led by our communities. They are also shared stories. We can't keep perpetuating the silencing and forgetting . . .

Since it was first proposed in 1834, the State Library of South Australia has adapted and worked hard to fulfil its role and purpose in the South Australian community, a process complicated by arguments over who should have financial responsibility for it – the state or the individual. But responsibility extends beyond finances. Even before the colony's establishment, the Library was created to educate and provide culture to a European community far removed from its lands, a community attempting to establish 'civilisation' on lands already occupied by another culture, a different people who had much to share and teach the colonists. Over the generations these opportunities were ignored in favour of the kind of culture the Library was mandated to replicate and promulgate, irrespective of whether the settlers wanted it or not. The early public debates remind us that what the first leaders of the Library wanted to cultivate and distribute was not necessarily what the public wanted. Today, members of the public are again demanding change and once again the Library is responding by creating the sort of site where people can gather freely to exchange and share, confront and learn, not only with respect, but with love and understanding, the basis of every successful relationship built up over time. Natalie remains positive and sees opportunity and potential in the latent value of the State Library and Records collections, which is awaiting activation:

It's really about building relationships and making those grounded connections with community, so all of those cultural sites of knowledge production and story creation on North Terrace can do something dynamic, responsive, creative and unique. This can be transformative work, and I'm hopeful. We're certainly not there yet. These are powerful public cultural institutions that can still be very damaging and exclusive and misrepresent Aboriginal people's experiences and truths. Fundamentally, these cultural institutions of knowledge production are located on the stolen lands of Kaurna people. These lands were never ceded. I think the State Library has a responsibility to make these stories and its Indigenous collections as accessible and transparent as possible. Our Elders deserve the right to access material about their lives, for archives to be repatriated where possible, the right of reply to set the record straight if needed, and the right to tell their stories in the ways they want for future generations. The responsibility to get it right can only come about through committing to a decolonising policy mandate in the archives sector that's led by our communities. There can be no truth-telling without access to our archives. These are our stories and lives, and there is so much work to be done.

The story of colonial contact in South Australia is not just the history of the Indigenous past. *It belongs to everyone.* As Natalie suggests, 'this is everyone's family history'. South Australians cannot miss this opportunity to resolve the conflicts and challenges of our colonial past, which, if unreconciled, will continue to plague future generations. The responsibility to learn from the past and take informed steps towards the future belongs to all of us. The State Library is already showing leadership in this field through its implementation of the recommendations of the Tandanya-Adelaide Declaration. In doing so, the Library is also leading the state towards a more authentic and trusting relationship with all members of the community – becoming the democratic and reflective institution it has always aspired to be.

Our stories and our lives

Not all creative or scientific pursuits have predictable results. I've discussed with colleagues the similarities between arts practice and scientific research. The final goals and outcomes are usually unclear until the exploratory practice and the processes of experimentation, consultation and refinement are resolved or abandoned. Both the arts and sciences require years of practice, research, funding, patience and networks of supporting allies. They also need time, lots of it, given that recognition of the relevance and value of some of the most important breakthroughs may be a long process. Integral to such pursuits is that *the process itself* is as valuable as the outcome. Critically, both sets of practices require imagination – the ability to conceive and then work towards a better understanding, to follow an idea and create a new way of seeing, or to contribute a minor element to what may become a major new story. Along the way, scientists and artists may discover, recognise or conjure something they could not have imagined, had they not commenced the process. The *process* is usually the *point*. What we do, here and now. We may be long dead before the outcomes of our actions are realised.

As points of engagement between the public and the public service, cultural institutions facilitate access to and recognition of quality resources – for learning, inspiration, understanding and identity formation. This service builds the common ground in which the seeds of our dreams can be cultivated, now and into the future. The voices of the public I've shared here – people from around the world and our own backyard – describe a range of possibilities, lofty aspirations and specific goals and desires. Each one of them brings as much to the Library as they gain from it. Life, energy, assistance, thought, stewardship and hope. They come with a need, a dream or a purpose and build a community; a faith that the Library will always be there for them when they need it, like a hospital or a police officer. The State Library has striven to achieve this purpose throughout its history, providing members of the public with the materials they need to fulfil their intellectual and research needs and to foster their imaginations while ensuring the protection and preservation of the collection items for future use.

The requirement for evidence of economic outcomes is relatively new in our culture and underpins the current evaluation frameworks demanded of government agencies around the world to justify the expenditure of public funding. The return on their investment needs to be viewed and measured within a given and limited timeframe, and that is as it should be. Everyone responsible for spending public funding needs to be accountable. The requirement only becomes problematic once numbers become the sole means of evaluation of the outcomes of pursuits that may not be visible or felt for years to come.

Financial and visitor numbers should be accompanied by narrative evaluation and feature the voices and views of the public. Under current reporting requirements, each of the survey respondents and interview subjects presented here would have been reported as a mere number. But, as history reminds us, without their voices, they become dehumanised and meaningless. And as economist Sanne Blauw suggests, 'numbers are like soap: if you squeeze them too hard, they slip from your fingers'.[22] The public perspective provides the authentic narrative context that gives meaning to quantitative data and not only reflects the cultural value of the State Library but how that value is enlivened.

Viewed through the eyes of the interview subjects, the Library adds value to their daily lives in Adelaide and the life of the community. The reciprocal, iterative and functional relationship between the Library and its public is highly prized and, like many human relationships, largely taken for granted. However, the notable exceptions were Joseph and Edward, who grew up in cultures and political environments where citizens have limited or no democratic political engagement or free access to information. Some governments, including at times our own, believe so completely in the transformative power of information that they do not trust what their citizens might do with it, and so access is limited.

The State Library provides an everyday space where the value of new knowledge and creativity is activated through public engagement with staff, volunteers and the collections, preserved by generations of librarians for the public of tomorrow. The value is realised today, even if the book or document was collected and preserved decades ago: it was always waiting for the right person at the right time. This is cultural value made manifest. It is deeply personal and ultimately intangible, enjoyed quietly, or possibly amplified, celebrated in families and communities and available every day throughout the year. The State Library of South Australia is not a special occasion; it is a way of living. The value of such cultural institutions to their public is so powerful and precious that they have the potential to change the world.

Little wonder that the question of their value warrants so much attention.

Chapter 6

Reclaiming common ground for the common good

This book has focused on two key questions: what cultural value does the State Library of South Australia generate for the public; and can this value be expressed, captured and reported in a way to both meet regulatory requirements and retain meaning and significance for the public. The answer to the first question can be found in the words of the public themselves; these voices tell us that the Library means many things, these being variously precious, life-affirming and collectively invaluable.

The second question is a little trickier, and perhaps has more than one answer, which is frustrating, yet also acceptable. The *process* of investigating the cultural value of the State Library has been the point of this work, and the following sections explore my conclusions. Rather than limiting our thinking about cultural value and the reporting of it to numbers and economic outcomes, I've discovered that we need to identify alternative approaches to building policies, funding mechanisms and reporting frameworks, which incorporate and are steered by how the public values their cultural institutions and what they mean to their communities. These conclusions explain why we need to stop demanding only measurable outcomes from our cultural institutions, or risk missing out on the best part of the story.

History, heritage and the importance of continuity

Several respondents identified the special connection they believed existed between the heritage of the State Library and the history of South Australia. Others also spoke of how the institution builds trust in the community, supporting their sense of identity by reinforcing both personal and collective memory. The international human rights lawyer and advocate for civil liberties Geoffrey Robertson describes heritage objects as items that have been witness to history, objects that symbolise and enliven the past: 'they have a meaning that a replica could not – well, replicate'.[1] The heritage value experienced by visitors to cultural institutions such as the State Library does not appear in the lists of attributes previously identified as part of intrinsic audience experiences.[2] This new value theme – confirming the Library's heritage value as part of the visitor experience – is a complex element of the public's relationship with the institution, reflecting a continuity of an individual's experience within the site, which connects members of the public to their personal histories and at the same time, to the history of South Australia. The State Library's heritage goes beyond an appreciation of architectural aesthetics: it is also something subjective for many visitors, a symbolic and formative part of their lives, linking them to their past and that of the state, neither of which can be replicated.

Heritage value and the sense of both collective and individual continuity contribute to the State Library's institutional value. Institutional value, which I argue underpins all other forms of cultural value, fosters the trust, inclusion and authenticity experienced by many of its visitors; however, the opposite may be true if those personal or community memories were negative or traumatic. Heritage value is theme was bolstered by transgenerational family connections, with these informing personal memories and aspirations for the future. Visitors may not visit regularly, but they also value the knowledge that the Library will be there when they need it. The physical collections reflect how value, meaning and significance can evolve, is activated and accrued. This longitudinal form of value is constructed over time and shared across generations of Library users, volunteers and stewards, strangers with whom today's visitors identify and collaborate in the co-creation and exchange of knowledge, value and experience. Through the Library's collections and the potential of ongoing collective use, stewardship and public experience, the State Library consolidates and mediates the cultural memory of the state.

Cultural memory is more than the passive collection of objects. It relies on both the careful selection of important canonical items – such as those relating to the foundation of the state and specialist collection areas – and the vast archival holdings, which form the 'basis of what can be said in the future about the present when it will have become the past'.[3] This view was repeated almost verbatim by one survey respondent, who asserted that the Library is 'a link to our past and our future'. Survey respondents and interview subjects perceive that the collections are rich with memory and potential, a perception that is subjective and dependent on the experiences of the community across time. The State Library is considered by the public to be the site where South Australia's cultural memory was formed and is maintained, and that this is one of the institution's most critical functions.[4] From their individual perspectives, the collective public recognises and appreciates the heritage value of the State Library and the sense of continuity it provides. But within that collective appreciation, personal perspectives vary from precious and positive, to traumatic and frustrated. All must be considered when addressing the State Library's contribution to the community.

The historical overview of the Library presented earlier in the book assists in an appreciation of what the institution symbolises to the public today, from equal access to knowledge, mutual support and lifelong education, to the mixed legacies of the colonial experience. The State Library has come to symbolise the value of an informed democracy and Adelaide's distinct cultural identity, consolidated by its location in the North Terrace Cultural Precinct and the more recent moves to improve its operations and practices for all members of the community.

If the State Library and all it represented was a single collection item being evaluated for insurance or for sale, its record of ownership and symbolism, as well as its accessibility and potential, would add to its value. Such a record is known in the arts and cultural sectors as 'provenance'. Reconstructing the influences and inspiration that lie behind the establishment of the State Library demonstrates that many of these values and aspirations, whether accurate or illusory, inform the public's experience today. The record of the Library's ownership has remained unbroken since 1856, when the new colonial government accepted the 'permanent responsibility to provide a library for the public'. This unbroken record of ownership on behalf of the public, and the responsibility it entails, should be considered as evidence of how the citizens and the representative officials of South Australia are obliged by legislation to value the State Library.[5] We all benefit from government support of cultural institutions, support that adds value to the standard of living in the state and to the relationship between citizens and their government. Rather than being an onerous financial burden on the public purse, our cultural institutions represent an enviable way of life.

Why we need a different approach

By dividing cultural value into three separate subcategories of value – intrinsic, instrumental and institutional – and identifying corresponding stakeholder groups – practitioners, 'bean counters' and administrators – John Holden may have oversimplified the concept. I think the Cultural Value Triangle has unfortunately also led to a division of thought and an argument in which the stakeholders who are aligned with the two most immediate values – intrinsic and instrumental – dominate. Intrinsic and instrumental values are more likely to be measurable, readily recognised and policy-friendly and satisfy the short-term solutions required to develop strategies to address perpetual funding crises – be they in the UK or Australia. Institutional value, which underpins the others, accrues over time and is perhaps the most difficult to measure, is overlooked or lost. In recent decades institutional value may also have been damaged by scandals and crimes in other forms of public institution, such as banks and churches. Furthermore, some cultural institutions can be less culturally sensitive and slow to address their roles, for example, as keepers of colonial archives, placing them at odds with many in the community. Attempting to define the cultural value of an institution of the age and complexity of State Library of South Australia is to grapple with a 'wicked problem'.[6] The goal of this book has not been to solve this problem but to understand this complexity and demonstrate that other forms of evidence – stories from the public – can present a more complete narrative of value, one capable of supporting quantitative reports and economic impact statements, by strengthening their capacity to convey meaning. Such an authentic narrative context, based on what the public values, is essential for the future of institutions. By not listening to the public, we are ignoring the reason for the very existence of these cultural institutions.

Current reporting practices are no longer a comfortable fit. Despite the vast evidence provided by cultural institutions, by way of reliably careful budget management, stable visitor numbers or innovative artistic or curatorial practice, we've seen that organisations do not escape budget cuts. This has been illustrated over the past decade by the policy-driven imperatives imposed on the State Library and other South Australian cultural institutions to meet efficiency dividends. Time will tell if and how this unsustainable practice will continue in South Australia – or whether it might change for the better through the influence of *Revive*, the Australian Government's first cultural policy in over a decade, released in the first term of the Albanese Government.

Placing how the public values their public institutions at the heart of evaluation strategies is the best measure of success we have. To understand what the public values, they need to be counted and their voices heard. And for that to happen, the public must be given a chance to speak.

We need to get along with economists

One of the most surprising and heartening experiences I've had on this project is coming to the realisation that many national and international scholars of accounting and economics are the loudest advocates in support of diversifying how we record and speak about value. As explored earlier, changes to government policies and priorities over the last 30 to 40 years have influenced how libraries have been valued at different points in their history, and why the concept of 'cultural value' has been abstracted beyond the point of practicality.

The slow creep of economic rationalism, which began its determined march through every corner of our lives in the 1980s, has gained apace of late. The practice of imposing standardised commercial and competitive processes across all sectors of government is proving to have its limitations. Indeed, some of the most rigid approaches are counterintuitive to some community sectors that are essential to our way of life – our health systems, our aged care and social services, and tertiary education sectors. The cultural sector has long felt the implications of this operational change of focus from service delivery to value for money. However, some sectors are also displaying a growing awareness of the need to shift away from the focus on market imperatives towards a more values-based approach to spending public monies. During the pandemic, the time spent at home, together, isolated, insecure, possibly under threat and concerned with the future brought what matters most to us to the fore: time with friends, family, community and cultural engagement. We had a chance to miss what we had always taken for granted. The human capacity to share knowledge and our talent for survival have seen the resurrection of the concept of 'common good', bringing about a reassessment of our value systems; that is, how we treasure the experiences and connections that make us human within a sustainable environment. This change of public heart has led to more than one change of government in Australia and gives many hope for a more human and sustainable future.

The ability to gather, learn, share and commune within a cultural setting makes life worth living, according to the cultural economist Arjo Klamer:

> *Culture is all that gives meaning to shared lives. With our actions in the company of others, like family members,*

*colleagues, fellow citizens or professionals, we generate and
sustain cultures. Those cultures define who we are; they provide us with a context of meanings, with a sense of belonging,
with inspiration hopefully. When we are groping in the dark,
we will inevitably end up needing culture.[7]*

Klamer returned to the ancient roots of the word 'economics' to
explain the importance of an individual's personal perspective
when determining value. He uses the example of how we value a
home (*oikos* in ancient Greek) as distinct from a house; the latter,
a bricks-and-mortar structure that can be assessed, measured and
valued for its market potential:

*Houses are important but homes are what define us: it is the
home that really matters to me. Even if the house were to fall
down, the home will remain standing, at least so I presume . . .
My home stands for everything that I share with my wife and
kids. It evokes the atmosphere in our house with its furniture,
decorations and special places. Also with the memories that
we generated there and now cherish together, the shared stories, the dogs and cats buried in the back yard, the party that
we gave last year, the Christmas celebrations, the dramatic
scenes, the door posts where we measure the height of the kids
throughout the years (gosh, how they've grown!). Not to forget
the gatherings with friends and families, and so much more.[8]*

The State Library is more than a building providing access to
information. Undoubtedly, a quantity surveyor could estimate the
cost of materials required to rebuild it, but as Geoffrey Robertson
might say, it cannot be replicated. The State Library is enjoyed and
valued for the associations it holds, everything it represents to
its users, which include the memories of discovery and pleasure,
inspiration and assistance, peace and security, and the social interactions and leaps of imagination that have already occurred – and
those yet to take place – within the Library's diverse structures
and spaces. For people living on the streets, it may be the closest
they have to a home.

Klamer's argument also supports the qualitative narrative-based approach I've used to explain how the public values the Library, which basically adopts the same terms as Klamer when he values his home:

> *The economic discussion nowadays tends to focus on the numbers, on the things that can be bought and that therefore are measured in monetary terms. The numbers convey a sense of concreteness and practicality. A house is good for numbers. A house is concrete . . . A house is a product that can be sold and bought. The oikos [or home] is another matter altogether. It makes for an entirely different discussion, a discussion without many numbers and without the appearance of concreteness and practicality of a house. It is the quality of the oikos that I really care about.[9]*

Klamer's description of *oikos* mirrors the quality of the relationship between the public and the State Library: like a home, its worth and meaning are comprised of a complex communal system of memory, experience and values. With each visit, these are reinforced by the precious moments alone or with family and strangers, the recognition of shared values and common language, and the myriad interactions that support a sense of welcome, stewardship and belonging. This concept of *oikos* also explains the early colonists' need for a public library and access to books, which were intended not only for their education but also to foster order and resilience and to improve the colony's chances of survival by maintaining the community's identity, *values*, culture and imaginations. The collection of books and the promise of a library were intended to replicate the culture and community they'd left behind, and, as seen in the survey responses, continue to inform how some visitors and locals define the South Australian identity.

The Library continues to provide support to the South Australian community, assisting new arrivals in an unfamiliar community with their transition to new lives and identities, while also furnishing them with opportunities to engage with familiar landscapes of memory and belonging. For other visitors, the State Library anchors them in the social world, enabling them to interact with others in a neutral civic space. For those who have enjoyed libraries elsewhere at other times, the Library offers a similar experience, building on their knowledge and identity and improving their communication skills and confidence. For students and researchers – professionals and amateur enthusiasts – the Library is a gateway to answers, objects and strange new worlds, where they may venture freely to compile, confirm and recast disparate facts into new works to inspire others, or to simply build understanding of their own family and their place in the world. For most, these are not new experiences, but represent the continuity of existing relationships built up over time.

An agreement is voluntarily struck between members of the public and the State Library. This mutual compact of trust and shared values ensures the ongoing regeneration of institutional value, activating the latent possibilities of the collections and fuelling the potential of the public. Visitors invest their time and energies to give meaning and significance to the collections while fostering their sense of ownership of the public resource, the community asset. As Kate suggested in her interview, the public has a responsibility to use the Library, to continue to reaffirm its value and to ensure it will be available for the future. A sort of 'paying forward' of cultural value to future generations. The Library belongs to all members of the community, a place where they find a sense of belonging, where, as one respondent suggested, 'citizens from all walks of life [come] to share the learning space together'. These responses are all values-based statements and reflect how their relationship with the State Library is *a part* of their personal heritage, *a part* of their life, *not apart from it*. More importantly, they count on its being part of their future. Like a place to call home.

Bread and circuses or bricks and mortar?

The cultural policy environment in today's South Australia was designed in the early 1990s to favour arts festivals.[10] This structure is so normalised that even some of our car number plates declare us to be living in 'The Festival State'. The dominance of festivals is a perennial source of debate in South Australian creative circles. While Adelaide's festivals are indeed rich and wonderful experiences, most headline acts originate from across state borders – and even overseas. A large proportion of the South Australian arts budgets supports artists and arts companies from other states and countries, who for a few weeks a year travel to Adelaide to perform for the benefit of largely South Australian audiences. While some workshops and showcases may be offered for local practitioners, is this the most effective way to invest in culture? The present approach has negative impacts on the development and expectations of the local artists, arts audiences and cultural sector in South Australia: the current cultural policy is not equally supportive of the development and promotion of South Australian culture, stories and audiences through the permanent local institutions, collections, companies and artists. It is generally accepted that the most successful model for promoting and presenting culture in Adelaide is to market it as a festival of one type or other: it will be visible, measurable and relatively cost-effective, packaged alongside similar experiences, even if they number in the hundreds. Those with the biggest budgets rise to the top of the public's consciousness – and earn more because of it. As Holden suggests, festivals have become our culture 'because culture is what gets funded'.[11]

I wonder when or if the funding policy priorities will become more balanced between local and visiting artists, short-term fleeting experiences and the ongoing service and responsibilities of collecting institutions like the State Library. All experiences are important for a dynamic cultural ecology and for the development of informed and creative communities, but only some are made available to everyone throughout the year. As we've seen in the survey responses, the relationships between the public and the Library are mutually supportive and self-perpetuating, but they require a basic and reliable level of sustenance to ensure this system does not collapse. Following the pandemic, a number of policy discussions were held to investigate longer-term funding structures to support the local SA arts community, although the outcomes of these discussions will take some time to be implemented; they will also be influenced by cultural policy developments at the national level. I look forward to a time when more South Australian stories and voices are heard and our local issues explored and celebrated across all artforms, underpinned by a cultural policy context developed from the audience perspective – a neo-institutional view – responding to the values and needs of local audiences and artists. A time when the cultural value of the treasures in the state collections can be accessed, activated and realised for the South Australian public in a creative cultural economy, generating experiences and innovations that will attract not only tourists but significant economic investment into South Australia. What could that do for community identity, our cultural memory, and our long-term productivity?

Adelaide is one of the few cities in the world where the major cultural institutions – Library, Gallery, Museum, and, perhaps one day, an Indigenous Cultural Centre – are lined up, accessible on foot and only a few metres apart. I dare to imagine these cultural institutions as freed from efficiency dividends and with adequate funding levels restored, showcasing their cultural value to locals and visitors alike – a rich, stimulating and creative common ground available to welcome, entertain and support the community all year round *and* representing an ongoing, multi-layered and complex, yet overwhelmingly positive, return on public investment in culture.

As a public institution within this rich cultural environment, the State Library generates and facilitates trust for and in the South Australian Government, becoming a support mechanism enabling direct engagement with the public and representing a sense of authority; it also channels the government's trust in the Adelaide community and between members of the public, encouraging the development of social cohesion for the benefit of users and non-users alike, an important institutional value that must be taken into account when considering the contribution made by the Library to the state of South Australia.

Adelaide's cultural institutions shouldn't be forced into an unequal and inequitable competition for government funding with one another. Nor should they need to compete with the quantifiable successes of festivals, whose rise to prominence, along with their ever-increasing budgets, mirrors the advance of economic rationalism. An experience held *for a limited period of time* and creating a *limited measurable economic impact* cannot be compared with an invaluable well-established community resource and heritage site, which is embedded into the social fabric of the state all year round and whose *impact and value accrue over generations* and, for many, *defines their way of life*.

The profound fundamental differences between these two cultural entities should be reflected in distinct funding models. And for the models to be authentic, they should be guided by the public, not political preferences.

Culture, value and the State Library of South Australia

Two decades ago, the Australian cultural economist David Throsby confirmed what now seems glaringly obvious, that 'it should not be difficult to accept that cultural value is a multiple and shifting thing which cannot be comprehended within a single domain'.[12] That said, policy-makers and platform-developers around Australia continue to create and apply standardising cultural evaluation tools. My research has demonstrated that qualitative techniques – especially those that include the viewpoint of the public – represent the most direct route to understanding the meaning of culture and assessing its value. Unlike many of those who insist that digital methods authentically capture cultural value, I took a different approach, recognising that value, meanings and connections are imparted across generations through the use of narrative and stories to evaluate and assess, a process that offers 'a dynamic ordering of information that can cope with time'.[13]

There is much we can learn by listening to the public. We come to understand that the State Library is an active participant in the collaborative process of creating community identity – as well as subjective inspiration and social cohesion – over decades. The public's stories capture their personally transformative and imaginative interactions with the site's heritage, the experienced team members and the collections. This recognition of the State Library's value extends beyond the boundaries of the institution and contributes to the public's larger relationship with the North Terrace Cultural Precinct, a precinct understood to reflect the history, identity and potential of the South Australian community.

The quality and value of the public's experience is influenced by the physical and digital sites, the geographical location, their personal relationship with the institution – what it means to them – and their interactions with the collections. Above all, the public's perception of value comes from their trust in the current stewards of the State Library. Thus, the institution is positioned as both a keeper and producer of longitudinal cultural value in the public realm, where 'people become citizens, not just consumers'.[14] Members of the public recognise the State Library's civic contribution to South Australia's culture in the ethnographic sense, as a 'cognitive map of meanings',[15] as exemplified by the public's stories of belonging and social cohesion, or their absence. These neo-institutional values benefit all South Australians, regardless of their current level of engagement with the State Library. They confirm the institution as a site of symbolic interaction with the public, supporting how they 'define, interpret and give meaning to situations, and then behave in response', thereby informing the quality of our society and way of life.[16] These final words on cultural value come from John Holden:

> It is not the existence of a theatre or a museum that creates these values; they are created in the way that the organization relates to the public to which, as a publicly funded organization, it is answerable. Trust in the public realm, transparency and fairness, are all values that can be generated by the institution

in its dealings with the public . . . it is through recognizing these
values, and, crucially, deciding for itself how to generate them,
that the moral purpose of an organisation becomes apparent,
and where organisational rhetoric meets reality.[17]

Shortly after the opening of the Institute Building in 1860, Adelaide's need for European cultural experiences flourished, with the gradual establishment of the Public Libraries Association, the Art Gallery of South Australia, the South Australian Museum and the University of Adelaide along North Terrace. Over the years, the cultivation and diffusion of useful knowledge in South Australia saw the formation of niche arts and scientific societies and membership organisations, such as the South Australian Geographic Society and the Royal South Australian Society of Arts, Writers SA, the Royal Society of South Australia, and many others, some of whom are tenants in State Library buildings today. The recent inclusion of Indigenous voices and cultural practices in the care and custodianship of records to ensure the preservation of the Indigenous experience of colonial and more modern Adelaide offers a hopeful pathway and contribution to overdue truth-telling.

The collections of the State Library offer an exemplary record of the state's progress, and the extent to which the community has evolved – or perhaps not in some areas. These collections, which can be endlessly revisited, are as valuable as we wish to make them: their value is made manifest by the public's need, interest and connection. As with any book, or a library of them, its covers need to be opened before the story can be revealed, and only then its relevance or value judged. The vivid, thoughtful, challenging, warm-hearted and surprising statements made by members of the public highlight the many ways by which the meaning and value of the State Library can be recognised and assessed, a value that has been a source of debate for almost two hundred years. Today's State Library represents a continuation of the original offer of support from South Australia's imperfect British founders. The institutions of Adelaide's North Terrace Cultural Precinct evolved with the society that grew around them. They exemplify decades of changing attitudes and practices, learning to co-exist, adapting to political and economic shifts and technological leaps.

The public will continue to value the State Library of South Australia and what it represents for individuals and the community, regardless of the political persuasion of the government of the day. It is part of who we are and how we see our world.

Epilogue

Capitalism is a difficult force to resist, its logic so icy-cold that it is inviolable, despite the nightmarish environmental, social, intellectual and spiritual wreckage left in its wake. Like questioning the encroachment of technology on all corners of our lives, capitalism is hard to challenge without being called naive, a Luddite, someone who just doesn't understand.[1] But I persist: I've never been too comfortable with any form of absolutism. Instead, I find hope in human nature.

During the COVID-19 pandemic, as countries, cities and states were locked down and dislocated from their way of life, arts and culture stepped in to fill the void – to help pass the time and to stay connected, provide solace and give voice to frustration, and to enable people to explore new aspects of themselves. Culture may be, as Holden said, what gets funded. But regardless of politics, I believe culture is also what people will reach for and turn to in times of crisis; culture makes us, and keeps us, human.

In response to the pandemic, the State Library of South Australia closed between 25 March and 9 June 2020, which prompted a dramatic loss of numbers through the door – but an increase in online access (up by 37.5%). In March 2020, the South Australian Public Library Network released a report, titled *The Answer is Libraries: The value of public libraries in South Australia*.[2] Having completed similar studies in Victoria and Queensland, the independent consultants commissioned to undertake the report concluded that the value of the state's library network is estimated to provide a net community benefit of $163 million dollars, which is $95 per capita and equates to a return of $2.80 for every dollar spent. These may be considered good numbers, but they're unlikely to change the current funding levels. These numbers alone also fail to tell the whole story. Good numbers have had little impact on governments at any level in recent decades, but perhaps new cultural policy initiatives at both the federal and state levels, which recognise artists and arts workers like me as providers of valued services, offer some cause for hope.

When the State Library closed its doors during the first wave of the pandemic, I wondered what had happened to the homeless men I'd interviewed. When the country closed its borders, I thought of the international students so obviously attached to the institution and their determination to find within it their 'sense of blongness'. Who would the volunteers talk to, to preserve their voice? As our lives became more circumscribed, discontent and distrust in government became amplified, fired by misdirected imagination and misunderstanding. These are the times our libraries are most important, as transmitters of critical and active expertise, understanding and comfort. In this post-pandemic world, however, their role remains just as important as a source of trusted information, with their previous value – community, discovery, creativity, learning alongside our peers – restored. As old tensions return and the consequences of global conflicts creep closer to home, reclaiming and preserving our common ground for the common good will only grow more vital to maintaining our way of life.

A quest for resurrection

Jane Gleeson-White's story of Anthony Clarke refusing orders to destroy Sansepolcro during the Second World War, recounted at the beginning of this book, has stayed with me. It remains the most illustrative example for me of the many issues around cultural value – along with all that is wrong with our current methods for evaluating it. As I was writing the thesis that formed the basis of this book, many people asked if my conclusions would change anything, and what I intended to do when I had finished. My outlook was uncharacteristically bleak, and I responded honestly: I did not know, but the arts and cultural sector needed a clean policy slate, and I was in need of resurrection.

Not long after I had submitted my thesis, I travelled with my husband to Italy. We landed in Bologna and then set out for Arezzo, Tuscany's third largest city, uncrowded and rich in the art and architecture of the Renaissance. No special event or festival determined or restricted our timing. We were constrained only by the limits of our energy, budget, my interest in Piero's works and the charming hillside town itself. We visited the house and garden of the sixteenth-century artist and architect Georgio Vasari, without whose book *The Lives of the Most Excellent Painters, Sculptors, and Architects* we would know little of Piero della Francesca or most of his colleagues. (For my scientist husband, I retold a story of sitting excitedly in the hallowed hush of the State Library of Victoria, reading a copy of Vasari's book during my arts degree.) On our third and final day, we hired a car and set off for Sansepolcro.

We made our way along cobble-stoned streets to the well-signed Museo Civico. Smaller than I'd imagined and embedded into the plaster of the walls was Huxley's 'Best Picture', Clarke's reason for not destroying the town – and our goal at the end of my research journey to understand the meaning and value placed on culture in our world.

Assessing the financial value of *Resurrection of Christ* (1458) would be an impossible task, although there are likely those who couldn't appreciate it any other way. The image is redolent with Christian symbolism but encourages a range of humanist interpretations. The central figure is muscular, strident, and almost recognisably normal in form, rather than idealised or deified. The model's decedents could easily have been outside on the street – perhaps that's why he looked so familiar. He appeared to me more like a warrior reborn than a victim of sacrifice, or perhaps stronger because of it. He is bare-chested with a loose shroud hanging from his shoulder, standing with one foot on the edge of his tomb as he prepares to leap out of the frame and back into the world. The background to the *Resurrection* is a landscape divided by the main figure: one side is redolent of life and of Spring, fecund and replete with possibilities; the other is stark, stripped of life and devoid of colour. Black and white. Guards lie asleep in the foreground, exhausted by their duties or perhaps drunk, either way oblivious to the miracles going on around them. I recalled that art historians wrote of the foreshortening and perspectival tricks used to create the sense of depth. I thought of the virtual reality shadow play we'd seen in the basement of Piero's house, showing the profile silhouettes of Piero and Luca Pacioli – the artist and the promoter of double-entry bookkeeping – arguing about the mathematical formulas and precise measurements that may have gone into the painting's construction. The work could not exist without either these techniques or the creative vision that had composed it. This balanced approach created the master-work that came to define the town and eventually saved it from destruction; it also gave rise to a style of painting that fostered depth and perspective, influencing art and culture across Europe. Pacioli's balanced approach to financial record-keeping supported the economic boom that funded the artists of the Renaissance.

No miracle of insight leapt from the traces of Piero's hand, only a comforting recognition that the value of culture, and my contribution as an arts worker to it, is immeasurable and resides somewhere between me, my colleagues and the members of the public who'd come to share the various experiences we'd created. The value of culture and its impact, like the value of *The Resurrection*, resists measurement through traditional numbers-based methods, even though it continues to build and grow with every interaction. The value lies in this process – the collaborations and the common belief of having contributed to something bigger and better than ourselves, so that we may make the world a better place, even if only for half an hour – or perhaps a lifetime. There may even be economic benefits gained along the way. And, for my part, that has all been well worth pursuing.

* * *

Following his Italian sojourn and disturbed by growing fears and anxieties about a future dominated by technologies, totalitarianism and loss of individuality, Aldous Huxley wrote the dystopian classic, *Brave New World* (1932). Anthony Clarke survived the war and migrated to South Africa, where he became an influential and much-loved antiquarian bookseller, revered for providing banned texts to brave students during the dark years of apartheid. Clarke's Bookshop still operates on Long Street in Cape Town. Clarke is also remembered by the people of Sansepolcro, who named a street after him in gratitude for his actions, which saved its people and its priceless treasures. For when it mattered most, he'd by chance recalled something he'd once read in a book.

References

Introduction – How an artwork saved a town

1   J.M. Wood, *The Cambridge Companion to Piero della Francesca*, University of Illinois, Urbana-Champaign, ILL, 2002, p. 244.

Chapter 1 – Culture and value

1   J. Holden, *Cultural Value and the Crisis of Legitimacy*, Demos, London, 2006, p. 11, https://www.demos.co.uk/files/Culturalvalueweb.pdf.

2   ibid.

3   ibid., p. 15.

4   ibid., p. 12.

5   J. Holden, *Capturing Cultural Value: How culture has become a tool of government policy*, DEMOS, 2004, https://demos.co.uk/wp-content/uploads/files/CapturingCulturalValue.pdf

6   Holden, *Cultural Value and the Crisis of Legitimacy*, p. 15.

7   ibid., p. 14.

8   The Adelaide Fringe is a spectacularly successful event for the city and gives prominence to its economic impact in their reporting of its success; see https://2016-assets-adelaidefringe-com-au.s3.amazonaws.com/production/2018/06/14/07/02/10/f63d3bd2-7035-4938-ade9-79ad18a91a18/2018_AnnualReview_Digital_01.pdf.

9   Holden, *Cultural Value*, p. 16.

10   ibid.

11   I wonder if the logic of instrumentalism works both ways: would the same indicators be used as evidence of negative effects of events if the numbers decreased rather than improved? As a hypothetical, could a reduction in restaurant or hotel bookings in the city also be attributed to a festival's poor programming choices, in the same way that increases in these indicators are used as evidence of a festival's success? This thought experiment shows the dangers festival organisations face as they become more dependent on instrumental indicators to demonstrate their worth.

12   Holden, *Cultural Value*, p. 18.

13   'Co-creation' is a term I've borrowed from the museum sector to describe

the collaborative partnership between a cultural institution and its visitors, which creates value for both parties; see P. Barnes & G. McPherson, 'Co-creating, co-producing and connecting: museum practice today', *Curator: The Museum Journal*, vol. 62, no. 2, 2019, pp. 257–67. https://onlinelibrary.wiley.com/doi/abs/10.1111/cura.12309.

14 J. Holden, 'How we value arts and culture', *Asia Pacific Journal of Arts and Cultural Management*, vol. 6, no. 2, 2009, p. 454.

15 D. Gillman, *The Idea of Cultural Heritage*, Cambridge University Press, Cambridge, Eng., 2010, p. 39.

16 M. Patton, *Qualitative Research & Evaluation Methods*, 3rd edn, Sage Publications, Thousand Oaks, CA, 2002, p. 437.

17 R. Towse (ed.) *Handbook of Cultural Economics*, 2nd edn, Edward Elgar Publishing, Cheltenham, Eng., 2003, p. 5.

18 See R. Missingham, 'Libraries and economic value: a review of recent studies', *Performance Measurement and Metrics*, vol 6, no. 3, 2005, pp. 142–58.

19 M. Norman, 'Frail, fatal, fundamental: the future of public libraries', *Public Library Quarterly*, vol. 31, no. 4, 2012, pp. 339–51, DOI: 10.1080/01616846.2012.732491.

20 J. Meyrick & T. Barnett, 'Culture without "world": Australian cultural policy in the age of stupid', *Cultural Trends*, vol. 26, no. 2, 2017, pp. 107–24, p. 14.

21 Holden, *Cultural Value*, p. 21.

22 C. Scott (ed.), *Museums and Public Value: Creating sustainable futures*, Routledge, London, Eng., 2013, p. xiii.

Chapter 2 – How the arts became an industry

1 J. Pick, M.H. Anderton & R. Ajala, *The Arts in a State: A study of government arts policies from ancient Greece to the present*, Bristol Classical Press, Bristol, Eng., 1988, pp. xiv–xv.

2 ibid., p. xiv.

3 ibid., p. xi.

4 ibid.

5 G. Monbiot, *How Did We Get Into This Mess? Politics, equality, nature*, Verso, New York, 2017, p. 15.

6 M. Blyth, *Austerity: The history of a dangerous idea*, Oxford University Press, Oxford, Eng., 2015, p. 155.

7 ibid., p. 155.

8 Robert Gordon from the US National Bureau of Economic Research also questions the myth of constant and inevitable economic growth and suggests that the US economy, still the most influential in the world, is facing six headwinds to growth: 'demography, education, inequality, globalization, energy/environment and the overhang of consumer and government debt'.

9 N. Horne, *Background Note: The Commonwealth efficiency dividend: an overview*, Parliamentary Library, Parliament of Australia, Canberra, 2012, p. 2.

10   P. Hamilton, 2013, *Budget Review 2014–15 Index: Australian Public Service staffing and efficiencies*, viewed 23 September 2019, https://www.aph.gov.au/About_Parliament/Parliamentary_Departments/Parliamentary_Library/pubs/rp/BudgetReview201415/APS.

11   D. Carroll, 2018, 'What sponsors want from the arts', *ArtsHub*, viewed 23 September 2019, https://www.artshub.com.au/news-article/features/grants-and-funding/diana-carroll/what-sponsors-want-from-the-arts-255672https://www.artshub.com.au/news-article/features/grants-and-funding/diana-carroll/what-sponsors-want-from-the-arts-255672.

12   R. Denniss, 'Dead right: how neoliberalism ate itself and what comes next', *Quarterly Essay*, no. 70, Black Inc., Carlton, Vic., 2018, p. 7.

13   Australian Major Performing Arts Group & Creative Partnerships Australia 2018, *Tracking Changes in Corporate Sponsorship and Donations 2018*, https://www.ampag.com.au/article/sponsorship-and-donations-revenue-up-but-volatile-and-uneven.

14   Such arrangements also prevent the company and their associated contractors from publicly voicing dissent against the policies and practices of the sponsoring company or government department. Public servants are bound by the terms of their contracts not to publicly voice dissent. This is also the case in state institutions, as outlined by Judith White in the case of NSW where employees agree to a code of conduct 'forbidding public comment on contentious matters' (*Culture Heist: Art versus money*, Brandl & Schlesinger, Blackheath, NSW, 2017, p. 28).

15   L. Waldhuter, 'State Library of South Australia to shed 20 full-time jobs due to '$6 million budget cut', *ABC News Online*, 2016, https://www.abc.net.au/news/2016-08-10/20-full-time-jobs-cut-from-sa-state-library/7718048. https://www.abc.net.au/news/2016-08-10/20-full-time-jobs-cut-from-sa-state-library/7718048.

16   Ibid.

17   Monbiot, *How Did We Get Into This Mess?*, p. 17.

18   J. Radbourne, '*Creative Nation*: A policy for leaders or followers? An evaluation of Australia's 1994 cultural policy statement', *The Journal of Arts Management, Law and Society*, vol. 26, no. 4, 1997, p. 272.

19   J. Garnham, referring to Adorno and Horkheimer, 'From cultural to creative industries: an analysis of the implications of the "creative industries" approach to arts and media policy making in the United Kingdom', *International Journal of Cultural Policy*, vol. 11, no. 11, 2005, p. 17.

20   J. O'Connor, 'After the creative industries: why we need a cultural economy', *Platform Papers*, no. 47, Currency House, Strawberry Hills, NSW, 2016, p. 7.

21   E. Belfiore, 'Auditing culture: the subsidised cultural sector in the New Public Management', *International Journal of Cultural Policy*, vol. 10, no. 2, 2004, pp. 183–202, p. 184.

22   M. Banks, & J. O'Connor, 'Inside the whale (and how to get out of there): moving on from two decades of creative industries research', *European Journal of Cultural Studies*, vol. 20, no. 6, 2017, pp. 637–54.

23 Banks & O'Connor, 'Inside the whale', pp. 637–54.

24 M. Banks, 2015, 'Valuing cultural industries', in K. Oakley & J. O'Connor (eds.), *The Routledge Companion to the Cultural Industries*, Routledge, London, 2015, p. 39.

25 ibid. Mark Banks and Justin O'Connor, professors of cultural economy, tracked the rise and fall of the UK's creative industries policy platforms, which promoted such links between creative populations and the regeneration of urban areas and communities ('Inside the whale', 2017, op cit). This questionable causal relationship led to what became known as the 'Bilboa effect': cultural institutions and the moneyed 'creative classes' attracted by them would increase the desirability of the neighbourhood, benefit from improved employment levels and drive up housing prices. Richard Florida, who developed the theory behind the effect has since retracted his original creative industries treatise and found that the town of Bilboa had been flooded with tourists or pilgrims since the Medieval period, when each year thousands would stop over as part of the pilgrimage trail to Santiago de Compostela. The Bilbao Museum simply provided a means of counting them; see also A. Franklin, 'Journeys to the Guggenheim Museum Bilbao: towards a revised Bilbao effect', *Annals of Tourism Research*, vol. 59, 2016, pp. 79–92, 80.

26 See particularly E. Belfiore, 'Auditing culture: the subsidised cultural sector in the New Public Management', *International Journal of Cultural Policy*, vol. 10, no. 2, 2004, pp. 183–202; E. Belfiore, 'On bullshit in cultural policy practice and research', *International Journal of Cultural Policy*, vol. 15, no. 3, 2009, pp. 342–59; C. Gray, 'Commodification and Instrumentality in cultural policy', *International Journal of Cultural Policy*, vol. 13, no. 2, 2007, pp. 203–15.

27 Belfiore, 'Auditing culture', p. 184.

28 S. van Thiel & F. L. Leeuw, 'The performance paradox in the public sector', *Public Performance & Management Review*, vol. 25, no. 3, 2002, p. 267, DOI: 10.1080/15309576.2002.11643661.

29 T. Christensen & P. Lægreid, 'New Public Management: puzzles of democracy and the influence of citizens', *The Journal of Political Philosophy*, vol. 10, no. 3, 2002, pp. 267–95, https://doi.org/10.1111/1467-9760.00153, p. 268.

30 ibid.

31 van Thiel & Leeuw, 'The performance paradox', p. 267.

32 ibid.

33 van Thiel & Leeuw, 'The performance paradox', p. 269.

34 J. Caust, 2003, 'Putting the "art" back into arts policy making: how arts policy has been "captured" by the economists and the marketers', *International Journal of Cultural Policy*, vol. 9, no. 1, 2003, p. 60.

35 C. Madden, 'Using "economic" impact studies in arts and cultural advocacy: a cautionary note', *Media International Australia, Incorporating Culture & Policy*, no. 98, 2001, p. 161.

36 ibid.

37 ibid.

38   ibid.

39   ibid.

40   C.D. Throsby, 'Assessing the impacts of a cultural industry', *The Journal of Arts Management, Law and Society,* vol. 34, no. 3, 2004, pp. 188–204, DOI: 10.3200/JAML.34.3.

41   F. Chiaravalloti, 'Performance evaluation in the arts and cultural sector: a story of accounting at its margins', *The Journal of Arts Management, Law and Society*, vol. 44, no. 2, 2014, pp. 61–89, DOI, 10.1080/10632921.

42   ibid.

43   I've wondered about the influence digital project management tools have had upon public service thinking and delivery, given their co-evolved relationship to the NPM model. Tools I have enjoyed working with such as MS Project demand specified goals and outcomes as part of setting up, managing milestones and evaluating a project. Much government work is by necessity considered as a project, tied to short-term funding rounds and measured and evaluated against predetermined policy goals and outcomes. I've worked with some great project leaders who use these tools well in a government context, but the limited timeframes and budgets mean it is 'beyond scope of the project' to consider or incorporate longer-term goals at the expense of the immediate KPIs. All government work, even endeavours that extend beyond a political term, like culture, health, infrastructure and education, seems to have been turned into a series of limited and disconnected policy projects.

44   Scott, *Museums and Public Value,* p. 4.

45   J. Radbourne, H. Glow & K. Johanson (eds.) 2013, *The Audience Experience: A critical analysis of audiences in the performing arts*, Intellect, Bristol, UK, p. 5.

46   My own experience has included having to outsource the compilation of an economic impact estimate, required as part of a funding application, to a friendly contact at a local business school. The funding body, when asked, did not have a standard model or formula for establishing estimates of economic impact, even though all applicants to the fund would be judged by the estimates they would provide and be required to acquit against them at the end of the funding period. When I expressed concern, I was told to 'just make a good story with the numbers you have'.

47   For example, in their annual review of the 2019 Adelaide Fringe Festival, the organisation first thanks their teams before reporting the following: 'Last year, Adelaide Fringe increased tourist attendance by a whopping 72%! This led to an overall visitor-related expenditure increase of 24% to $36.6 million and a total of 150,257 visitor bed nights being generated by the interstate/international audiences and artists who came to visit Fringe (an increase of 53% per cent)'; see https://adelaidefringe.com.au/annual-review-2019.

48   Madden, 'Using "economic" impact studies in arts', p. 173.

49   D. North, *Institutions, Institutional Change and Economic Performance*, Cambridge University Press, Cambridge, Eng., 1990, p. 21.

50   ibid., p. 11.

51   ibid., p. 3.

52   ibid., p. 11.

53   A. Hatton, 'The conceptual roots of modern museum management dilemmas', *Museum Management and Curatorship*, vol. 27, no. 2, 2012, p. 129.

54   Cultural economists Steven Hadley and Clive Gray pulled no punches as to the unfairness: 'Crude instrumentalization (in the sense of a simple imposition of the concerns of other policy sectors onto those of cultural policy) depended for its effect on the willingness of exogenous policy actors. These included national governments enforcing their preferences on cultural policy actors, particularly at the regional and local levels, where central power holds less sway. As such, the greater the pressure to prioritise central policy expectations . . . concerned with non-cultural sets of policy priorities, the more difficult it would be for outright resistance or more subtle forms of policy management to have effect' ('Hyperinstrumentalism and cultural policy: means to an end or an end to meaning?', *Cultural Trends*, vol. 26, no. 2, 2017, p. 96, https://doi.org/10.1080/09548963.2017.13238362).

55   E. Belfiore & O. Bennett, 'Determinants of impact: towards a better understanding of encounters with the arts', *Cultural Trends*, vol. 16, no. 3, 2007, p. 185.

56   E. Belfiore, 'On bullshit in cultural policy practice and research', p. 348.

57   P. Landman, 'Inside the Powerhouse', *Meanjin: On Museums*, vol. 40, no. 4, 2001, p. 38.

58   B. Walmsley, 'Whose value is it anyway? A neo-institutional approach to articulating and evaluating artistic value', *Journal of Arts and Communities*, vol. 4, no. 4, 2013, p. 2.

59   J. Caust, 2005, 'Privilege or problem: the distinct role of government in arts development in South Australia', *Journal of Arts Management, Law, and Society*, vol. 35, no. 1, 2005, p. 27.

60   ibid., p. 31.

61   These objectives for the new plan are points 7 and 8 of a list of 8 prescribing the government's future direction for the arts and cultural sector in South Australia. The full proposal is available at https://dpc.sa.gov.au/responsibilities/arts-and-culture/arts-plan.

62   R. Hewison 2006, *Not a Slide Show: Leadership and cultural value*, Demos, London, Eng., 2006, p. 21.

63   Office for the Arts, Australian Government, 12 December 2024. https://www.arts.gov.au/news/highlighting-value-our-cultural-and-creative-activity

64   D. Whitelock, *Festival!: The story of the Adelaide Festival of Arts*, published by the author, Adelaide, 1980, p. 173.

65   Caust, 'Privilege or problem', pp. 29–31.

66   D. O'Brien, 'Cultural value, measurement and policy making', *Arts and Humanities in Higher Education*, vol. 14, no. 1, 2015, p. 84, doi: 10.1177/1474022214533892.

67   Walmsley, 'Whose value is it anyway?', p. 6.

68   ibid., p. 2.

69   ibid., p. 12.

70   North, *Institutions, Institutional Change and Economic Performance,* p. 11.

71   B. Walmsley, 'Deep hanging out in the arts: an anthropological approach to capturing cultural value', *International Journal of Cultural Policy*, vol. 24, no. 2, 2016. 'Deep hanging out' was a research approach undertaken to evaluate audience experience of an arts festival in the UK, where researchers accompanied audience members over an extended period of time. I found it interesting and applicable for the library experience because of the interpersonal connection and shared experiences that can be drawn out through direct conversation.

72   Walmsley, 'Whose value is it anyway?', p. 6.

73   Holden, 'How we value arts and culture', p. 454.

Chapter 3 – Libraries, literacy and a distinctive state of mind

1   A. Black, 'Lost worlds of culture: Victorian libraries, library history and prospects for a history of information', *Journal of Victorian Culture*, vol. 2, no. 1, 1997, p. 99.

2   J. Caust, 'Privilege or problem', 2005, p. 21.

3   H. Reynolds, 'South Australia: between Van Diemen's Land and New Zealand', in R. Foster & P. Sendziuk (eds), *Turning Points: Chapters in South Australian history*, Wakefield Press, Adelaide, 2012, p. 30.

4   ibid., p. 21.

5   I particularly recommend Carl Bridge's book *A Trunk Full of Books: History of the State Library of South Australia and its forerunners* (Wakefield Press, Adelaide, 1986) for those who wish to explore the history of the State Library up to 1986 in more detail.

6   R.B. Kinraide, 'The Society for the Diffusion of Useful Knowledge and the democratization of learning in nineteenth-century Britain', doctoral thesis, University of Wisconsin, Madison, WI, 2006, p. 2.

7   Black, 'Lost worlds of culture', p. 99.

8   ibid.

9   J. Rose, *The Intellectual Life of the British Working Classes,* Yale University Press, London, Eng., 2010, p. 17.

10   ibid., p. 7.

11   D. Pike, *Paradise of Dissent: South Australia 1829–1957*, Longmans, Green & Co., London, Eng., 1957, p. 495.

12   ibid., p. 495.

13   J. Beddoe, 'Mechanics' institutes and schools of arts in Australia', *Australasian Public Libraries and Information Services*, vol. 16, no. 3, 2003, p. 123.

14   J. Booth, 'Emigration, economics or strategy? The British government and the *South Australia Act 1834*', *Journal of Australian Studies*, vol. 27, no. 80, 2003, p. 157.

15   Reynolds, 'South Australia', in Foster & Sendziuk (eds.) *Turning Points*, p. 26.

16   K. Goldsworthy, *Adelaide*, NewSouth Publishing, Sydney, 2011, p. 3.

17 . P. Sendziuk & R. Foster, *A History of South Australia*, Cambridge University Press, Cambridge, Eng., 2018, p. 2.

18   Reynolds, 'South Australia', in Foster & Sendziuk (eds.) *Turning Points*, p. 27.

19   Foster & Sendziuk, *Turning Points*, p. 24.

20   Reynolds, 'South Australia', in Foster & Sendziuk (eds.) *Turning Points*, p. 26.

21   ibid., p. 26.

22   N. Draper, 'Recording traditional Kaurna cultural values in Adelaide – the continuity of Aboriginal cultural traditions within an Australian capital city', *Historic Environment*, vol. 27, no. 1, 2015, p. 81.

23   A. Nettelbeck, *Indigenous Rights and Colonial Subjecthood: Protection and reform in the nineteenth-century British empire*, Cambridge University Press, London, 2019, p. 125.

24   M. Talbot, 'A re-evaluation of the South Australian Literary and Scientific Association Library', *Australian Academic & Research Libraries*, vol. 39, no. 4, 2008, p. 278.

25   W.H. Langham, *In the Beginning*, Hassell Press, Adelaide, 1936, p. 8.

26   Bridge, *A Trunk Full of Books*, p. 1.

27   Kinraide, 'The Society for the Diffusion of Useful Knowledge', p. 1.

28   Rose, *The Intellectual Life of the British Working Classes*, p. 50.

29   R.D. Hill & F.D. Hill, *The Recorder of Birmingham: A memoir of Matthew Davenport Hill: with selections from his correspondence*, Macmillan, London, 1878, reissued 2015 by Forgotten Books, London, p. 80.

30   Rose, *The Intellectual Life of the British Working Classes*, p. 23.

31   Bridge, *A Trunk Full of Books*, p. 4.

32   According to Talbot (2008, p. 272), the collection also included philosophical and religious texts, as well as historical and literary works, such as a ten-volume set of Shakespeare's plays.

33   Hill & Hill, *The Recorder of Birmingham*, p. 32.

34   M. Horsburgh, 'Her father's daughter Florence Davenport-Hill, 1829–1919', *International Social Work*, vol. 26, no. 4, 1983, p. 2.

35   M. Talbot, *The Library of the South Australian Literary and Scientific Association: A combined short-title list arranged by contributor*, State Library of South Australia, 2008, p. 7, https://guides.State Library.sa.gov.au/ld.php?content_id=17256669.

36   D. Moss, 'Sir Rowland Hill and postal reform', *History Today*, vol. 29, no. 9, p. 590.

37   ibid., p. 589.

38   D. Gorham, 'Victorian reform as a family business', in A.S. Wohl, *The Victorian Family: Structure and stresses*, St. Martin's Press, New York, 1978, p. 129.

39   Moss, 'Sir Rowland Hill and postal reform', p. 590.

40   Talbot's 2008 list of the collection of the SALA notes that the SDUK 'gave

References

£10 worth of their books, to be selected at pleasure. To date no details of the selection are available'. My search of the surviving SDUK papers held at the National Archives in Kew, outside London, uncovered correspondence to Thomas Oakes esq. from Rowland Hill at the SAA offices at Adelphi Terrace in London, headed 'Respecting Cap Hindmarsh etc'. The note reads 'the present is no doubt intended for the South Australian Literary and Scientific Society – the company is a trading association with which we have no [illegible]. Do you allow [illegible] or the Captain any voice in the selection of the books?'. This indicates that Rowland Hill was considered an appropriate go-between to clarify the SDUK's query regarding who would make the selection of books for the colony. Unfortunately, many of the SDUK papers were destroyed in the Second World War so a final list may not be recovered. There are however several SDUK publications remaining in the State Library Special Collections.

41   M. Talbot, 'A re-evaluation of the South Australian Literary and Scientific Association Library', p. 278.

42   Bridge, *A Trunk Full of Books*, p. 6.

43   ibid., p. 7.

44   ibid.

45   G. Sutherland, *The South Australian Company: A study in colonisation*, Longmans, London, 1898, p. 35.

46   R. Haines, 'Indigent misfits or shrewd operators? Government-assisted emigrants from the United Kingdom to Australia, 1831–1860', *Population Studies*, vol. 48, no. 2, 1994, p. 234.

47   P. Sendziuk, 'No convicts here: reconsidering South Australia's foundation myth', in Foster & Sendziuk (eds), *Turning Points*, p. 35.

48   T. Dolin, 'First steps toward a history of the mid-Victorian novel in Colonial Australia', *Australian Literary Studies*, vol. 22, no. 3, 2006, p. 276.

49   C. Falke, 'On the morality of immoral fiction: reading Newgate novels, 1830–1848', *Nineteenth-Century Contexts* vol. 38, no. 3, 2016, p. 184, https://www.tandfonline.com/doi/full/10.1080/08905495.2016.1159810.

50   C. M. H. Clark, 1973, *A History of Australia III: The Beginning of an Australian civilisation*, Melbourne University Press, Melbourne, p. 59.

51   ibid., p. 54–5.

52   Bridge, *A Trunk Full of Books*, p. 8.

53   Talbot, 'A Re-Evalutation of the SALSA Library', p. 271.

54   Bridge, *A Trunk Full of Books*, p. 13.

55   The Adelaide money lender's name was Mr Da Costa, according to Bridge in *A Trunk Full of Books*, p. 12.

56   ibid., p. 14.

57   ibid., p. 15.

58   ibid.

59   ibid.

60   Ibid., p. 17.

61   Clark Papers, Special Collections, State Library of South Australia.

62   Bridge, *A Trunk Full of Books*, p. 25.

63   ibid.

64   Sendziuk & Foster, *A History of South Australia*, p. 55.

65   Bridge, *A Trunk Full of Books*, p. 30.

66   ibid., p. 20.

67   Dolin, 'First steps', p. 283.

68   Bridge, *A Trunk Full of Books*, p. 32.

69   ibid., p. 38.

70   ibid., p. 39.

71   See the comprehensive work by M. Talbot, *A Chance to Read: A history of the Institutes Movement in South Australia* (Libraries Board of South Australia, Adelaide, 1992); see also, Heidi Ing, 'Subscription in South Australian libraries' (Master's thesis, University of South Australia, Adelaide, 2011).

Chapter 4 – How the public values the State Library

1   The data collection for this case study is based on the scholarship and recommendations of arts audience evaluation commentators, especially Radbourne, Glow & Johanson (eds), *The Audience Experience*; C. Scott (ed.), *Museums and Public Value: Creating sustainable futures* (Routledge, London, Eng. 2013); P. Kaszynska, 'Capturing the vanishing point: subjective experiences and cultural value' (*Cultural Trends*, vol. 24, no. 3, 2015, pp. 256–66); and two works by B. Walmsley ('Whose value is it anyway?, pp. 299–15, and 'Deep hanging out in the arts').

      These theorists suggest that the audiences and publics of cultural institutions and the performing arts have much to contribute towards determining and assessing cultural value.

2   M.Q. Patton, *Qualitative Research & Evaluation Methods*, 3rd ed., Sage Publications, Los Angeles, 2002, p. 21. Patton suggests that 'The purpose of gathering responses to open-ended questions is to enable the researcher to understand and capture the points of view of other people without predetermining those points of view through prior selection of questionnaire categories . . . To capture participants "in their own terms" one must learn their categories for rendering explicable and coherent the flux of raw quality. That, indeed, is the first principle of qualitative analysis.' This approach is indeed time-consuming and complex, but cuts right to the heart of what this book and qualitative research are about – that which is worth doing is worth the effort.

3   D. O'Brien, 2015, 'Cultural value, measurement and policy making', *Arts and Humanities in Higher Education*, vol. 14, no. 1, p. 93. O'Brien, one of the leading figures in cultural economics, confirms that the arts sector already has enough trouble making ends meet, without the added expense of new technologies to communicate what they are already well placed to know.

References

4   According to correspondence with Culture Counts (dated 8 October 2019), the annual subscription to the platform costs $1500.00 and is accompanied by a range of confidentiality clauses.

5   The Western Australian Government announced in 2019 that the Culture Counts app saved arts organisations in receipt of recurrent government funding $950,000 per year in consultant fees. This sum is an indicator of the amount previously spent in WA on external evaluation consultants each year in order to report back to government funding bodies. Culture Counts is supplied free of charge to WA cultural organisations as part of their funding arrangements with Department of Culture and the Arts.

6   This was an analysis techniques aligned with the principles of inductive analysis described by V. Clarke & V. Braun, 'Thematic analysis', *The Journal of Positive Psychology,* vol. 12, no. 3, 2016, p. 298. Most of the organising themes were adapted from similar themes developed by Walmsley, and others from the Melbourne arts-evaluation scholars, Radbourne, Glow & K. Johanson (*The Audience Experience*). The only theme not covered in their book was heritage value, which is a category of value that related more to collecting institutions of some longevity, such as the State Library, and emerged as part of my doctoral research.

7   Walmsley (2016) shifted the conversation from 'what is the value of culture' to 'how is cultural value manifested' in his study on the Deep Hanging Out approach. I've found it a more useful and enlightening basis for the conversation around cultural value and am indebted to his work.

8   This goal was based on Scott's description of public value as 'outcomes which add benefit to the public sphere' and taps into the relationship between public value and cultural value.

9   G. Born, 'Making time: temporality, history, and the cultural object', *New Literary History*, vol. 46, no. 3, 2015, p. 368.

10   Holden, *Cultural Value*, p. 18.

11   Walmsley, 'Deep hanging out in the arts', p. 287.

12   Completed in 1884, the Mortlock Wing is a three-levelled polychromatic stone and brick Romanesque building, housing significant historical collections of South Australiana. According to the State Library website (http://guides.slsa. sa.gov.au/c.php?g=410288&p=2795746), the building was originally intended to be one wing of a mixed collections quadrangle facing North Terrace, and was intended to house the National Gallery, Public Library and Museum of South Australia. Although economic circumstances prevented the completion of all three wings, the building opened with all three institutions in residence in June 1884, 11 years after construction had begun and 23 years after the need for more space at the Institute Building had become apparent (Bridge, *A Trunk Full of Books*). The original chairs and other features are still in use today. This building is one of Adelaide's leading tourist attractions.

13   Dolin, 'First steps', p. 283.

Chapter 5 – Narratives of value, in the words of the public

1   For a full explanation, sources and methodology behind this research, you can read the full chapter in my thesis found at https://theses.flinders.edu.au/view/39d1a0b5-a2e1-4935-9903-6671c837d98e/1

2   The names of all but one of the interview subjects have been changed and an alias applied, out of respect for their privacy.

3   Volunteering Australia, 'National Standards for Volunteer Involvement', https://www.volunteeringaustralia.org/resources/national-standards-and-supporting-material/.

4   United Nations Volunteers, *State of the World's Volunteerism Report*, 2011, p. 4.

5   Kaszynska, 'Capturing the vanishing point', pp. 256–66.

6   Born, 'Making time', pp. 361–86.

7   J. Gleeson-White, 'Erasure: Hey Utopia!', *Griffith Review*, vol. 73, 2021, p. 43.

8   Holden, 'How we value arts and culture', p. 454.

9   T. Holmes (ed.), *A Perpetual Flow Of Benefits: Wilderness economic values in an evolving, multicultural society*, US Department of Agriculture Forest Service, Washington, DC, 2022, https://doi.org/10.2737/WO-GTR-101.

10   S. Saxena & A. McDougall, 'Estimating the economic value of libraries', *Prometheus: Critical Studies in Innovation*, vol. 30, no. 3, 2012, p. 368.

11   Based on the Old Royal Adelaide Hospital site on the eastern of North Terrace, Lot Fourteen is home to the new Australian Space Agency, a data project from Massachusetts Institute of Technology (MIT) and the University of Adelaide. The precinct is also home to 'a number of start-up and medium-sized companies on site as it attracts firms working in its strategic themes of space, defence, cyber security and creative arts technology'. The SA State Government is partnering with a range of local and international universities, the Australian Government and commercial interests to develop Lot 14. This project is being described as an engine to reinvigorate the South Australian economy through, amongst other initiatives, the collection of data. This data will 'inform decision making for government projects, industry projects and future prosperity. It will improve productivity and, most importantly, create more jobs right here in SA'. Another proposal put forward by the state government is for the development of a new Gallery of Indigenous Art and Culture, drawing on the collections of the State Library, SA Museum and Art Gallery of South Australia. At the time of writing, the future of this project is unclear.

12   I produced a case study of such latent long-term value activation. The State Library held for over a century a collection of archival documents from the Red Cross. These documents were transformed from administrative records to an internationally recognised online experience connecting countries and families over time and across the world. Physically, they had travelled only a stone's throw from where they were originally compiled (in the Verco Buildings on North Terrace, diagonally opposite the State Library), but had been ferried through time as part of the collection. It was 100 years before their latent value

was realised as part of the commemorations of the Anzac Centenary. They were transformed and reinterpreted using digital technologies. Publishing these records online connected them to similar archives around the world, creating a universal story of war, loss and love through the eyes of South Australians. This localisation of international experiences through the collections is reflected in Grant's description of the State Library's functional role as 'a cultural anchor' (J. Meyrick, R. Phiddian & T. Barnett, *What Matters?: Talking value in Australian culture*, Monash University Press, Clayton, Vic., 2018).

13   A. Castledine & C. Chalmers, 'LEGO robotics: an authentic problem solving tool?', *Design and Technology Education,* vol. 16, no. 3, 2011, pp. 19–27.

14   The Australian Bureau of Statistics, accessed 17 October 2023, https://www. abs.gov.au/statistics/people/housing/estimating-homelessness-census/ latest-release

15   D. Yaffe-Bellany & J. Stern, 'Yale students aren't ready to close the book on the school's libraries just yet', *Washington Post Higher Education*, 2019, https://www.washingtonpost.com/education/2019/04/21/yale-students-ar- ent-ready-close-book-schools-libraries-just-yet/?noredirect=on.

16   Denniss, 'Dead right', p. 50.

17   Walmsley, 'Deep hanging out in the arts', p. 17.

18   The Gladys Elphick Collection is embargoed for cultural reasons, meaning that access permissions will be granted under appropriate conditions, set by the Indigenous community and currently determined by senior community members once a thorough assessment has taken place.

19   From the Preamble of the Tandanya – Adelaide Declaration from the International Council of Archives Expert Group on Indigenous Matters, 2011, https://www.archives.sa.gov.au/__data/assets/pdf_file/0006/830283/SRSA- Response-to-the-Tandanya-Declaration-Action-Plan-Final-V1.0-A263011.pdf

20   ibid., p. 2.

21   State Library of South Australia, Media release, 10 March 2022, https:// www.slsa.sa.gov.au/news/press/2022/03/aboriginal-reference-group-meets- for-first-time.

22   S. Blauw, *The Number Bias: How numbers lead and mislead us*, Sceptre, London, 2021, p. 40.

Chapter 6 – Reclaiming common ground for the common good

1   G. Robertson, Who Owns History? Elgin's loot and the case for returning plundered treasure, Penguin Random House Australia, Sydney, 2019, p. xiii.

2   See Walmsley 'Whose value is it anyway?'.

3   A. Assman, 'Canon and archive', in A. Erli & A. Nunning, A (eds.), Media and Cultural Memory Studies: An international and interdisciplinary handbook, Walter de Gruyter, Berlin, 2008, p. 102.

4   'The storing of documents and artefacts of the past that do not meet all these standards [of the canon] but are nevertheless deemed interesting

or important enough to prevent them from vanishing on the highway to total oblivion. While emphatic appreciation, repeated performance, and continued individual and public attention are the hallmark of objects in the cultural working memory, professional preservation and withdrawal from general attention mark the contents of the reference memory. Emphatic reverence and specialized historical curiosity are the two poles between which the dynamics of cultural memory is played out' (ibid., p. 101).

5   Bridge, A Trunk Full of Books, p. 30.
6   Interaction Design Foundation (IxDF), 'What are wicked problems?', https:// www.interaction-design.org/literature/topics/wicked-problems
7   A. Klamer, Doing the Right Thing: A value based economy, Ubiquity Press, London, 2017, p. 9.
8   ibid., p. 5.
9   ibid.
10   Caust, 'Privilege or problem', p. 31.
11   Holden, 'How we value arts and culture', p. 449.
12   C. Throsby, Economics and Culture, Cambridge University Press, London, 2001, p. 28.
13   Meyrick, Phiddian & Barnett, What Matters?, p. 100.
14   Hewison, Not a Slide Show, p. 21.
15   K. Punch, Introduction to Social Research: qualitative and quantitative approaches, 3rd edn, Sage Publications Inc., Los Angeles, 2014, p. 127.
16   ibid., p. 127.
17   Holden, Cultural Value, p. 18.

Epilogue

1   A. Yeatman 'Restoring wholeness: hey utopia!', *Griffith Review*, vol. 73, 2021, p. 131. The coincidence of those two sectors resisting challenge is due to the normalisation of neoliberal principles such as economic rationalism, and the rise of subjectivism which Yeatman suggests 'fosters interventionism, the belief that the all-powerful human subject is the one in control and can sort things out. The delusional nature of this belief is obvious'.
2   SGS Economics and Planning, which has offices in Canberra, Melbourne, Hobart and Sydney. The full report can be found at: https://www.sgsep.com. au/assets/main/SGS-Economics-and-Planning_The-value-of-public-libraries-in-South-Australia_FINAL.pdf

Index

Index

Wakefield Press is an independent publishing and
distribution company based in Adelaide, South Australia.
We love good stories and publish beautiful books.
To see our full range of books, please visit our website at
www.wakefieldpress.com.au
where all titles are available for purchase.
To keep up with our latest releases, news and events,
subscribe to our monthly newsletter.

Find us!

Facebook: www.facebook.com/wakefield.press
Instagram: www.instagram.com/wakefieldpress

www.ingramcontent.com/pod-product-compliance
Lightning Source LLC
Chambersburg PA
CBHW040254290326
41929CB00051B/3374